A Practitioner's Guide
to Rational-emotive Therapy

A Practitioner's Guide to Rational-emotive Therapy

Susan R. Walen, Ph.D.
Raymond DiGiuseppe, Ph.D.
Richard L. Wessler, Ph.D.

OXFORD UNIVERSITY PRESS
New York   1980   Oxford

Copyright © 1980 by Oxford University Press, Inc.

Library of Congress Cataloging in Publication Data
Walen, Susan R
  A practitioner's guide to rational-emotive therapy.
  Bibliography: p.
  Includes index.
    1. Rational-emotive psychotherapy. I. DiGiuseppe,
  Raymond, joint author.   II. Wessler, Richard L., joint
  author.   III. Title.
  RC489.R3W34   616.8'914   79-9121
  ISBN0-19-502667-5
  ISBN 0-19-502668-3 pbk.

Printed in the United States of America

Dedicated with love to
Andy
Audrey
Alec

Foreword

Although rational-emotive therapy (RET) has now become one of the most popular modern psychotherapies and is at the core of the new movement that favors cognitive-behavior therapy, there are as yet relatively few works for professionals who want to learn how to practice it—most of them, for better or worse, written by me. And some of these leave much to be desired. The seminal work in the field, *Reason and Emotion is Psychotherapy*, which I published in 1962, deliberately emphasized the cognitive aspects of RET and gave few details about its emotive and behavioral aspects. The same could be said about *Growth Through Reason*, which I published in 1971 and which included verbatim transcripts of cases by Ben N. Ard, H. Jon Geis, Paul A. Hauck, John M. Gullo, Maxie C. Maultsby, Jr., and myself. Most of these cases were actually seen in the 1960's; again, they emphasized cognitive restructuring and omitted many important aspects of RET.

While I published many papers giving some of the details of the emotive and behavioral aspects of RET in the 1960's (Ellis, 1968, 1969a, 1969b), most of this material did not begin to appear in book form until the mid-1970's when such works as *Youth: Toward Personal Growth, A Rational-Emotive Approach* (Tosi, 1974); *Rational-Emotive Therapy* (Morris and Kanitz, 1975); *The Counseling Process: A Cognitive-Behavioral Approach* (Lembo, 1976); *Handbook of Rational-Emotive Therapy* (Ellis and Grieger, 1977), *Brief Psychotherapy in Medical and Health Practice* (Ellis and Abrahms, 1978), and *Theoretical and Empirical Foundations of Rational–Emotive Therapy* (Ellis, 1979b) were published.

Even these books, in number and in popularity, are almost a drop in the bucket when compared to the large number of mass market books on RET that have thus far appeared—some of which, like *Your Erroneous Zones* (Dyer, 1976), *Fully Human, Fully Alive* (Powell, 1976), and *A New Guide to Rational Living* (Ellis and Harper, 1975) have achieved immense popularity with the reading public. People sometimes ask me why I and other writers have concentrated so heavily on writing best-selling books about RET rather than on professional publications; and one answer that I give is that whereas most systems of psychotherapy are too abstruse and complicated to be stated in simple form that will be useful to the average reader, RET is a form of therapy that can easily be made available to almost anyone who can read; and since there are many more potential readers of self-help literature in the world than potential clients of psychotherapy, it is highly important that they be reached by a simple, understandable, and (I naturally believe) yet profound system of self-help with their emotional problems. Moreover, as Drs. Walen, Di-Giuseppe, and Wessler nicely illustrate in this book, RET almost invariably includes bibliotherapy as well as other cognitive methods; and I am happy that many suitable texts, including some of my own authorship, are available for this important purpose.

With all the current interest in RET by both therapists and the public, a definitive work explaining in detail exactly how neophyte and more experienced therapists can use its many cognitive-emotive-behavioral methods has yet to be written; the present text by Drs. Walen, DiGiuseppe, and Wessler comes closest to that goal. It is quite comprehensive, including almost all the major facets of RET and applying them to individual psychotherapy, marriage and family therapy, and various other aspects of psychological treatment. It is clear, exceptionally precise, and replete with realistic applications of RET to actual psychotherapeutic treatments.

In surveying the RET literature, including the many excellent points made in this book, and in thinking over my own quarter of a century practice of rational-emotive therapy, what are some of the main characteristics of a good or competent rational-emotive therapist? As I pointed out some time ago, in rebuttal to Carl Rogers' (1957) paper "The Necessary and Sufficient Conditions of Therapeutic Personality Change," "there is probably *no* single condition which is absolutely necessary for the inducement of changed attitudes and behavior patterns" (Ellis, 1959, p. 538). I have similarly contended that there are no necessary and sufficient characteristics that a good therapist has to possess to be effective with clients (Ellis, 1974a). Nevertheless, there are several characteristics that, in my opinion, are highly desirable for any therapist, and particularly for a rational-emotive therapist (Wessler and Ellis, 1979). Let me briefly list some of these.

Intelligence. Although many highly intelligent people, including highly intelligent therapists, are emotionally disturbed, I think that there is a distinct tendency for bright people to draw sensible conclusions from their own experience and to pick up and utilize the practical and rational solutions to their problems that others, including their therapists, may present to them. If so, it is highly desirable for any therapist, including one who practices RET, to have a considerable degree of intelligence, and preferably to be as bright as or brighter than most of the clients that s/he is likely to see.

Therapeutic knowledge. RET is one of the few modern psychotherapies that consciously, on theoretical as well as practical grounds, includes a dozen or more cognitive, emotive, and behavioral techniques, each of which has many possible subheadings. RET therapists, as Arnold Lazarus (1976) has emphasized, had therefore better have a wide knowledge of the general field of psychotherapy and the ability to effectively employ many different therapeutic methods—as long as these methods do not primarily help their clients to feel better rather than to get better (Ellis, 1972).

Empathy. RET practitioners do not overemphasize the kind of empathy that has been so often stressed by Rogers (1951) and his followers (Carkhuff, 1969), which largely consists of reflecting the negative feelings of clients about themselves and the world—and thereby often implying that their lives really *are* miserable and that they have little choice but to be anxious and depressed. However, RET therapists tend to be considerably more empathic than other therapists in that they deeply sense what basic philosophies (and particularly self-sabotaging philosophies) lie behind clients' communications and significantly create or contribute to their disturbed feelings. RET-oriented empathy, therefore, is in many respects deeper and more profound than other kinds of therapist-instituted empathy. It gives the clients the feeling not only that they are being listened to and understood, but that their therapists understand some of their feelings *better* and more *helpfully* than they themselves do. Consequently, they can *listen to themselves* much better after a few RET sessions and are more in touch with their own feelings than they ever were before. RET practitioners, partly through their understanding and continued use of RET theory, had better acquire this unique kind of empathy that is so important in helping many clients.

Persistence. Therapy clients are the way they are not only because they easily and naturally disturb themselves (as perhaps do virtually all human beings) but also because they *indulge* in their dysfunctional feelings, thoughts, and behaviors and refuse to persist in the hard work that is usually required to change them. If therapists are equally indulgent and permit their clients (and themselves) to get by with half-hearted attempts to change themselves, little will be accomplished. RET practitioners, therefore, had better work *hard* and *persistently* to show their clients how they are disturbing themselves and to keep after them, with various behavioral as well as cognitive-emotive methods, to correct themselves again and again.

Interest in helping others. Even if psychotherapy is becoming something of a science as well as an art, it normally requires a real interest in helping others—and, we might add, an *enjoyable* interest. An effective RET therapist, therefore, had better *like* people, *desire* to see them get along better in life, and have a real *interest* in talking them out of their nonsense and supervising their work in feeling and acting in a more functional manner. Unfortunately, perhaps, many therapists greatly enjoy the drama or the excitement of various kinds of ineffectual therapy (such as psychoanalysis, psychodrama, or encounter groups). They therefore engage in this kind of treatment mainly for their own sake rather than for the satisfaction of their clients. The problem is for therapists to employ an effective procedure and *also* to enjoy using this procedure with others. If they cannot solve this problem satisfactorily, perhaps they had better turn to some nontherapeutic vocation or profession.

Scientific outlook. As Eysenck (1964), Yates (1970), and other therapists have pointed out, the process of efficient psychotherapy overlaps significantly with the process of scientific inquiry and experimentation. Every time therapists see clients, they come to the sessions with a theory about how people disturb themselves and how they can be helped to change; they then attempt to apply this theory to a particular client at a particular session. This is especially true of RET, which tries to be a scientifically based theory and practice that is relatively free of dogmas and overgeneralizations, and that is continually being tested and changed as old methodologies are found wanting and new ones produce better results. Successful RET therapists, therefore, do not assume that any RET position is absolutely true or valid for all time to come. They test their specific hypotheses about clients and general hypotheses about RET, and keep changing their outlook and procedures. RET itself has changed considerably over the years—notably by the addition of many cognitive, emotive, and behavioral methods that were hardly invented when I first started to employ it early in 1955. Therapists who follow RET principles will continue to add new theories and practices to its present armamentarium and help its steady growth and development.

Personal Use of RET by the Therapist.   I agree with Carl Rogers' (1951) remark that it is desirable but not necessary for client-centered therapists to have some individual client-centered therapy themselves. It is highly desirable for RET therapists to be in individual or group RET for some period of time—for they will then learn it better, see its advantages and disadvantages, and be able to understand their own clients' resistances to therapy in general and RET in particular. I have noticed, over the years, that the most effective RET practitioners tend to be those who, through their reading of the literature or actual experience as an RET client, have used RET on themselves and have benefited considerably from so doing. I think the recent tendency of many traditional behavior therapists to become cognitive-behavior therapists or RET-ers has largely stemmed from the fact that they have found orthodox behavior therapy to be relatively useless in their own lives but have found RET to be immensely helpful in overcoming some of their own longstanding emotional problems. In any event, in training our Fellowship candidates in RET at the Institute for Rational-Emotive Therapy in New York, as well as in training our Primary Certificate and Associate Fellowship candidates in the practica which we sponsor in various parts of the United States and in Europe, we find that their use of RET in solving their personal problems is one of the most important aspects of their training. So, we see that this part of RET is never neglected.

These are some of the main characteristics of an effective RET therapist, but of course, they are not the only ones. Nor does anyone have to possess them ideally. One of the best points of the present book is that it highlights and gives salient information about how people who want to use RET can help themselves achieve or improve on some of these traits and increase their therapeutic efficiency. For one of the main principles of rational-emotive therapy—as Drs. Walen, DiGiuseppe, and Wessler keep emphasizing—is that human beings have, largely though not completely, the power to *choose* their own reactions and to *make themselves* more or less effective in their professional and personal lives. One of the main ways that therapists using RET can increase their own knowledge and ability is to study, and do their best to carry into practice, the highly relevant and useful material in this book. Almost any counselor or therapist who takes the book seriously—and himself or herself not *too* seriously!—will benefit considerably from it.

Institute for   Albert Ellis, Ph.D.
Rational-Emotive Therapy

Preface

There are currently many books and articles on rational-emotive therapy (RET). Albert Ellis, the founder and most articulate spokesman of RET, has written or co-authored more than forty books. The majority of these are written for the patient and are useful as self-help manuals. Both clinical reports and some psychological research have indicated that bibliotherapy may often be quite effective for many patients (Ellis, 1977a, 1978b). Often, however, troubled people can use additional processing and rehearsal of the written material in constructive work with a therapist. The present manual is designed as a supplement to the available literature on RET and is directed not at the client but at the RET therapist-in-training.

Explaining the basic principles of RET is not difficult. In outline, the format is simple and the concepts, as articulated by Dr. Ellis, are catchy (e.g., "*Mus*turbation leads to self-abuse!"). After reading *A New Guide to Rational Living* (Ellis and Harper, 1975), one can easily give an engaging lecture. In fact, many patients can give the lecture; however, although they may parrot the principles quite appropriately, they may be unable to apply them consistently to their own problems. Leading a client successfully through the RET maze often sounds a lot easier than it actually is.

We recall our own initial confusions in discriminating rational beliefs from irrational beliefs, in pinning down the specific emotions in the complaints of some clients, in the ease with which we as beginning therapists became mired in slippery disputations. In other words, therapist-client interchanges are not always as clear-cut in an actual therapy session as they are made to seem in texts. The fuzzy predicaments brought in by clients don't seem to follow the scripts.

Over the years, many therapists have come to the Institute for Rational-Emotive Therapy for direct training in RET. Even in the brief but intensive five-day practicum offered by the Institute, significant progress in therapist behavior can be seen from day one to day five as practice therapy tapes are made and supervised. In addition to rehearsal and feedback, a large factor in this therapist behavior change is the influence of a strong oral tradition in RET. Supervisors give their students, who in turn may become supervisors, a wealth of helpful hints in doing RET. As is common in oral traditions, the original source of a hint may be lost but the useful information continues to circulate. Some of the bits of clinical lore in the present manual, for example, have been derived from a legacy left by supervisors such as Bill Knaus, Ed Garcia, Jon Geis, Janet Wolfe, Ginger Waters, Larry Moodie, Howard Kassinove, Bill Golden, Rose Oliver, Albert Ellis himself, and a host of others whom it would take too much space to credit.

The purpose of the present manual, therefore, is to codify some of these traditional oral teachings. We have tried to include many of the common stumbling blocks and basic confusions of the new therapist as reconstructed from our own experience or the experience of helping others. These confusions seem to fall easily into the basic ABC model of RET. So, too, do the battery of hints, aphorisms, examples, explanatory devices, and others which form the bulk of the oral tradition.

We have organized the chapters in this book for easy referencing of therapist problems. For example, patients may present difficulties in focusing on an A (Activating event); they may complain that "everything hurts" or that nothing is wrong but they merely want to become self-actualized. What does the therapist do? Chapter 3 has some helpful suggestions. Perhaps the therapist has identified a "should" but is not sure how best to dispute it; Chapters 6, 7, and 8 may be useful. Thus, at its core, this manual is meant to be a *practical* guidebook—something to reach for when you, as a therapist, feel "stuck."

In writing this manual, we found ourselves confronted with problems of language. Sexist language has been a particularly troublesome issue. We have tried to follow various guidelines for nonsexist language, although occasionally we have settled on the use of "he" or "she" in order to make a point clearly and without unnecessary clumsiness of style. We hope the reader understands that our choice of language does not reflect a sexist bias on our part.

A similar problem arose in choosing a word to identify the consumer of the therapist's services. For political reasons, some individuals object to the term "patient," believing that it is perjorative and labels the individual as sick. The word "client," as an alternative, has not yet received widespread usage. Our solution has been to use both words interchangably, simply for variety in language.

This book focuses primarily on the use of rational-emotive therapy with adults. While RET has effectively been used with children and adolescents, we believe that these populations require special sets of skills and knowledge which are desirable, yet beyond the scope of the present book to teach. If you are already skilled in treating these populations, the present book will be of help to you. If you are not, we strongly recommend that you receive specialized training before working with youngsters or refer these clients to another therapist who is more appropriately trained. Similarly, there are other specialized problems that a general rational therapist will be ill equipped to handle unless he or she has received specialized training. One such specialized area is sexual counseling. The field of sex therapy contains a great deal of information about human sexuality, its function, dysfunction, and treatment. Without this specialized information, the general counselor may be doing clients a disservice by assuming he or she can handle their problems. Again, when you are confronted with a client who presents these kinds of problems, we recommend that you either get specialized training or refer the client to another therapist who has done so.

There are a number of other specialized problems which, while amenable to some mental health interventions, are not well treated with rational-emotive therapy. One population for whom RET is of limited use is the psychotic patient. Rational therapy or any psychotherapy will be unable to overcome, though it may help ameliorate, psychotic processes which may well be a function of biochemical, physiological factors. The psychotic patient, however, may also have neurotic problems or may be emotionally upset about the psychotic process itself. For these problems, rational therapy is indeed useful. Clients with neurological damage are in a similar category. RET will not improve the neurologic impairment, but will help the client cope with it and help him deal with his neurotic problems about this handicap as it would with other kinds of handicaps.

This manual is aimed at practitioners new to RET, but since RET is a broad cognitive-learning therapy, we assume the reader has some knowledge of psychological principles, behavior modification tools, and general counseling skills. Without these, RET, like any other system of psychotherapy, runs the risk of being conducted mechanically—which, although not awful, is probably of less value to the patient.

In any case, if you have not already done so, we encourage you to begin your study of RET by reading the first six chapters in *The New Guide to Rational Living* (Ellis and Harper, 1975) and Ellis' classic text, *Reason and Emotion in Psychotherapy* (1962).

Therapists-in-training at the Institute for Rational-Emotive Therapy tape-record virtually all of their therapy sessions, of course with the client's permission. You, the reader, will be asked to perform many self-checking exercises throughout this book so that in addition to obtaining peer supervision, you will be able to supervise yourself. Therefore, if you are not already in the habit of taping your therapy sessions, *begin now.*

We wish to acknowledge our appreciation to the following people who read and commented on earlier versions of this manuscript: Dr. Albert Ellis, Dr. George Spivack, Dr. Aaron Beck, Dr. Barry Bass, Dr. Morris Roseman, Dr. Lawrence Donner, and graduate and undergraduate students at Towson State University and Hofstra University.

June 1979   S. R. W.
                                               R. D. G.
                                               R. L. W.

Contents

A Practitioner's Guide
to Rational-emotive Therapy

1 Basic Principles of RET and How to Get Them Across

The writings of Albert Ellis (e.g., 1962, 1976, 1978a) encompass three basic areas: rational-emotive *theory*, rational-emotive *philosophy*, and rational-emotive *therapy*. The theory deals with Ellis' conceptions of the causes of human emotions; the philosophy is one of humanistic hedonism and concerns itself with nothing less than the purpose of life; and the therapy is a pragmatic clinical system. We have organized the present chapter according to this tripartite system, turning first to rational-emotive theory.

Rational-emotive Theory

There are three main psychological aspects of human functioning: thoughts, feelings, and behavior. All three aspects are intertwined and interrelated, since changes in one will often produce changes in the others. Thus, if individuals change the manner in which they think about an event, they will most likely feel differently about it and may alter the way they behaviorally react to it. Behavioral psychologies focus on changing environmental contingencies to alter behavior, and cognitive psychologies focus on altering thought content, but few psychologies deal directly with emotions because they are difficult to influence directly. RET theory is perhaps unique in this regard since it takes as its focus the cognitive-emotive interface. Thus, the first and most *basic principle* of rational-emotive theory is that cognition is the most important determinant of human emotion. Simply stated, we feel what we think. Events and other people do not make us "feel good" or "feel bad"; we do it to ourselves, cognitively. Therefore, past or present external events contribute to but do not directly induce or "cause" emotions in us. Rather, our internal events, our perceptions and evaluations of these external conditions, are the more direct and powerful sources of our emotional responses.

A second major principle of rational-emotive theory is that dysfunctional emotional states and many aspects of psychopathology are the result of *dysfunctional* thought processes. The characteristics of dysfunctional thinking include the following: exaggeration, oversimplification, overgeneralization, illogic, unvalidated assumptions, faulty deductions, and absolutistic notions. The term that Ellis uses to describe these cognitive errors is *irrational beliefs*. Ellis has categorized certain irrational beliefs common to our culture, which are hypothesized to account for much emotional disturbance. For example, one widely held belief is that human beings must be loved and approved of by virtually every significant person in their environment (Ellis, 1962, p. 61). This belief is irrational because it is obviously impossible for all significant people to approve of us; there will probably always be someone who does not. Even if we could get everyone to approve of us, we would always have to be concerned with keeping their approval. Thus, the belief in the necessity for others' approval is a direct cause of anxiety.

Most irrational beliefs fall into four basic categories: (1) *awfulizing statements*, which exaggerate the negative consequences of a situation, (2) *shoulds, oughts,* and *musts*, which reflect unrealistic demands on events or individuals, (3) statements of *evaluation of human worth*, either of oneself or others, which imply that some human beings are worthless or of less value than others, and (4) *need statements*, which are arbitrary requirements for happiness or survival. Thus, whenever we are emotionally disturbed, we begin with a wish which gets blocked or thwarted in some way. The wish itself is harmless, but disturbance comes about because the wish becomes escalated into a pernicious demand, which is the root of the disturbance. These demands or commands form the core irrational beliefs and are recognizable by cue words such as "should," "ought," "must," "need," and "have to."

Ellis often leads clients through the following vignette, which illustrates this model of emotional disturbance:

T: Suppose, as you left the house this morning, you said to yourself:
    "I'd like to have $5 with me today. It doesn't have to be any more
    than $5, and it's not that I must have it, but I'd prefer to have that
    much money in my pocket." Then later you check in your pocket
    and find that you have only $4. How do you think you'd feel?
C: Well, disappointed, I suppose.
T: Right! You'd feel disappointment or regret, but you wouldn't have
    to kill yourself over it. Now, suppose instead, when you left the
    house you had said: "I *must* have $5 with me today. It doesn't have
    to be any more than $5, but I've *got to* have that much in my
    pocket *at all times.*" Then later if you reached into your pocket and
    found $4, how do you think you'd feel?
C: I guess I'd be pretty upset.
T: Sure you would, if you didn't have what you thought you MUST
    have. Now, suppose you were still saying you *must* have $5 with
    you at all times, but you reached in your pocket and found $6! How
    do you think you'd feel?
C: Happy. Maybe ecstatic?
T: Yes, you probably would feel happy, but very shortly after, you'd
    feel anxious again. Do you know why?
C: No.
T: Well, suppose you lost $2, or spent $2, or got your pocket picked!
    So you see, you're miserable both ways when you think you MUST
    have something. You're anxious when you don't have it, and anxious
    when you do!

Since the basic notion of rational-emotive theory is that *we feel
what we think*, to break out of an emotional problem, we begin with an
analysis of thought. If distress is a product of distorted thinking, the best
way to conquer distress is to change our thinking.

Another assumption of rational-emotive theory is that *multiple
factors*, including both genetic and environmental influences, are
etiologic antecedents to irrational thinking and psychopathology. While
all human beings probably have a tendency to easily learn irrational
beliefs, as witnessed by the fact that they are so widespread, the culture
in which we live furnishes the specific content that we learn.

Like many contemporary psychological theories, rational-emotive
theory places its emphasis on present rather than historical influences on
behavior. Another tenet of rational-emotive theory, therefore, is that
while hereditary and environmental conditions are important in the

acquisition of psychopathology, they are not the primary focus in under-standing its *maintenance*. People maintain their disturbance by self-indoctrination. The contemporary adherence to irrational beliefs, rather than how they were acquired, is the cause of emotional distress. Thus, if individuals reevaluated their former thinking and abandoned it, their current functioning would be quite different.

Yet another principle of rational-emotive theory is that contemporary *beliefs can be changed*, although such change will not necessarily come about easily. Irrational belief elements are changed by active and persistent efforts to recognize, challenge, and revise one's thinking, thereby reducing emotional distress.

MYTHS AND MISCONCEPTIONS

At this point, we would like to dispel a few of the more common misconceptions of RET. "Rational" does not mean "unemotional"; rational-emotive theory does *not* say that all emotions are to be banned; rather, that it is not inevitable that one feel terribly upset or emotionally disturbed. Even when thinking rationally, the individual may experience discomforting negative emotions, albeit to a more moderate degree. The distinction between the consequences of rational and irrational thinking is reflected in the *frequency, intensity,* and *duration* of the negative affect rather than its presence or absence.

Emotions are important motivators for behavior in general and for behavior *change*. The classic Yerkes-Dodson law, described in most gen-eral psychology texts, attests to the relationship between levels of emo-tion and behavior. When people experience no emotion or, at the other extreme, excessive emotion, behavioral efficiency is lost. For example, the student who is extremely anxious may do poorly on a test; the student who has no concern at all may never be motivated to study and will also do poorly.

Another misconception is that if people do not believe that events are "awful," they will not be motivated to change them. "Rational," however, does *not* mean passive acceptance of events. There are two general kinds of events: those we can possibly change and those we cannot. Accepting an unfortunate reality and not getting overly upset about it implies the following: acknowledging that reality exists, that it *is* unpleasant, and that it would be irrational to *demand* or *insist* that it should not have happened. One can certainly be determined and vigilant in trying to prevent similar events from happening again. When we are feeling upset, however, we may not be very adept at problem solving and may not work effectively at changing our environment.

In summary, the basic principles of rational-emotive theory are as follows:

1. Cognition is the most important, though hardly the only, determinant of emotion.
2. Irrational thinking often produces dysfunctional emotional states.
3. We have a natural tendency to think irrationally and upset ourselves, which gets reinforced by the environment.
4. We perpetuate our own emotional distress by repropagandizing ourselves with our irrational beliefs.
5. The most effective way to reduce emotional distress is to change our thinking and our behavior, a task accomplished by persistence and practice.
6. Rational thinking leads to a reduction in the frequency, intensity, and duration of emotional disturbance, not to flat affect or the absence of feeling.

Rational-emotive Philosophy

The application of rational-emotive theory is based on strong philosophical underpinnings. Ellis has selected a quotation from Epictetus, a Stoic philosopher from the first century A.D., as the starting point of RET:

"Men are disturbed not by things, but by the views which they take of them."

Our view of things is a function of our perception and our evaluation, which in turn reflect our individual value systems. Thus, as in other philosophies, rational-emotive philosophy emphasizes: (1) *epistemol-*

ogy, a theory of knowledge, (2) *dialectics*, the art of reasoning, (3) a system of *values*, and (4) *ethical* principles.

EPISTEMOLOGY

How do we know a thing to be true? What are the most reliable and valid ways of obtaining knowledge? Rational-emotive philosophy suggests that it is through the methods of science that we can best obtain knowledge about the self, others, and the world. Whereas religion typically acknowledges revelation and/or divine inspiration as the sole or most important way of knowing, RET advocates scientific thinking in arriving at conclusions. For every belief expressed by a client, the appropriate RET question is, "Where is the evidence that what you believe is true?" In RET, we seek to make good scientists of our clients so that they can acquire correct information, use evidence logically, and construct sound, self-helping beliefs.

Science starts with questions about what is, and then proceeds to question the relationship between events. Hypotheses are formed to answer the questions, and observation and measurement are conducted to test the hypotheses. If the observations are consistent with the hypotheses, the hypotheses are accepted and we say that we know something to be true. The emphasis on the observable tends to eliminate mysticism and magic. In addition, acceptable observations are to be verified by more than one observer, to eliminate the use of "special powers" of intuition or inspiration.

How, then, do we know a thing to be true? We determine the *probability* of its truth through repeated verification by observable data. Of course, we hope to do more than confirm isolated facts; we hope to build them into a coherent picture or theory of reality. From the theory we can predict new occurrences of the same thing by deducing new hypotheses to fit different circumstances.

We have taken this brief venture into the epistemology of science to show some important characteristics of RET. We want our clients to know that a thing is true, not because of faith in us as surrogate clergy or by virtue of our authority as experts in human relations but because they know how to obtain accurate evidence and think with logic. From such evidence, we hope that they will construct a more realistic picture (or theory) of themselves and of the world in which they live.

DIALECTICS

The art of logical thinking is not easy to acquire; most people seem to be expert at illogic. A typical bit of self-deprecating illogical reasoning goes like this:

I should be perfect.
I just made a horrible mistake.
That proves I'm imperfect and therefore worthless.

Would this reasoning stand up to scientific scrutiny? Not at all. Where is the evidence for the statement, "I should be perfect"? There is none, although there is ample evidence that I, like everyone else, am *im*perfect and thus, in a sense, "should" be imperfect, not perfect.

How about "I just made a horrible mistake"? It can be demonstrated that I made a mistake (although I'd better be careful not to rush to judgment here, for it may be too soon to tell whether it *was* a mistake), but how can I prove that any mistake is "horrible"? How bad does something have to be before it crosses the boundary between extremely bad and horrible?

That I am imperfect is surely proven by my mistake, but does it follow logically, therefore, that I am worthless? Obviously not, although people who are thinking dichotomously will say that it does. In dichotomous thinking there are only two categories, such as "perfect" and "worthless."

Clients are rarely aware of the major premises in their thinking or the syllogistic flow of their thoughts. Most commonly, they focus only on the conclusion—which, if it is illogical, is likely to produce emotional problems. Rational thinking, then, involves logical reasoning from empirically verified or verifiable statements. If we think rationally, we are not likely to reach conclusions that lead to extremely disturbed feelings.

VALUES

Two explicit values in the philosophy of RET are widely held by people but not often verbalized. These two major values are *survival* and *enjoyment*. The ideas one holds can be evaluated against these values in the search for rational thinking. Anything that promotes your survival and happiness can be defined as rational. Anything that works against your survival and happiness is, by definition, irrational. Our commonly held goals, therefore, are to live the only life we are sure of having with as much enjoyment as possible given the limitations of the human body and the physical and social world; to live peacefully within our chosen group; and to relate intimately with certain people of our choosing. These are the explicit values advocated by RET.

ETHICS

Rational-emotive philosophy suggests that dealing fairly with other people can be based upon human reason, anticipating the consequences of our actions. What is ethical, then, is specific to each situation; there are no absolute rights or wrongs. In fact, the self-imposition of absolute rights and wrongs is precisely what leads to guilt, shame, anxiety, and depression, as well as to hostility and intolerance of other people.

Experience shows that if we treat others unfairly (lie, cheat, steal, cruelly criticize, etc.), they will eventually retaliate. What happens is obvious when you examine the norm of fair play (more technically, the "norm of reciprocity"). The norm or unwritten rule is that people shall deal fairly with each other. While it is often difficult to determine what constitutes "fair," people usually have an implicit understanding of what is fair and what is not. If you break this norm, the same social processes are likely to occur as when other norms are broken. First, other people try subtly or directly to influence the norm breaker to conform. This process may include attempts to teach, threats, and even punishment. If the norm breaker continues, he or she will be expelled from the group. Since most of us have as one of our happiness goals that of relating to many people compatibly and to a few people intimately, the threat of rejection is enough to keep us from breaking norms. Thus, it is not in our own best interests to act unfairly, inconsiderately, or selfishly.

Hence, according to the ethical principles of rational-emotive philosophy, it is wrong to exploit and act harmfully toward other people. It is not wrong in an absolute sense, for that smacks of the very dogmatism that RET opposes. It is wrong in the sense that it is wrong for the individual, because it may defeat his or her goals. The ethics that RET advocates are not based upon rigid dogmatism. In fact, RET holds that rigidity, authoritarianism, dogmatism, and absolutism are among the worst features of any philosophic system and are the very styles of thinking that lead to neurosis and disturbance.

RET seeks to help the individual use *reason* in solving ethical dilemmas, to evolve a nondogmatic, nonabsolutistic philosophy of living that is socially responsible. The ethical principles derive from answers to the question, "Will my actions harm other people?" not "Does this act violate some God-given rule?" Ethically responsible acts are both prosocial and proself; that is, they harm neither others nor yourself. In essence, the ethics of RET sound very much like the Golden Rule: Act in ways that set good examples for other people, or do as you would have others do.

RESPONSIBLE HEDONISM

The philosophic stance of RET is frankly hedonistic. However, unlike the blindly compulsive hedonism of the Freudian id, the hedonism of RET is both guided and individualistic. Whereas in the concept of the id we are all driven by the same impulses that originate in bodily processes, in RET, individuals are recognized as enjoying and therefore seeking a wide variety of enjoyable pursuits. Thus, RET does not prescribe *how* to enjoy or *what* to enjoy, but it does hold that enjoyment, along with survival, is a main goal in life.

Hedonism can be thought of as merely seeking pleasure and avoiding pain, but such a principle would not necessarily lead to *continued* enjoyment. If you derive pleasure from something that has harmful side effects, you clearly will not enjoy the pleasure very long. Thus, if you drink or use drugs to excess, you may experience considerable pleasure in the short term but more pain than pleasure in the long term. Because short-term pleasures may actually work against the other main goal, survival, RET often teaches (yes, advocates) moderation.

The term for moderation is *hedonic calculus*, a concept taken from the pragmatic philosophers of the nineteenth century. It is not a true calculus, of course, because no numeric values are assigned to our various pleasurable pursuits. Rather, hedonic calculus refers to the rational habit of asking ourselves whether the pleasure we experience today is likely to backfire in some way tomorrow, next week, or even years from now. Conversely, if we live only for the future, we might pass up a good deal of current enjoyment, and that too would be irrational. So, as you can see, the pursuit of the simple hedonic goals of survival and happiness can be quite complicated. Both immediate gratification and delay of gratification have their advantages and disadvantages. In RET we advocate noncompulsively seeking an optimum solution that sacrifices neither the present nor the future.

There is a special form of hedonism that deserves careful consideration. That is when one avoids present pain, discomfort, and inconvenience and in so doing cuts oneself off from a desirable outcome. A person may want to do something but be unwilling to work toward a long-range goal. In RET, this avoidance is called *Low Frustration Tolerance*, or *LFT*. Clients show it when they refuse to do that which they agree would be beneficial for them, citing reasons such as "It's too hard," "I'd be too scared," or "I can't stand it." LFT is perhaps the main reason that clients do not improve after they have gained an understanding of their disturbance and how they create it.

LFT is a philosophy. It is a personal rule that states, in effect, "I shouldn't have to do anything that is unpleasant or uncomfortable, and I'd sooner maintain the status quo than risk discomfort." While people clearly have a right to live by such a philosophy, it can lead to unhappiness by blocking them from goals they seek to attain.

Does the frank hedonism of RET lead to irresponsibility and anarchy in human relations? No, not if the person has thought through the consequences of his or her behavior—which include getting cut off from future opportunities to pursue happiness. Exploitation of other people is hardly in our long-range best interests.

ETHICAL HUMANISM

In humanism, the reasoning individual is the source of wisdom, not the almighty God. The existence of God is questioned or even denied entirely, since God is not needed to explain the creation of things (that is the job of science), nor is He needed to create an ethical code (for that can be done by clear thinking). Ellis himself is clearly an atheist, and in several articles has postulated that while religion (that is, a philosophy of life) may be rational, religiosity (that is, dogmatic and absolutistic faith unfounded in fact) is not merely the opiate of the masses but a major cause of psychopathology. He contends that it is the acceptance of absolute notions of right and wrong, and of damnation for doing wrong, which leads to guilt, shame, anxiety, and depression, as well as hostility and intolerance toward other people.

While Ellis is an unabashed hedonist, humanist, and atheist, one can retain a form of religion and practice good RET. Many Christian and Jewish clergy do just that, although they do not share Ellis' atheism. It is also not necessary to have clients give up all forms of religious belief, although it is frequently useful for the client to give up the most extreme forms of religious orthodoxy in order to increase enjoyment of life, self-acceptance, and toleration of others.

RATIONALITY AS A PERSONAL PHILOSOPHY

As you can see, when RET practitioners begin to explore a client's belief system, they will encounter some rules of living that the client has been trying to follow. These personal rules or philosophies of living may rest upon parental teachings, religious teachings, widely held common wisdom, or highly idiosyncratic statements about how life should be lived. These rules, because they are dogmatically held, rigidly self-enforced, conflicting, or otherwise maladaptive for individuals, are the basis of their disturbance. When the personal rules of living hinder clients' attainment of the goals of happiness and survival, they are fair game for examination and change.

What the RET therapist hopes to do is to help the client evolve a new philosophy of life, one that will help to reduce emotional distress and lead to an increase in happiness. The therapist holds the view that people are thinking creatures who can either add to their misery with illogical and unscientific thinking or promote their enjoyment with careful reasoning from evidence. The goals of a rational philosophy are to establish beliefs and habits that are congruent with:

Survival

Achieving satisfaction with living

Affiliating with others in a positive way

Achieving intimate involvement with a few others

Developing or maintaining a vital absorption in some personally fulfilling endeavor

RET therapists know and help patients remember that *all* persons are fallible, forever destined to fail and err. They help disturbed people give up their demands for perfection and strive to help them develop constructive self- and other-acceptance. In its best form, this change comes about by scientific/logical thinking which results in deep philosophical/attitudinal change.

Rational-emotive Therapy

The therapeutic system evolved by Ellis over the years is a pragmatic and efficient clinical discipline, useful with moderately dysfunctional neurotic adults, severely disturbed adults, psychotic individuals, and children as young as four to five years. The therapist takes a persuasive, active-directive role, yet patient and therapist share in working toward common goals. In addition, RET uses an educational approach, and as in school, encourages the patient to do reading and homework assignments to help the patient incorporate the therapy into living and enjoyment outside the therapy sessions.

RET does not claim to undo the mental and emotional effects of physiologically induced dysfunctions, such as those attributable to hormonal deficits, seizure states, or psychoses due to biochemical imbalances. Importantly, however, patients often have a neurotic overlay to these problems which *is* amenable to rational-emotive therapy. For example, manic-depressive patients, even when controlled by medications and not in a depressed state, often worry about when their depression will strike again. While RET does not cure psychosis, it may be extremely helpful in dealing with such neurotic problems about being psychotic. When used in conjunction with psychotropic drugs, it may be distinctly valuable in helping to ameliorate psychotic states (Ellis and Abrahms, 1978).

THE ABC MODEL

Ellis has conceived a simple conceptual schema to illustrate the role of thinking processes in emotional disturbance. He calls this schema the *ABC's* of RET. In this system, the A stands for *Activating event* (or Activating experience), which is usually some obnoxious or unfortunate environmental occurrence. C stands for the emotional and behavioral *Consequences*; it is this uncomfortable affective reaction which, in fact, propels the patient to the psychotherapist's office. The B is the patient's *Belief System*. The Belief System consists of two parts: rational and irrational beliefs. It is the latter cognitions which will be the therapist's focus.

Belief systems, and irrational beliefs in particular, will be taken up in detail in Chapter 6, but for now we can summarize them briefly into the three Major Musts:

1. I must do well or get approval (and I'm a worm if I don't).
2. You must treat me nicely and kindly (and you're a louse if you don't).
3. The world must give me what I want quickly, easily, and with great certainty (and it's awful if it doesn't).

These three Musts almost invariably lead not only to the parenthetical evaluations above but to the following derivative cognitions:

Things are awful.

I can't stand it.

I'm (or you're) a rotten person.

Small wonder that anyone uncritically believing these ideas would be upset. Since rational-emotive philosophy assumes that a major goal in life is to live and be reasonably happy, it also assumes that such disturbing cognitions and emotions are incompatible with this goal.

Patients, when they believe that the A event is directly responsible for C, their emotional upsets, are ignoring, or more likely are unaware of the presence and impact of their cognitions, attitudes, philosophies, and beliefs. Patients in psychotherapy are experiencing debilitating and disturbing emotions. Since they are disturbing themselves, presumably they can also refuse to disturb themselves. In other words, the patient has a *choice* of feelings and, perhaps without quite knowing why or how, has decided to suffer. It is a primary task of the therapist to teach the client that his or her psychological problems result from the cognitive processes of misperception and mistaken thinking.

This basic principle, easy enough to state, is often difficult for patients to grasp. Our everyday language is filled with examples antagonistic to this concept. How often do we say or hear phrases such as, *"He* made me so mad!" or *"It* has got me so upset!" More correctly, we could say, *"I* made me mad" and *"I* got me upset." How strange these sound to our ear! Yet the common ingredient in the corrected statements implies an important concept: that we are responsible for our emotions. Thus, emotions are not foisted upon us or injected magically into us, but result from something we actively do. Specifically, emotions result largely from what we tell ourselves. Clients come to therapy firmly believing that A causes C, and this belief is reinforced by virtually every important person with whom they come in contact. You, the therapist, will be teaching quite a revolutionary idea: that B causes C; it is your first teaching responsibility to help your client understand and believe this notion.

TEACHING THE CLIENT THAT EVENTS DO NOT CAUSE FEELINGS

How can the therapist illustrate to clients that internal rather than external factors are primarily affecting their feelings and actions? One way to explain the B-C connection is to ask clients how a hundred people, similar to themselves, would react to their problem. For example, a client has just discovered that his wife would like to get a divorce, and he is very depressed. The therapist would ask him how a hundred men would react to the same event. Clients usually respond with, "Well, most of them would be depressed." (If the client answers, "100 percent," the therapist can point out how unrealistic such an estimate is.) The therapist persists, and asks, "But what percent would be depressed—40, 50, 60 percent?" After the client has answered, the therapist leads the client to examine the other possible reactions that the remainder of the population would have. In this way, the client is faced with the fact, by his own admission, that while possibly 50 percent of the sample might be depressed, some of the remainder would only be sad, others would be a little displeased, some would be neutral, a few relieved, and a small percentage would be downright exuberant. At this point, when other emotional options have been set forth, the client is confronted with the crucial question: "If Activating events (A) do, in fact, cause emotional Consequences (C), then how do you explain that the same event led to so many different emotional reactions within this hypothetical sample?" Most clients respond at this point with something like, "Well, I guess A doesn't really cause C" or "They're all different, so they react differently." The about-to-be-divorced client has given the therapist an opening, for he has mildly and ever so slightly hinted that A did not cause C. The therapist can reinforce the client for this insight and for reaching it on his own and then explain further, "That's correct; they all *are* different; they all reacted differently because they *evaluated* it differently." The therapist has now gotten a foot in the door and can use it to further elaborate on the point.

A story such as the following may help to make the ABC connections clear:

> Suppose you are driving and you come to a red light. Does this make you stop? If red lights make you stop, you would brake at all red lights, not just those in traffic signals. And if all red traffic lights *made* you stop, no one would ever go through them or get traffic tickets for doing so. Do you *always* stop when you come to a red traffic light? No, not always. Perhaps it is the wee hours of the morning and the streets are deserted. Perhaps you are in a great hurry. Perhaps you are driving to the hospital with your wife, whose labor pains are two minutes apart. In other words, red lights do not always make us behave in a predictable fashion. Other factors can intervene, and these are our attitudes or cognitions about the event—the way we interpret it.

TEACHING THE CLIENT THAT OTHER PEOPLE DO NOT CAUSE FEELINGS

Commonly, patients object that other people in their environment do, in fact, cause them to be upset. A popular tune expresses this notion well:

"You made me love you, I didn't want to do it. I didn't want to do it."
How on earth could such an idea be true? If you really didn't want to
love him or her, then you wouldn't, because your thoughts, beliefs, and
attitudes are what cause feelings to occur. There is no way for people to
force you to love them. They might coerce you into *pretending* that you
love, but your evaluations are your own private thoughts which they
cannot magically control. And it is your evaluations of them which
produce the love that you feel—or do not feel.

The use of "experiments" and analogies help to get the point across.
As an experiment, the therapist might suggest the following:

> OK, Marsha, if people can give you emotions, let's see if I can
> do it right now. (pause) Marsha, I really like you and I want you to
> feel good forever. Now—how do you feel?

Analogies such as the following might be useful:

C: She makes me feel so guilty!
T: No, Marsha, they're *your* guilt buttons. She may be pushing on
     them, but you're in charge of the electronic wires. If you learn to
     disconnect them, she could push all she wanted and you wouldn't
     have to respond.

Another way of disputing the notion that other people give us
feelings is to point out the incongruency between this particular irrational belief and another cognition that Americans, particularly religious
ones, usually have: the concept of free will. Most Judeo-Christian reli-
gions train people to believe that human beings are different from the
rest of the animal species because we have intellect and free will, thus
strongly professing "freedom" and "self-determination." The therapist
might ask: "If someone made you angry, you therefore had no say in it.
Well, do you believe in free will and self-determination, or do you
believe in strict determinism?" By phrasing the question in this way,
or in a manner understandable to the client, the therapist can point
out the fact that the individual is holding two contradictory beliefs at
the same time. Sometimes clients believe that they control their own
destiny and behavior and are free human beings, and at other times
they believe that they are pawns and puppets. Which is the truth? Many
individuals in our society have such a strong religious or philosophical

commitment to a sense of free will that they quickly disavow any concept that suggests that they are controlled by others. By consistently pointing up this contradiction to patients whenever they slip into deterministic language, the therapist may help clients to abandon the notion that A directly causes C.

There are a number of other ways of illustrating that the A-causes-C hypothesis is incorrect. Here are some alternate therapist strategies:

T: Well, John, if your father really is the cause of your anger, we'd better terminate therapy. You see, if the cause of the anger is *outside* you, how can I help you? You'd better send your father to me instead, and let me change him!

The following example involves teaching this point to young children:

T: Johnny, it sounds to me like you believe everyone controls you. No matter what happens to you, it's someone else's fault. They make you angry, they make you sad, they make you unhappy. Well, I have a great idea! Why don't we create a Johnny doll? We could probably get Mattel to market it. You know, we have this little doll with a set of remote controls and every time we press a button we can make it happy, we can make it sad, we can make it depressed, we can make it dance or sing. But we control the doll, just like a remote control. Or maybe we can make a puppet and call it a Johnny puppet. Other people pull the strings and Johnny does it. What do you think about these ideas?
C: (laughs) That's funny. But that's not how it is. I don't sound that way!
T: Oh, yes you do. You sound as if you believe you're a puppet and other people control you.

Ed Garcia, formerly co-director of training at the Institute for Rational-Emotive Therapy, uses dramatic procedures to point out to his clients their self-imposed powerlessness:

C: (Complaining about how other people controlled her, made her feel badly, etc.)
T: (Opens desk drawer, pulls out a large box or bag, and hands it to client.)

C: What's this?
T: This is your power. I'm giving it back to you. Obviously you've been walking around without it for a long time. You keep telling me how this person made you angry, and this person made you upset, and this person made you love him, and this person made you this and that. You go on and on telling me how other people are controlling your life. You must have left your power here one day when you ran out in a hurry. I really think you had better take it back now. Maybe you can get some more control over your life.

Once clients grasp the idea that thinking affects what they feel, the corollary task for the therapist is to show them that *changing* this thinking can lead to a change in emotion. Rene Diekstra, an RET therapist from the Netherlands, has pointed out that we often preplan how we will behave in a particular situation. We commonly script our verbal behaviors in everyday life in order to affect *other* people's reactions; we preplan in order to maximize the probability that we will get the reaction we want. This planning is customary and socially acceptable. We rarely spend any time, however, examining and preplanning how we talk to *ourselves.* It might be pointed out to the client that how we speak to ourselves will affect our own reactions as surely as how we speak to others affects their reactions. Similarly, we often ask ourselves, "How can I say this *to him* so that my message will be clear and I will have communicated correctly?" How often do we ask ourselves the same questions about our internal dialogues?

TROUBLE-SHOOTING THE CLIENT'S OBJECTIONS

Not uncommonly, patients find it difficult to understand that the correction of current thinking patterns is a prime focus of therapy. The difficulty arises because many patients believe that their past history causes their present behavior, and thus, they are either helpless to change or must first discover the "roots" of their disturbance. If clients have spent many months or years in a therapy which emphasized this belief, it may take a lot of convincing to disabuse them of this idea. Unfortunately, it is not only former therapy patients who suffer from the belief that the past fixedly determines the present. This misunderstanding of Freudian theory seems to have sifted down through the culture. It is popularized on television and in the movies, and is heard from even very unsophisticated clients.

As part of this therapeutic logjam, clients may believe that change is impossible because of the past. The client might assert, for example, "But I can't change; I've always been that way!" A therapeutic challenge would then involve correcting the client's language and thereby the concept. For example:

> You mean you haven't changed *so far*. Even if that's been true up to now, does that mean you won't change tomorrow? That's my business, you know—showing you how to change.

Depending on the sophistication of the client, the therapist may also wish to discuss the literature on early influences on development in order to present some scientific data. Few studies show any specific personality traits that are unchangeable, yet the client who firmly believes that he or she *cannot* change may be stating a self-fulfilling prophecy, which ironically will be self-defeating. Analogies might be instructive:

T: If you go into a ball game believing "I can't win, I can't win, I can't win," you'll find that attitude very self-defeating. If you go into therapy believing "I can't change—my early experiences fixed me permanently," that's also self-defeating and you may not change.

If clients insist that they need to discover the roots of their pathology by recalling the factors that have shaped their lives, the therapist can point out that recall is never accurate; it is a reconstructive rather than a reproductive process. Cognitive psychologists such as Neisser (1967) have indicated that our memory processes do not work like copy machines which take pictures of events and file them away for review. In effect, if an event occurred ten years ago, the way we remembered it a year later, five years later, and then today will all be different recollections of memory and will be a function of the present environmental, cognitive, and emotional experiences we are having at the time of recall. Thus, the basic hypothesis that one can search for past events, recall them accurately, and use these recollections to rearrange the personality is incorrect.

A useful challenge to the notion that the past determines present distress is to point out that although past events may have had an important role in contributing to past distress, they *continue* to be a problem only because the client continues to think about them in the same way. It is present cognitions, not past events, which affect us. Thus, although your mother may have worked hard to convince you that you were a worthless no-goodnik, it is only because you continue to take her seriously *today* that you upset yourself with this notion. Merely leaving home will never solve the problem, because you'll figuratively take your mother with you wherever you go unless you dispute your irrational thinking. Thus, if clients believe they are no good, and believe they hold this opinion because it was taught to them, the therapist might respond with questions such as:

And you believed it?

Why did you believe it?

If you were told so today, would you believe it?

The important point, therefore, is that past beliefs continue to be a problem because patients *currently reindoctrinate* themselves with these beliefs. An analogy such as the following might be useful to teach this point:

Suppose you had learned to play basketball very well in high school, but did not play again for twenty years. If you then went out on the court to play again, you wouldn't play basketball very well at all. You would have lost a lot of the skills because you hadn't practiced them, right? It's the same with being neurotic. If you learned to think irrationally when you were young, and didn't practice it for twenty years, then right now you wouldn't be all that neurotic. But you keep practicing it over and over again, reindoctrinating yourself, and that's what keeps you so *good* at being neurotic!

SYMPTOM STRESS

A unique aspect of rational-emotive therapy is its focus not only on the ABC structure of emotional distress but on the client's ability to upset himself about being upset. Frequently, emotions or behaviors which would be classified under C themselves become new A's. Essentially, clients watch themselves behaving ineptly and then "put themselves down" for this ineptitude. To illustrate, consider the following cycle:

Activating Event (A) = Client's mother kept bitterly complaining about the client's behavior.

Rational Belief (RB) = I wish she wouldn't act that way.

Irrational Belief (IB) = Since I don't like it, she *shouldn't (must not)* do it, and she's a bitch for acting that way.

Emotional-Behavioral Consequences (C) = Feeling angry at mother and yelling at her.

↓

Next Activating Event (A_2) = The client's anger and yelling.

Next Rational Belief (RB_2) = I wish I were better at "keeping my cool."

Next Irrational Belief (IB_2) = I *should (must)* be able to "keep my cool," and *I'm* a bitch for blowing up like that at my mother.

Next Consequence (C_2) = Anger at self or feelings of shame.

Clients will often become anxious about their anxiety attacks, depressed about their depressions, angry at their temper tantrums, and generally give themselves problems about their problems. We refer to these as *symptom stress*. It is important for the therapist to deal with these second-level symptoms first, for the added layer of distress will prevent the client from working most efficiently on the basic ABC. (Second-level symptoms will be discussed more fully in subsequent chapters.)

EXPANDING THE ABC MODEL

The ABC model of RET helps to explain to clients the source of their emotional distress; in its expanded form, an *ABCDE* model, it illustrates how they can reduce this distress. D stands for *Disputation*, in which clients learn to challenge and debate with themselves, cognitively and behaviorally, about their own irrational thinking. When successful, then at E they will experience a new Effect—a more rational philosophy and a level of affect which is compatible with effective problem solving. Thus, the RET therapist works not only at helping change beliefs but also at helping change activity, and often makes use of behavioral homework assignments to accomplish both ends.

Once clients have mastered a disputation and developed a more rational coping philosophy, there may still be work to be done; unpleasant activating events may remain to be confronted. Even when clients are not disturbing themselves, they will probably be less happy when unpleasant activating events frequently impinge on their life space. Since the therapist cannot insure that clients will always live in a stress-free environment, however, the preferred strategy is to first teach them how to cope with their unpleasant environment. As long as they remain upset, their problem-solving skills will tend to be adversely affected, and their ability to get what they want will be impaired. When disturbance is reduced, interventions can focus on teaching clients how to choose or change their environments to minimize aversive conditions.

Ultimately, of course, a goal of therapy is to have patients learn to be their own therapists. It is with these skills that patients can decide and implement the decision to not upset themselves. We now move on to discuss how one teaches the ABC's of RET.

New therapists often ask whether it is necessary to teach the ABC's directly to the patient or to include these in the active therapeutic vocabulary. The answer is that it is not necessary to do so, but it may be highly desirable, since the patient may use this clear conceptual schema in order to do structured cognitive homework assignments and to aid him in generalizing beyond the course of therapy. Some experienced RET therapists, including Ellis, occasionally or often omit these descriptive devices. For the *new* practitioner, however, we strongly recommend the formal adoption of the ABC system for use in listening, speaking, and teaching work with clients.

Appendix

As an overview of the basic tenets of RET, we include a highly condensed version of a therapeutic demonstration given by Dr. Albert Ellis at one of the Institute's five-day practicum courses. The client was a young professional who attended the course and wished to discuss the difficulties of beginning a new practice. In outline, A = wanting to try new professional activities, such as giving workshops, and C = inertia. The therapist asked the client what she was saying to block herself; the response was:

C: I might flub it.
T: And what would that do?
C: People might think I'm a crummy teacher.
T: And that would do what?
C: I wouldn't like it.
T: Just *that* evaluation wouldn't make you upset.
C: I can't stand it.
T: Why can't you stand their thinking you're a lousy teacher?
C: (long silence) . . . I think I have to be a good teacher in their eyes.
T: And why *must* you be a good teacher in their eyes? I'm a scientist—prove it (grinning).
C: (long silence)
T: As long as you believe that *must*, how will you feel?
C: Anxious.
T: *Must* they all like you?
C: No.
T: Then why must—
C: Because I want them to!
T: Whatever I want, I *must* get? Where will *that* command get you?
C: Scurrying around—
T: Right! Anxious, depressed. Now suppose you *get* it—they all adore you. You know you'll still be in trouble? (pause) How do you know you'll get it the next time? Aren't you asking, *demanding* for guaranteed adoration?
C: Hmmmm. Yes.
T: You'll be anxious as long as you believe that. How could you *not* believe that? How could you get so that you desire, but you don't *need* their approval?

C: Give some workshops?

T: Take some risks, right. What else? (pause) "If they don't approve, I could stand it. What would that make me as a human if they don't like my teaching?" Suppose you're just lousy at giving workshops? Too bad! Can you be a happy human even if certain things you want you don't get?

C: Ye-s-s-s-s-s (tentatively)

T: See how mildly you said that? How could you say that even stronger? (models): "Goddamn it! I'm determined not to put myself down even if I *never* do many things well!" Rating yourself as OK is also wrong. Why are you OK? Proving you are OK is just as impossible, empirically, as proving that you are a bad person. "I am I. Nancy. Now how the hell do I *enjoy myself* without trying to *prove myself*?" You see, you can choose not to label yourself at all. You don't need a grade for yourself—a continual report card. You can rate your behaviors in the workshop, because it will be pleasurable to do well.

2 Therapist Strategies: The Basic Dos and Don'ts of Doing RET

Beginning the Work with a Client

A profitable question to ask new clients before beginning therapy is whether they have been to previous therapists. One benefit is that the therapist can assess the client's expectations of therapy. A positive expectancy increases the chances of a positive therapeutic effect, while incongruency between the client's expectations and the therapist's view of therapy decreases therapeutic efficacy and increases the dropout rate (O'Leary and Borkovec, 1978). It is helpful, therefore, for the therapist to take time to outline what is expected from the client (e.g., keeping appointments on time, doing homework) as well as what the client can expect from the therapist (e.g., introducing the client to the therapist's cognitive-behavioral model of therapy). This explanation is best given during the first session, usually after the client has presented some major problem(s).

Patients often view therapy as "pouring your heart out" to the doctor and getting sympathy. Although such a procedure may provide some relief in the manner of a confession, it is a palliative solution, for the patients will not have taken the important step of understanding that they are responsible for their own emotions. It is often quite important, therefore, especially for the new client, for the therapist to describe what therapy is like and what procedures will be taken.

T: I'll be showing you how you can control many bad feelings and emotions. I'll be doing that by pointing out some of your misperceptions, asking you to reevaluate some of your perceptions of the world, correcting some of your belief systems, giving you homework assignments to help you change your thinking or your problem behavior, and asking you to read books and listen to tapes. Your active role in therapy is what is *most* important for you to reap the most benefit. I'm a therapist, not a magician. I can help you and I can advise you, but you will do the work.

A second benefit to knowing about previous therapy is that it may help the therapist to avoid unnecessary mistakes. As a rule of thumb, don't do something that a previous therapist has already tried unsuccessfully, or, at least, present it differently. If the therapist who used the technique was not skilled at it, it may be possible to use it again; to avoid an expectation of failure by the client, change its label. So, be sure to ask: "What did you do with your former therapist? What do you think helped you?" and "What do you think wasn't helpful?" Occasionally, the client will report, "The other therapist never talked about what was really bothering me." This may give the therapist a good opportunity to ask, "What was that?" If the client replies, for example, "I was raped when I was fourteen," the therapist may respond: "Then let's talk about that. It seems a good place to begin."

RET, like behavioral therapies, is problem-oriented, and this focus may be communicated to the patient in the early exchanges with the therapist. The therapist may say, for example, "You say that you've been feeling depressed lately. Let's find out what's going on there." If the patient has listed a number of areas of difficulty, the therapist may simply ask: "Which problem would you like to begin to talk about?" In succeeding sessions, the therapist can begin by asking, "What problem would you like to work on today?" or "Last week, we were discussing such-and-such a problem; how have you been working on that this week?" Opening remarks such as these are preferable to more general questions (e.g., "How was your week?") because they set the problem-oriented tone and help keep the sessions focused.

Many RET therapists attempt, even during the first session, to help the patient learn to conceptualize his problems in RET terms: to uncover some of the irrational ideas which are causing the troublesome behaviors and emotions, and to help the client begin to discover what he is doing to disturb himself. Ellis himself is particularly active and directive in his initial sessions with patients. Perhaps because of his temperament, his many years of clinical experience, his eminence in the field, and his diagnostic acumen, Ellis sets a fast pace which many new RET therapists assume they must follow. Such an assumption would be incorrect, however, since the novice may not be able to replicate Ellis' performance, nor may it always be desirable. Other RET therapists have different yet effective styles.

The best rule, perhaps, is for the therapist to recall his own first session with a psychotherapist or, if he has not had this experience, to try to put himself in the patient's shoes. Imagine coming into new surroundings, facing a complete stranger, and then trying to discuss your most difficult or embarrassing problems. What would you be feeling just then, and would that emotion be compatible with open discussion?

Self-disclosure is a prerequisite for psychotherapy, yet self-disclosure of the sort and extent necessary for psychotherapy is considered inappropriate behavior in most social situations. Clients may, therefore, not be accustomed to self-disclosure or may not know how to do it. In many families there is little talk of emotions and thinking, so that previous modeling may be lacking. Also, the self-disclosure which is required for therapy may be suppressed by fear. For children and adolescents, self-disclosure may be particularly difficult. It is often not until late adolescence, when close friendships or love bonds develop, that children begin sharing personal secrets.

Psychotherapists frequently fail to recognize this discrepancy in expectations for self-disclosure. Some therapists expect their patients to freely discuss their personal problems, while the patient may have quite a different agenda. Failure to self-disclose may be viewed by some therapists as resistance or deep psychological disturbance, but we suggest that you avoid such preconceptions. Be willing to consider multiple hypotheses—specifically, that problems in self-disclosure may also be a result of a repertoire deficit or suppression by fear.

If self-disclosure is initially absent, make use of encouragement and example. Encourage the client whenever he or she self-discloses and show by your own self-disclosure that it is safe and desirable. In addition, the therapist would do well to allow an adequate chance for reduction of the fear to take place; this will be difficult if the therapist is too active and appears to be impatient.

Relax. It is not necessary to solve the patient's problems right away. In order to assess the problems, take some time to get to know the client and sample his or her thinking. The patient is more likely to discuss personal problems if he or she believes that the therapist is truly interested in listening. So, for the new RET practitioner who has had only the model of Dr. Ellis to follow, a warning: sometimes it is better to slow down and let the client talk.

> As an active-directive therapist, you may occasionally find yourself feeling uncomfortable in this initial role; you may feel impotent if the cues to the client's irrational beliefs are weak or initially absent. In this case, you may profitably turn to your own cognitive structure. Are you upsetting yourself by *demanding* that the client "open up"? Are you harboring the irrational notion that the patient *must* get better—and *swiftly*?

Discomfort in self-disclosure may be particularly evident if patients view their problem behaviors as socially unacceptable. Issues such as homosexuality, promiscuity, even suicide may fall into this category. The therapist may have to spend a number of sessions establishing a climate of trust before such problems are brought up. Alternatively, clients may repeatedly work on "easy" problems for most of the therapy session and, just when time is up, "casually mention" an emotionally charged issue. With patience, encouragement, and gentle confrontation, the client will usually shorten these hesitancy delays across sessions.

Thus, in RET, the development of a good rapport between patient and therapist may be an important ingredient in maximizing therapeutic gains. What qualities can the therapist project to build rapport? Below we list some therapist characteristics defined by Rogers (1951) and Carkhuff (1969). Each is followed by a description of how these attitudes are communicated by the RET therapist.

1. *Empathy*. Empathy is the ability to perceive accurately what another person is experiencing, and to communicate your perception. The empathic therapist will be attuned not only to the words of the

clients but to the nonverbal aspects of their behavior in order to perceive accurately their feeling state. By return communications, the empathic therapist lets the clients know that he or she is aware of the clients' positive feelings and emotional discomforts.

The empathic *RET therapist* lets clients know that he or she understands not only what the clients are feeling but also what they are *thinking*. For example:

T: It sounds like you're really unhappy, and you're thinking it would be awful if you *did* fail.

When both the thought and the emotion are reflected, the client has an option to begin dealing with either; emotive reflecting alone, however, precludes this option. Often clients are startled by such dual reflections and appear amazed that the therapist has "read their mind."

2. *Respect.* Respect is evident when the therapist indicates a deep and genuine acceptance for the worth of the clients, separate and apart from their behavior. The mere fact of the clients' existence justifies this respect. The therapist respects the right of clients to make their own decisions, even if they are in error, for much can be learned from failure. As a respectful therapist, you are neither rejecting nor overprotective. Instead, you foster client independence, self-confidence, and self-reliance.

The *RET therapist* shows clients that they can be respected despite their disagreement with the therapist over certain philosophical issues. Thus, the RET therapist clearly discriminates between the clients and their dysfunctional thoughts and behaviors.

3. *Warmth.* Warmth is communicated to the client by appropriate use of touching, smiles, and other nonverbal gestures of appreciation, as well as by positive comments of concern and affection for the client.

The *RET therapist* also demonstrates concern and caring for the client in some of the following ways: by carefully attending to the client's behavior, by frequent questions for clarification or therapeutic intervention, by recall of personal details about the client and his or her problem, by use of gentle humor, and by quick, active attempts to help the client solve difficult issues.

4. *Genuineness.* To be genuine, do not be phony or try to play roles. Make your verbal and nonverbal behaviors congruent. Your be-

havior in the counseling relationship need not be dramatically different from that outside the relationship.

As an *RET therapist*, you construe your role in much the same way but are likely to go a step further. Active confrontation requires genuineness, and genuineness, in turn, requires honesty. Thus, the RET therapist is likely to openly disagree with the client, to directly ask for clarification when confused, and to respond to client questions with no hesitation.

5. *Concreteness*. Concreteness refers to specificity in the therapist's work on the patient's problems. Attention to detail is evident; the therapist will ask for concrete details (the what, why, when, where, and how) of the patient's experience. Concrete therapists often ask for specific examples and lead the client through a comprehensive examination of these situations.

The *RET therapist* agrees, and places importance on concrete details of the patient's *perceptions, cognitions,* and *emotions.* Do not encourage the client to supply details only about external circumstances (A), but focus primarily on the belief system.

6. *Confrontation*. Confrontations are used when the therapist detects discrepancies (a) between what the clients are saying and what they have said before, (b) between what the clients are communicating verbally and nonverbally, and (c) between the way the clients view their problem and the way the therapist views it. Confrontations take courage, yet are among the most powerful and valuable tools of the therapist. For example, the therapist might say: "You say you aren't angry, Mary, yet you are sitting there with your fists clenched!" Or: "You say you have no problems, Fred, but what are you doing here in jail?"

Carkhuff (1969) has outlined various levels of confrontation strategies, ranging from very mild to frontally assertive. The *RET therapist*, however, typically operates at the top of this hierarchy, at the most direct levels. This decision is based on a number of theoretical assumptions: (a) there is no concept of "readiness" of the client for confrontations or insights, as in other therapies; (b) by confronting clients with aspects of their behavior that are not in their awareness, problems can be quickly brought into focus; and (c) clients are unlikely to be devastated by confrontations and do not need to be overprotected. Thus, by confrontations, the RET therapist adds to his or her expressions of respect for the client. However, we advise that a good working relationship be established before confrontations at the top of the hierarchy are used.

Three additional qualities that are important in building rapport are self-disclosure, the use of humor, and an active-directive style. *Self-disclosure* brings human sharing to the communication. Therapists can expose their own thoughts, ideas, feelings, and attitudes at special times for the benefit of the client. For example, the therapist might say: "I know what you are going through, Joe. As a matter of fact, some years ago I went through the same thing, and here's how I dealt with it." The therapist model, in such instances, may provide hope since the therapist is suggesting that he or she has known a similar problem and success-fully grappled with it. Thus, the therapist can model rationality, demon-strating appropriate thinking and behavior in dealing with a specific problem. In addition, the therapist is modeling self-disclosure itself, and thereby demonstrating trust in the client; this behavior reverses the typical one-way street of therapy. Self-disclosure is useful, however, only when it is relevant; the therapist may check on relevancy by asking himself, "What is the payoff for the client from this self-disclosure?" Keep in mind, in addition, that the rationale for self-disclosure is primar-ily the building of rapport and modeling of cognitive and behavioral strategies.

In addition, RET therapists are encouraged to develop and utilize a healthy *sense of humor*. Obviously, the patient is never the butt of a joke, but by gently poking fun at the irrational beliefs or events which the patient views as catastrophies, the therapist may put problems into a more realistic perspective. A few small examples of the use of humor in RET may be instructive:

T: You seem to have a healthy case of perfectionism. It doesn't do you much good, but it's nice to know it's well developed!

In attempting to point out a client's demandingness, the therapist may suggest: "You seem to be using the Reverse Golden Rule. Remember the Golden Rule? Do unto others as you would have them do unto you? The Reverse Golden Rule says others should do unto me as I do unto them!"

As Ellis (1977d, p. 269) has pointed out, "A sense of humor, in itself, will not cure all emotional problems. But the refusal to take any of the grim facts of life *too* seriously largely will."

Many therapists believe that being *active and directive* is incompatible with the development of rapport; we disagree. Remember that the basis for the therapeutic relationship is not friendship but professional competence, credibility, respect, and commitment to help the client change. Thus, rational therapists are not friends to their clients, although they could be, but rather concerned professionals. Rapport, therefore, *can* be developed when the therapist behaves directively. This point was particularly evident to us while co-leading psychotherapy groups with Dr. Ellis. As directive as he is, the group members frequently reported feelings of warmth and respect toward Al. When questioned by us, group members reported that he demonstrated his caring by his many questions, his complete attention to their problems, advocating an accepting and tolerant philosophy, and teaching them something immediate that they could do to reduce their pain.

A special problem in the development of rapport occurs in working with children and adolescents. These clients are usually not self-referred and have often been dragged into therapy by their parents. Children are not aware of the role of a psychologist, and sometimes do not even understand why they are seeing one. While the pace of therapy may be slower with children, the same directive, honest approach is recommended.

The first step in developing a rapport with clients in these age groups is to provide the youngster with information concerning the professional's role. Many children believe that since you are a doctor, you're going to jab them with needles, drill their teeth, or do the kinds of painful things which other doctors have done to them. Other children believe that only "crazy people" go to a "shrink" and refuse to cooperate because doing so would be an admission of such a diagnosis. Still other children believe you are a sort of super-disciplinarian whom their parents consult to determine the appropriate punishment for their misdeeds.

One can end some of these misconceptions by the following types of comments:

T: Johnny, I'm a psychologist. Do you know what that is?
C: No—well, the kinda doctor for crazy people?
T: Well, that's not totally true. Psychologists are doctors who study how people learn things and who help people learn things they have

been unable to learn. For example, some people have trouble learning to read and some psychologists help them learn to read better. Other children are anxious or depressed and haven't learned not to be. Psychologists help them learn not to be depressed. We help children with other problems like fears, anger, bed-wetting, and making friends. Do you understand?

C: Yes.

T: Well, what problem could I help you with?

Note that, first, a problem-solving tone is set, and second, the participants' roles are defined clearly. The child is not misled into believing that the therapist is a friend who is going to just play with him or her. Such deceptions are unfortunately common among child therapists, and while this is not done with malice, the net effect may be eventual loss of the child's trust.

Establishing the Problem Areas

To begin the work of rational-emotive therapy, much of the information other therapists look for is unnecessary. Background information is useful, but following a rigid pattern of elaborate history taking before initiating therapy may reduce client rapport. Some patients will feel threatened by so much self-disclosure; others believe that much of the material is irrelevant and that the therapist is wasting valuable time that could be used to help them. If patients are fearful and uneasy about exposing their real problems, they are just as likely to hide them during an extensive assessment as a shorter one. Patients will best be served by having the therapist work efficiently on an issue that they *are* willing to discuss, while transmitting nonjudgmental acceptance in the hope that they will come to view the therapist as a competent and trustworthy person to whom they can divulge their "secrets." Thus, you do not need to wait for the *"real* problem" or a list of *all* the problems to begin the work of therapy. Take whatever activating event or emotional consequence the patient is willing to present and use it to teach the ABC model. In this way, the patient will receive some help while being educated about RET theory.

Since RET is a cognitive therapy, it is to the therapist's advantage to assess some of the cognitive functioning of the client. A formal psychological assessment battery is recommended for most children but is not considered essential for adults. There may be some cases involving adults, however, in which a more formalized testing may be helpful in attaining information on cognitive functions. Cognitive deficits may have a neurological basis which may be responsible not only for the psychological problems but social skill deficits as well. This neurological base may often go unnoticed unless careful detective work and psychological testing are used. It might be wise for the RET therapist to keep in mind that George Gershwin spent years in psychoanalysis for the treatment of headaches and died of a brain hemorrhage.

Good diagnosis is the first step in good treatment. In RET, the major diagnosis focuses on identifying the dysfunctional belief systems which produce uncomfortable emotions, but diagnoses of other problems are also important in treatment. From the first session on, the therapist will be building up a picture of the patient's current level of functioning by amassing pieces of information about the client's life. Some of this information may have been gathered by a biographical data form or other pencil-and-paper measures, but much of it will emerge more informally in the interviews.

In addition to doing an ABC analysis of the patient's cognitive system (as described in the succeeding chapters), the therapist will want to do a careful behavioral analysis of the major problems. Good detective work is often required to establish the *antecedents* and *consequences* of specific target behaviors. For example, if the patient is requesting help with obesity, the RET therapist may follow behavior therapy prescriptions and request that the patient keep data on the following: where and when he ate, what he ate, his mood when eating, his thoughts when eating, and the immediate consequences (internal and environmental) of eating. The role played by significant others in the patient's life may also be important: does the obese patient's wife encourage him to eat second helpings? What motivates her behavior? What would it mean to her if her husband shed weight?

What kind of information is obtained in a behavioral analysis? Let's consider what you would want to ascertain about the agoraphobic as an example: How many times does the client go out of the house each week? Where does she go? Where is she willing to go? Where is she not willing to go? How far can she go? What happens to her when she tries to go out? Who buys her clothes? Who buys the groceries? What if a store had a sale; then could she go? Can she go to the movies or theatre? What happens when she tries to do these things? What is she afraid of? What would happen to her if she did try to go out? These are just samples of *some* of the questions one might ask.

Goals of Therapy

Within the first few sessions, the RET therapist will try to establish with the client the goals of therapy. Implicit or preferably explicit agreements will be made with the patient so that both parties will be able to determine when and if therapeutic progress is made. In fact, frequent reassessment of these agreed-upon goals encourages not only therapist responsibility but client involvement and commitment to the process.

A verbal commitment to goals also enables the therapist to refer back to them when the client is "goofing." For example:

T: By not doing X, aren't you hindering yourself from getting what you set out to achieve?

or

T: How can you accomplish your goal of marriage, Sam, if you don't go out and meet people?

Most therapists follow a professional code of ethics, which implies that they are there to help the client change what he wants to change. The therapist is not there to stamp out all irrational beliefs clients may have, but to work on their problems as their consultant. The therapist may see that clients have major problems which they haven't brought up, and may want to discuss them with the client: for example, "John, I think you have some other problems which you haven't brought up, and here's the reason why I think we'd better work on these." The ultimate decision, however, rests with the client. The first order of business, therefore, is: "What is it you want to work on? How can I help you?"

In addition to establishing long-range goals for therapy, we also recommend that you establish weekly treatment-plan goals. At the end of each session, you can review each of the problem areas listed, determine what the next step will be in working on the problem, remind yourself to check up on the progress of older problems, and outline the goals for the subsequent session. The use of formal treatment plans is taken up in greater detail in Chapter 12.

3 Getting at the A

Identifying the A

When patients describe a troublesome event in their lives, the therapist can think of it as containing three elements: (1) what happened, (2) how the patient *perceived* what happened, and (3) how the patient *evaluated* what happened. The first two elements are aspects of the A, the Activating Event; the latter relates to the client's belief system. For example, if at A the patient reports, "She said a horribly critical thing to me," the patient is confusing all three elements. The issue of what actually happened involves an objective description of what was said and the tone and manner in which it was said. That the comment was a criticism may be a perceptual issue, and whether criticism need be viewed as horrible is an evaluative issue.

We are making a distinction, therefore, between objective reality and perceived reality. *Perceived reality* is reality as clients describe it and as they presumably believe it to be. *Confirmable reality* refers to a social consensus of what has happened. If it were possible for many observers to have witnessed the same event, and they all described it the same way, we would have obtained confirmable reality. In our example above, if a group of people had heard the exact words and the manner in which they were said to our client, and a high percentage of the onlookers perceived the event as an insult, we would conclude that in confirmable reality our client had indeed been insulted.

A further distinction we are making is between two types of cognitions. The perceived reality entails clients' *descriptive* cognitions about what they perceive in the world. Rational and irrational beliefs are *evaluative* cognitions about descriptions of reality. To avoid confusion, realize that the term "belief" or "believe" is commonly used in our language to refer to both descriptive cognitions and evaluative cognitions. Here we shall use the term "belief" to refer only to evaluative cognitions, that is, rational and irrational beliefs. It will become clear in the next several chapters that it is important to make a distinction between these two types of cognitions when the word "belief" is used by the client.

In effect, therefore, the ABC model of RET can be expanded at this point as follows:

A (confirmable)—the activating event as it could be validated by a group of observers
A(perceived)—what clients perceive has happened; that is, their subjective description of it
B—the clients' evaluation of what they perceived
C—the emotional and behavioral consequence

For example, a male client may present a problem of depression because nobody in his office likes him. Further questioning reveals that co-workers interact primarily about business matters, that they infrequently chat or invite him to lunch, and when they do, he refuses. Thus:

A(confirmable):   "Few people ask me to lunch or attempt to socialize with me."
A(perceived):   "I think that no one likes me."
B: "It's terrible and awful that no one likes me!"
C: Depression

A crucial distinction for the new RET practitioner to understand at this point is that the client's *perception* of the activating event does not in itself cause upsetting emotional reactions. In the example above, clients could conclude that no one in their office liked them, yet not upset themselves about that perception. How would they do so? By choosing not to *evaluate* the A as something terrible. Thus, if at B they believed that not being liked was merely unfortunate or perhaps (less probably) that not being in the social circle had certain advantages, they could, at C, feel quite differently about the situation. Thus, although the perception of A does not cause C, the client who misperceives the A *and* holds irrational evaluative beliefs is more likely to be upset than the client who is merely irrational at B. Thus, the client who thinks that almost everyone dislikes him or her and who irrationally evaluates that as terrible will be upset more often than the client who does not make that interpretation of reality yet who also evaluates social disapproval as awful. The first client has more cues to set off his or her irrational thinking.

The client who thinks rationally at B, but who continues to distort reality at A, will not be terribly upset but, according to rational-emotive theory, can still experience negative affect. Let's return to the example above. If the client now believes that it's not awful but merely unfortunate that people at the office don't like him, he will still experience a negative emotional response, such as displeasure or disappointment. Thus, the cognitive element of the A does have an effect on the C, albeit a less significant one. Therapeutic work on these cognitive distortions is therefore an appropriate endeavor.

Before going on, we encourage you, the reader, to test your understanding of the crucial distinction between A and B. Examine the following client statements. For each, underline the activating event and circle the evaluative component (Answer Key is on p. 285):
1. "I did poorly on that exam. Oh, I'm such a failure!"
2. "No one talks to me. I just can't stand being so alone!"
3. "My mother's always picking on me. I know she hates me!"
4. "Doctor, the most terrible thing happened last week. My wife told me she wanted a divorce."
5. "I ate like a pig! You see, I know now that I'm really no good."
6. "I only make $30,000. Do you call that success? How can I be satisfied with that?"
7. "I had a marvelous time with George. It makes me feel so important that he loves me."

What are the options available to the therapist if both types of cognitions (distorted descriptive cognitions and irrational evaluative cognitions) are presented by the client? Two strategies are frequently recommended. Some cognitive therapists, such as Aaron Beck (1976, 1978), would begin by challenging the accuracy of the patient's perception of A. So, if a male client stated that nobody liked him, Beck would challenge the accuracy of this statement, calling into question the word "nobody" and the criteria the patient uses to determine how others feel about him. As he has escalated his belief in this unexamined A, the patient has presumably escalated his evaluation of its terribleness.

As you can see, Beck's assumption is that the work of cognitive therapy is accomplished by first tackling the distortions of A. Ellis (1977a, 1979a), however, refers to these attempts to correct perceptions of A as the empirical or "inelegant solution." He considers it inelegant because this strategy does not provide the patient with a coping technique to deal with his distress should reality ever match or approach his distorted version of it. For example, although unlikely, it is entirely possible that our client above may indeed find himself in a social environment in which no one likes him. He would be prepared to endure such a fate if in fact he believed it to be only unfortunate.

The rational-emotive school of thought suggests that the more elegant solution is to enable the client to assume the worst and not upset himself even if it were true. If the client insists that no one likes him, Ellis might say something like: "Well, we don't know if that's true, but let's just assume for the moment that it is. What do you tell yourself about that?" The assumption in this therapeutic approach is that if the client can deal with this distorted view of A, dealing with the reality will be even easier.

Which is the better way to proceed? There are no empirical answers since the crucial experiments have not been done. In addition, the question itself is perhaps misleading since both Ellis and Beck ultimately do lead the client through an assessment of the accuracy of A.

If the therapist elects to challenge the perception of A as an initial maneuver, we recommend that this be done thoughtfully. Some clients may react to an early challenge by feeling threatened, misunderstood, or unsupported by the therapist. Although these untoward reactions themselves reflect irrational beliefs and may be "grist for the RET mill," they may also weaken therapist-patient rapport.

In summary, the RET practitioner believes that assuming the worst and aiming for an elegant solution is valuable since, in real life, the A situation for the patient may worsen and new difficulties (new A's) arise. Consequently, we recommend that the new practitioner follow Ellis' model, reserving the challenge to the patient's perception of A until some work on disputation has been done. Some helpful hints on how to challenge A are found in Chapter 10.

Clarifying the A

UNNECESSARY DETAIL ABOUT THE A

As we stated in Chapter 1, patients typically come to therapy because they are upset in some way (C) and believe that they are upset because of some event (A). Usually patients have little difficulty in describing A and often want to spend a great deal of time sharing the details of the event with the therapist. Elaborate detail about the A is unnecessary, however, since the focus of therapy will be on B, the Belief system. Communicating this focus without appearing to be disinterested or un-sympathetic may occasionally be difficult, particularly with clients who have an expectation that it is appropriate to present elaborate detail about their past. Historical A's can never be changed, of course; only the client's evaluations of them are available for discussion, and evaluations can be presented succinctly.

The ability to speak succinctly is a problem for many patients; they tend to get lost in details of the A, as in the following example:

T: Well, Joe, what were you upset about this week?
C: Well, Doctor, let me tell you exactly what happened. It all started Saturday morning. I went over to visit my wife and children. I got out of my car and my kids came over and greeted me with a big hug. I wasn't doing all those things that usually upset my wife. I went into the house. I didn't say anything about the newspapers being all over the floor or the house not being clean. I didn't say any of those things like I usually do. But then I said to my wife ... (the client goes on for fifteen minutes describing all the details of what happened *and* what didn't! He finally concludes as follows:) And after I begged her to take me back, she didn't!

The therapist has allowed too much detail from the client. The patient's final point is really the most crucial one and is really the A about which he is upsetting himself. One strategy utilizing more appropriate therapist behaviors would have been to stop the patient's monologue earlier and directively lead the patient to the point, as in the following example:

T: Well, Joe, what were you upset about this week?
C: Well, Doctor, let me tell you exactly what happened. It all started Saturday morning. I went over to visit my wife and children. I got out of the car and my kids came over and greeted me with a big hug . . .
T: Is that what you were upset about?
C: No! Let me tell you some more.
T: Before you do that, Joe, let me point something out to you. You often give me a lot of extra details that confuse me rather than help me understand your problem. Try to tell me exactly what you are upset about in as few words as possible.
C: But if I don't tell you what happened, how will you understand?
T: We'll go back and get the details later, but for now, just try to stick to the question: exactly what happened just before you got upset?

A second strategy to deal with verbose clients is to train them to monitor and condense their own stories by giving them feedback that their present mode of communication is inefficient. With the patient above, the therapist could allow the story to run its course, and then intervene in the following manner:

T: Joe, you've just given me a great deal of information and detail. I'm confused about what's the most important part. Could you go back and tell me just what was the reason you got upset?

Note the manner in which the therapist allows the client to review his own report and learn to succinctly extract the relevant information. If the client has mistaken the forest for the trees and is unable to summarize the relevant incident, the therapist may reflect the critical portion for the client and thereby model condensed speech. For example:

T: Joe, it sounds to me that you're upset because even though you've tried to change, your wife won't take you back. Is that it?

VAGUENESS IN REPORTING THE A

Occasionally the therapist will encounter patients who have difficulties in presenting the A, being either vague or denying that a specific event triggers their disturbing emotions and behaviors. What are some possible reasons for this vagueness? The therapist may consider the following:

1. *Defensiveness.* The vagueness may be a way to avoid negative reactions from the therapist and significant others in the patient's life, which he or she fears.
2. *Style.* Perhaps the patient has learned to communicate in an ambiguous manner and does so habitually.
3. *Cognitive functioning.* The patient may really think in these vague terms and is not clear even to himself or herself.
4. *Life functioning.* The patient may lack a clear A because the problem is one of absence of meaningful relationships, constructive activity, or work enthusiasm. These voids may be difficult to verbalize.

Difficulty in locating an A is not uncommon in patients who have physiological or hysterical disorders, such as migraine or tension headaches. The patient may complain of headaches, for example, but insist that nothing is wrong in her life. Now, RET as a cognitive-change therapy depends on two preceding factors: (1) the belief that it is acceptable to self-disclose, and (2) the ability to recognize that a psychological problem exists. The former goal may be approached by remaining patient and empathic; active listening over a number of sessions will be helpful. The second goal may be approached in two ways. The first is to ask the patient not for problems but for information on how she could make her life even better or how she could become more self-actualized. Second, the therapist may help the patient learn problem identification skills and help her to recognize areas of conflict in interests, desires, and so on. The most constructive approach to problem identification entails getting a behavioral analysis. For example, the headache patient may be asked to keep a ledger in which she records overt and covert antecedents (events, thoughts, and feelings) as well as consequences of each headache episode. As these data accumulate over a number of weeks, patterns will usually unfold.

Some patients sound as if they are experiencing an "identity crisis." When asked why he came to therapy, Ted might respond, "To find myself—who am I?" The RET therapist would respond by asking the client to change the question "Who am I?" to "What do I enjoy and what do I value?" Little progress will be made unless the therapist can determine what characteristics the client would like to have. RET therapists would do well to communicate to the client that they do not teach self-discovery but self-construction. The RET therapist's view is that the client is not an entity to be found but rather an evolving process.

The use of pinpointing questions is helpful. Joan, a depressed patient, for example, may claim that she is depressed "all the time." The following questions may help her achieve some focus on her affective state: "When did the depression begin?" "When are you most often depressed?" "What seems to make the depression worse?" If the patient responds that she doesn't know, the therapist may initially refuse to accept this answer and press by gently insisting, "Yes, you do." If this tactic fails, logbooks may again be useful.

Another difficult A statement occurs when Jim simply but repeatedly complains, "Life is meaningless." A therapeutic clarification might entail asking, "What would it take for life to be meaningful?" Such a patient may be harboring the irrational notion that he needs noble motives or prestigious goals in order to be happy. For most people, however, their often unverbalized goals are simple and desire-directed (e.g., having sufficient money, relationships with others, interesting work). Such goals can be justified rationally because they bring pleasure or avoid discomfort. If the therapist can communicate the message that hedonism and self-pleasuring are acceptable, Jim may more readily identify his goals and his unfulfilling activating events.

The need to clearly identify the A events is particularly important in phobias; unless the therapist knows what the specific fears are, therapy may proceed along the wrong track. Marie may say she is afraid of subways, for example. Although this statement seems specific at first glance, careful probing may reveal a more core activating event. What is it about subways that is frightening? Perhaps the feeling of being closed in. What might happen then? Perhaps Marie fears she might faint. What might happen then? People on the train might look askance or disapprove of her. Thus, in this example, the patient's basic fear is of disapproval, not of trains.

The most severe problem of identifying A is presented by the patient who does not do so at all. Robert might report, for example, that he has been depressed for weeks but has *no idea* why. Patients faced with this problem frequently choose to reduce their discomfort with this void by creating an attribution for the depression. Understandably, the attribution that they often arrive at is that they are "simply depressives," thus giving themselves a new A about which they further depress themselves. When Robert does not identify an A at all, the therapist may frequently be helpful by asking pinpointing questions, such as, "Has anything changed in your life in the past few months?" "Do you anticipate any changes in your life in the next several months?"

In summary, when the patient's description of activating events is confused, vague, or absent, the therapist may keep in mind the following helpful hints:

1. Talk in the patient's language in drawing the data from his/her experience.
2. Pin down the patient with detailed questions.
3. Ask for recent examples.
4. Avoid abstractions.
5. Request logbooks of experiences.
6. Keep on track, not only to reduce the problem of scattered focus but to serve as a model for the patient.
7. Ask about recent or impending life changes.

TOO MANY A'S

Many patients come to therapy with multiple problems and a wide array of activating events to discuss. The initial therapeutic focus is on selecting a target problem on which to work. Therapist and client may list problem areas, and the starting choice may be offered to the patient. Alternatively, therapists may wish to make the choice. They may, for example, wish to select a small problem with minor affective consequences because (1) they think they can best teach the RET principles in a less complicated area, (2) they believe that progress can be made in a very few sessions so that their credibility and the patient's enthusiasm will bolster further success, or (3) they presume that one specific problem may be the cause of the others.

Take the case of a client, Sam, who is overweight and has low frustration tolerance problems in controlling his eating, is anxious about dating situations, and is guilty about not visiting his mother as frequently as she would like. It would be very difficult to work on his fear of dating situations, since he is unlikely to be successful in this realm if he is considerably overweight. Dealing with his low frustration tolerance may (1) help him to lose weight, (2) help him to go through the difficulties he may encounter in meeting women to date, and (3) help him to put up with his mother. Overcoming the LFT would, in effect, help overcome all three problems and would therefore be the target belief to work on first.

Is it wise to allow the client to bring up new problem areas before some resolution of old ones has been achieved? Usually, yes, since the patients typically spend only one hour a week in therapy and 167 hours in their normal environment. New problems and crises are bound to arise, and therapists who rigidly insist on sticking to the previous week's agenda may not only fail to be helpful but may jeopardize their relationship to the client. As a caveat, however, the therapist may be watchful for diversionary tactics by the patient. Is the presentation of a new problem a way to ward off discussion of difficult or troublesome topics? For example, a compulsive overeater may bring up a number of other problem areas to avoid the work of dieting; the diversionary behavior may thus be another example of low frustration tolerance. If new topics are repeatedly brought up over a number of sessions, the therapist would do well to confront the patient directly by pointing out and discussing this aspect of his or her behavior.

In some cases, the therapist may note a common theme in the new problems or a correlation between them and the original or core problem, and can use the new material as a wedge to the core. Consider, for example, the case of a young woman who presented problem after problem with the common theme of failing. She reported not being able to do well at a job interview because she believed she didn't deserve the job. She described sabotaging love relationships because she believed she wasn't good enough for her partners. She told of alienating friends because "no one could like a person like me." She seemed to believe that it was good for her to be in pain. After several sessions of listening to these Activating events, the therapist then asked her if she recognized a common theme in all of these examples: that she had to suffer because she was not good enough to reap any of these rewards. The patient replied that, in fact, she did recognize that theme and recalled how the other members of her immediate family had suffered greatly. Her sister died after a very painful car accident, her mother died after a bout with breast cancer, and her father after a sudden heart attack. Only she had remained alive and apparently believed that it was only right, proper, and moral for her to suffer equally.

A'S BEYOND THE THERAPIST'S EXPERTISE

Clients' problems usually have two components. One component is the practical problem, and the other is the psychological problem. If the practical problem is clearly outside the therapist's area of expertise (e.g., a medical problem), then he or she would do well not to deal with it and perhaps to refer the client to a specialist in the problem area. If the therapist is able to deal with the practical problem, he or she may elect to give the client advice about it. Remember, however, that the patient will most likely have a psychological problem *about* the practical problem; if so, the therapist had better deal with this *first*.

Since therapists' competence is in dealing with cognitions, emotions, and behaviors, they would do well to *refocus* the discussion back onto this area. Below is a suggestion for how this refocusing may be approached:

> "Look, Mary, you know that the information that you're giving me is outside my area of professional competency. I can't advise you about medical matters. You obviously have some pretty strong emotions about these issues, however. Why don't we talk about how you're *feeling* about the medical problems?"

C BECOMING AN A

One of the most important Activating events which the RET therapist will quickly seek is *symptom stress*. In other words, the patient's symptom (e.g., depression) becomes a new A and itself requires an RET analysis. A hallmark of rational-emotive therapy is its focus on these higher-level problems as a *first* order of business. The cycle of events can be described as follows:

A—Original symptom (e.g., depression)

B—"Isn't it awful that I have this symptom!"
"I shouldn't feel this way!"
"I must be able to get over my problem quickly and easily."

C—Further anxiety, guilt, or depression.

The patient can become upset about B's or C's in such a cycle. For example, patients may become angry or depressed about their irrational beliefs:

"There I go thinking irrationally again. Damn it, I'll never stop. What's the matter with me? I should've learned by now. . . ."

Similarly, patients may become anxious over the physical signs of anxiety, a problem which is particularly prominent in agoraphobia (Goldstein and Chambless, 1978). These clients appear to focus on the physiological symptoms of anxiety and believe that they are signs of impending death, doom, or unbearable discomfort:

"I'm terrified of panic. When I get in the car and I feel the anxiety come, I know I won't be able to stand it!"

Ellis (1978a, 1979c) has called this form of anxiety *discomfort anxiety*, to distinguish it from *ego* anxiety. Phrenophobia, fear of going crazy, is the most common example of such a problem. Some estimates of its occurrence are as high as 77 percent of the patients seen in an office practice (Raimey, 1975). Clients with this problem anticipate losing control of their minds, such that they will become raging homicidal maniacs. Raimey has identified symptoms which phrenophobics believe are signs of impending insanity or mental breakdown:

Constant feelings of anxiety

Any errors in reasoning or memory

Inability to concentrate

Irritability

Insomnia

Patients commonly upset themselves over their behavioral difficulties as well. Thus, the drug addict may suffer equally from guilt addiction, the overeater typically overindulges in self-blame, and the impotent male not only "can't get it up" but can't get it off his mind.

Primary focus on this secondary problem may be particularly important when dealing with seriously disturbed and/or psychotic patients. Psychotherapy of any sort may be difficult or even ineffective in ameliorating primary symptoms such as thought disorders or endogenous depressions which may well be a function of biochemical imbalances (Davison and Neale, 1974). Often, however, there is a neurotic overlay or secondary symptom—for example, depression about manic-depressive episodes. A most useful therapeutic goal may be to help patients learn to accept themselves with their handicap instead of depressing themselves about such handicaps. The same principle is true, of course, with less seriously disturbed patients. Consider again Sam, the compulsive overeater. Whenever he breaks his diet and overeats, he immediately begins to cognitively castigate himself, which inevitably leads to the uncomfortable feelings of guilt or shame. Once he is feeling bad enough, he is liable to "do something nice for himself" in an attempt to feel better, and that "something nice" may very well be another hot fudge sundae. Breaking the second-level shame and guilt cycle may be a prerequisite to helping Sam stay on task to achieve his long-range goal of weight loss.

Once a second-level stress has been identified as an A, RET therapy proceeds in the usual fashion: the C is clarified, the irrational beliefs are identified, and the client is assisted in disputing them.

ON CHANGING THE A

Broadly speaking, Activating events fall into two main classes: those that *can* be changed and those that *cannot*. To paraphrase the motto used in Alcoholics Anonymous, a job of therapy is to help the patient try to change those events that can be changed, to gracefully tolerate those that cannot be changed, and to try to discriminate the two types.

Generally, it is not profitable to try to change the Activating event first. Merely changing the A may make the patient feel better but perhaps for the wrong reasons. In other words, doing better is always nice, but a more useful accomplishment may be learning not to be self-downing or self-rating even when one is *not* doing well. As Ellis is fond of pointing out, "life" is really spelled H-A-S-S-L-E, and whether we like it or not, new and unpleasant Activating events will always appear on our horizons.

Additionally, RET therapists work under the basic assumption that when Activating events can be changed, doing so will require patients to use their problem-solving skills. They will be in the best position to solve problems once they are freed from debilitating emotional states by acknowledging and then challenging their core irrational philosophies. To understand how these preliminary steps can be accomplished, we turn in the next chapters to emotions and cognitions.

4 Getting at the C

Why do patients come to therapy? Usually because they are feeling bad; they are in emotional distress. The therapist will not want to lose sight of this focus. Patients usually don't just come in to talk or to rid themselves of irrationalities. It is the C, the affective Consequence, that typically brings them to the therapist's door.

Many RET therapists have found that clients can clearly explain their emotions about certain Activating events. In fact, it is not unusual for clients to begin sessions by discussing their feelings. Thus, the client may reply to the question, "What problem would you like to discuss?" by saying, "I feel very depressed lately." If the client does not volunteer the emotion, the advised strategy, in accordance with RET's emphasis on active-directive intervention, is to ask. After the client has described the Activating event, the therapist typically asks, "Well, how do you feel about that?"

More experienced therapists may be able to use a clinical hunch about the patient's emotional state and phrase the question in another way, such as, "Aren't you feeling anxious about that?" This technique may also serve as a strong rapport builder, for clients may conclude that the therapist truly understands their problem. We advise against *telling* your clients how they feel, however. Phrase your comment as a question and be prepared to change your mind when you have sufficient data that your hunch is wrong.

The more experienced therapist will also learn to recognize that certain emotional states are frequently associated with specific clinical problems. For example, avoiding certain situations usually indicates anxiety, assaultive or verbally abusive behavior generally points to anger, lethargy or inactivity probably means depression, self-injurious or self-deprecatory behaviors indicate guilt, and a recent loss is likely to lead to grief.

In other words, there are three ways that the experienced therapist can *infer* the presence of certain emotional states: (1) by using cues from the client's behavior, (2) by understanding typical emotional consequences to common life situations, and (3) by deduction from rational-emotive theory, so that from knowing a client's belief system one can infer a specific emotion.

A warning to new therapists: not all emotions are inappropriate or targets for change. RET theory does not say that emotions are undesirable; in fact, they are part of the spice of life. The distinction the therapist makes is between helpful and harmful emotions. A harmful emotion is one which impedes clients' ability to reach their goals, to enjoy themselves. Also, some emotions are physiologically harmful—such as anxiety, which can lead to psychosomatic disorders (e.g., colitis, duodenal ulcers, and hypertension), or anger, which at least knots up the stomach. Thus, while it is quite appropriate for a client to feel sad about a loss, when the sadness is prolonged or very debilitating, it then becomes a target for therapeutic intervention.

A common problem in the work of new therapists is the failure to accurately identify the C. Sometimes this problem arises because therapists simply do not take the time to clearly label the C or because the therapists assume that they and/or the client intuitively understand what the C is. Such an assumption is often wrong, of course. More often, perhaps, problems in identifying the C come not from therapist negligence but because emotions are a difficult and confusing problem for the patient. The following sections may help the therapist to trouble-shoot some of the reasons for the patient's difficulty with the C and offer some helpful hints to break the emotional blockade.

Trouble-Shooting Problems with the C

GUILT ABOUT THE C

Trouble in identifying the C may stem from guilt; patients may be unwilling to label their affect if they are experiencing a negative emotion for which they denigrate themselves (cf., "C becoming an A," p. 47).

For example, in family therapy, children may be unwilling to acknowledge their anger in front of their parents. A somewhat more subtle example was seen in the case of the wife of a devoted rabbinical scholar. She often felt compelled to interrupt his studies to remind him of his responsibilities to his parishioners, such as visiting the sick or bereaved. He would do as she suggested and received the thanks and approval of his flock; while she, being quiet and shy, was regarded as aloof and, of course, received no credit for her contributions. She stated her problem as one of wanting more support, understanding, and appreciation, yet she could not define a specific C other than to say that she felt she was overlooked and taken for granted. Again, the underlying C was anger, but as the wife of a cleric, she felt she was not entitled to such an emotion.

What might the therapist do in such cases to encourage the client to face the emotion? One of the following suggestions might be useful:

1. Try a Gestalt or psychodrama exercise, such as the empty chair technique. For example, the rabbi's wife might be asked to imagine her husband or one of the ungrateful parishioners sitting in an empty chair. She might then be engaged in a dialogue in which she plays one or both parts, perhaps moving between the two chairs as she exchanges roles. Loosening the usual stimulus constraints in this way may increase the likelihood that she will acknowledge her anger.

2. Try modeling. The therapist might say, for example, "Jim, if I were in your situation, I think I would be annoyed or even downright angry!"

3. Try using humor. By deliberate exaggeration, gently poking fun at the situation, or humorous analogy, the therapist may set the climate for a less threatening acknowledgment of anger. Examples: "I guess you really are a saint; most people would be boiling mad!" or "It's great how you let them walk all over you; everybody loves that!"

SHAME ABOUT THE C

Patients may not be in touch with their emotions because of a tendency to intellectualize their predicaments. Such individuals will avoid labeling their feelings and instead describe their thoughts. They may even deny that they experience emotions at all. Underlying this affectional anesthesia may be the belief that expression of emotion is weak, and avoidance prevents the patient from feeling foolish.

The key concept that the therapist will want to communicate in this case is that all emotion is justified in the sense that it exists. Emotion need not be validated as acceptable by pinning it to an external event, since emotions are internal and come from what a person is saying to himself *about* the outside events.

A useful goal for such a client may be to appreciate the extent to which all people react emotionally. As a homework assignment, the therapist may request patients to write down all the different "I feel _____" or "I'm in a _____ mood" statements that they hear others make in the course of a week. They can also monitor their own statements of this sort. In addition, the therapist could make use of the three techniques described above.

LITTLE OR NO AFFECT IN THE SESSION

The therapist may observe the lack of affect in the session. Assuming that the absence of affect is not a psychotic symptom, the therapist may want to check out two possibilities for this occurrence.

1. Clients may believe that they are "supposed to be serious" in therapy, that it is a solemn occasion requiring hard work and a no-nonsense attitude. The therapist will want to disabuse the client of such a notion by direct suggestion, modeling, and use of creative strategies to elicit more affect (e.g., encouraging disagreement with the therapist, asking patients to pantomine their problems or express them in song or poetry format).

2. The therapist's behavior may be fostering little affect. For example, the therapist may be making long-winded speeches, asking closed-ended questions, moving too fast and confusing the client, and so forth. Listen to your tapes with such a client and evaluate your own remarks that precede instances of minimal affect. Try to encourage verbal expression by asking simple, open-ended questions (e.g., "And then what?").

FLAT AND INAPPROPRIATE AFFECT

The patient may describe experiencing flat affect—an emotional anesthetic reaction ("feeling dead" is a common expression) or may show inappropriate affect—that is, an emotion that is socially unusual. Affective disturbances of these sorts often reflect a psychotic process, and RET alone may *not* be the appropriate tool to help with these emotional states. You can help most by making an appropriate referral for medication (Ellis and Abrahms, 1978).

PAINFUL EMOTION

Patients may not be aware of their feelings because they fear the emotion; the problem may thus be one of avoidance of affective states. For example, being depressed is, after all, an uncomfortable or even a painful experience. The patient may avoid discussing life situations which are evocative of this emotion.

The problem in this case seems to be one of LFT, low frustration tolerance, in which patients convince themselves that the emotional turmoil is more than they can stand. The therapist can encourage and support the client—for example, by pointing out that it is *normal* to have bad feelings and that it would be helpful to discuss the painful emotions. As has been found useful in the research on helping patients through delayed grieving or mourning states, the therapist can figuratively hold the patient's hand through more extended therapy sessions in which desensitization to the discomfort is allowed.

Another aspect of painful emotions is the shame patients fear if others see them emoting. The job of the RET therapist is to help the clients accept their own emotions, for shame may prevent them from confronting the emotion and doing an ABC analysis of it. For example:

C: (crying)
T: You're obviously in distress about something, Jean. What's going through your head right now?
C: I'm so scared that I'll cry at work. I might lose control of myself in front of the other people in my office.
T: Well, what would be so terrible about that?
C: I couldn't stand it!
T: Well, what's the worst thing you could imagine happening? If you lost control, would you run amok through the halls? Would you not be able to function at all?
C: (smiling) No-o-o. I guess I just wouldn't want them to think I was upset.

T: And if they did—would that be so bad?
C: Ummmm. No, you're right. It wouldn't.
T: OK, so can we give you permission to be quite upset while you're still upset?

CONFUSION OF B AND C

People in our culture frequently confuse thoughts and feelings. Sometimes you may ask a client to describe a feeling and he or she will respond with a belief. For example, the client may say, "When she said that, I felt dumb." At other times, you may ask a client to identify a belief and get a feeling for a response. You may ask, "What were you thinking then?" and the client may respond, "Oh, I was thinking I was anxious."

A difficulty that new therapists and patients often share is discriminating B's from C's, and this problem may relate in part to the imprecision in our language. The word "feeling," for example, may have many different meanings in everyday speech:

1. It may refer to a physical sensation ("I feel cold").
2. It may refer to an opinion ("I feel that taxes should be lowered").
3. It may refer to an emotional experience ("I feel happy").
4. It may refer to an evaluation ("I feel that it's terrible").

The therapist can carefully listen for the clients' meaning of "feel" and encourage them to use the term to describe emotional consequences rather than opinions and evaluations. This distinction will help clients detect the difference between their beliefs and emotional C's, which will be of greater value to them when they attempt to dispute their irrational beliefs. Thus, when patients mislabel a B as a feeling, it is often useful to stop and correct them. For example, if the therapist asks Tom, "How were you feeling?" and the patient says, "I felt dumb," the therapist will recognize that Tom (1) has a strong feeling of depression or guilt and (2) is making self-deprecatory statements. After acknowledging these two issues, the therapist would attempt to point out to the client that "dumb" is not an emotion but really reflects a thought: "I think I am dumb." In fact, Tom's statement "I felt dumb" is usually shorthand for

"I believe that I'm dumb and I feel depressed about that." It is important to make this distinction because the client may wrongly attempt to dispute his feeling of "dumb" or to justify his belief that he is dumb because of this so-called feeling. Feelings are not open to dispute; they are phenomenological experiences for which only the individual has data. You cannot argue with such subjective states, while thoughts, beliefs, and opinions are open to challenge. Thus, in the example above, the therapist would point out to Tom that he does not feel dumb; he feels depressed because he believes that he is dumb and that he must not be. The stage is now set for working on this irrational belief.

DESCRIPTIVE DEFICITS

When asked how she is feeling, Myra may state, or her behavior may imply, that she is *confused*. The confusion may result from the fact that she is experiencing a *mixture* of emotions or simply that she lacks an adequate *emotional vocabulary*. In general, the more the therapist can help her simplify and label her emotional problem, the more easily she will be able to grapple with it. Again, if Larry can only describe himself as feeling "down," the therapist may inquire what he understands by the word "depression." In other words, the therapist may want to take the opportunity to expand the client's vocabulary. A side benefit of this will be to increase the patient's ability to profit from bibliotherapy, since most books are written using terms such as "depression," "anxiety," and so on.

The therapist may help patients label their emotions by instruction and modeling. Initially, the difference between positive and negative emotions may be suggested (e.g., "Did you feel good or bad?"), after which more descriptive terms may be suggested and discussed. Some of the following exercises may be useful either in session or as homework assignments:

1. Here are the names of some emotions or feelings:
   happy
   angry
   proud
   embarrassed
   scared

nervous
relaxed
sad
disappointed
hurt
curious
frustrated
guilty
anxious

Pronounce each word to yourself; say it out loud.

Do you know what each word means?
Pantomime (act without words) each of the words that you
know. (Different people express the same feeling in different
ways, so there is no right way to do it!)

Are there any other feelings you can think of? If so, write
them here:

2. Orally or in writing, complete the sentence "I feel _____" in as
   many ways as you can.
3. Start a diary of "I feel" or "I felt" statements. At first, just write
   the statements. Later, begin to add "When such and such happened, I felt _____." For example, "I felt anxious when I
   started writing this diary."

DICHOTOMOUS THINKING

Many patients tend to categorize emotional states dichotomously; for
example, they believe that the only way they can respond is very negatively or as if nothing happened. In fact, however, emotions are on a
continuum of intensity, and it is important to assure that the client
understands that there is a range of emotions to feel and a range of
behaviors to express them. For example, if John has trouble in his
marriage and has only been able to feel *rage* and to express it by beating
his wife, he may not have the concept of *annoyance* or the skills to
express it. Imagery experiences, modeling, and direct training may be
needed to help him extend his conceptual schema of emotions in order to
discriminate between feeling annoyed and feeling angry.

   If the patient can envision and label various levels of emotion, he or she may also be able to envision ways (cognitions) to arrive at a more desirable or adaptive feeling state. The therapist might, for example, present a group of emotional labels to clients and help them to classify the words as *mild, moderate,* or *strong* emotions. It can then be pointed out that rational or helpful thinking usually leads to mild/moderate feelings or to strong feelings (like intense regret or sorrow) which are appropriate, while irrational or hurtful thinking leads to strong and debilitating emotions.

Dichotomous thinking about emotions can also occur on dimensions other than intensity. John may believe, for example, that once he learns how to get over his anger at his wife, he must never be angry again. A useful distinction here would be between appropriate irritation and annoyance versus inappropriate anger, the difference based on (1) his demand that his wife *must* not act irritatingly and annoyingly; (2) the length of time he was angry; (3) the effects of the anger on himself; and (4) the effects of his displays of anger on others in his life. In other words, it would be irrational for the patient to believe that he should *never* be angry, depressed, anxious, and so on. These are normal and overlearned reactions. Strong inappropriate emotions are problematic mainly when they persist for prolonged periods and thereby interrupt goal-directed behaviors.

MISLABELING EMOTIONS

Patients often mislabel their emotional states, so that it is a good rule of thumb to clarify the affective referent. The therapist would be wise to ask routinely for some explanation or expansion of the patient's emotional label (e.g., "What do you mean by guilty/anxious/bothered/ etc.?") and, if the client seems to be in error, point it out (e.g., "Sam, it sounds more like you're angry than anxious").

An interesting form of this error is seen in patients who mislabel their problem as ego-anxiety, when it may really be low frustration tolerance or discomfort anxiety (Ellis, 1978a, 1979c). For example, Gary may claim that he can't go to work because he is too anxious. What this statement boils down to is that he is not willing to experience the discomfort of going to work and has, perhaps, *sanctified* his avoidance of discomfort by labeling it as a "serious emotional problem." Obviously, we advise the therapist to also attend to material and social gains which may be encouraging Gary to maintain this view of himself.

UNCLEAR LABELING OF EMOTIONS

Clients may use a label which, although clear to them, may be unclear to the therapist. For example, May says, "I was so indignant!" Do you understand precisely what she means? Is this level of affect mild, moderate, or intense? Does it reflect a rational or irrational belief? The answers to these questions are best found by asking her clarifying questions: "What do you mean when you say 'indignant'?" or "That sounds like you're angry; on a ten-point scale, how angry are you?"

LACK OF APPARENT DISTRESS

Occasionally, one will interview a client who rattles off a list of problems but is not obviously in distress about anything. The therapist may want to consider the following as some possible explanations for this behavior. Perhaps the patient (1) is truly not in distress, (2) has come to therapy for companionship rather than help, (3) is worried about being "normal" and has come to therapy to find out and get reassurance, or (4) is engaging in avoidance maneuvers which prevent the appearance of negative affect. If despite the therapist's patience for allowing emergence of affect, no emotional distress is apparent, confrontation might be recommended. One or more of the above explanations may be discussed with the client so that appropriate goals for action may be set.

Avoidance maneuvers pose perhaps the trickiest problem, for if patients' behaviors effectively prevent them from experiencing negative affect, both they and the therapist will be in the dark about the C. If an emotional consequence is not evident but patients describe troublesome behaviors, it is often helpful to apply a learning theory model to the behavior problems. Quite simply, behavior can be viewed as maintained either by its pleasurable results or the avoidance of negative stimuli, and often the negative stimuli are the patients' own hidden emotions. Sometimes direct confrontation may break the blockade, as in the following instance. The client was avoiding taking a major exam, yet claimed he felt no anxiety over it.

T: Jerry, if that were so, if you had no anxiety at all, why would you *not* take the test?
C: But I don't experience any anxiety now.
T: Right, because as long as you stay away from that test, you avoid experiencing much anxiety. Do you see that something is blocking you from getting too close, and that something is your anxiety? Now what do you think would happen if you took the test and *failed*?
C: Wow! That's it. That's so simple, but that must be what I'm worried about. . . .

Often, a more extensive use of projective fantasy is called for in order to discover what the client fears. One client, for example, reported that she was concerned about the fact that she was dating only married men; she denied any particular negative emotion and stated that she was simply more attracted to married men. The therapist guided her through a fantasy in which she imagined herself out on a date with an attractive man who suddenly announced that he was single and, in fact, found her to be the only desirable woman he'd ever met. In another case, an obese client fantasized being very slim and out on a date with an attractive man. In both instances, the imagery exercise allowed the clients to get in touch with a great deal of interpersonal anxiety which their avoidance behaviors (dating married men or being overweight) had successfully blocked. The anxiety then became the focus of therapy.

A similar problem was presented by a male client who experienced no specific emotional problems except exhaustion. He complained of feeling tired almost all of the time, and no matter how much sleep he got, he never felt truly rested. Medical evaluation revealed no physiological basis for his fatigue. Extensive questioning revealed that he had a demanding yet fulfilling job, a full social life, and was active in athletic events. In all respects, he appeared to be "living the good life," yet on closer questioning, the client reported that he did not always enjoy all of his activities and occasionally did not want to do them. Thus, since the intrinsic pleasure of the activity was not always maintaining his behavior, we assumed that some of his busy schedule was actually avoidance behavior. The client was asked to fantasize a typical day in his life, omitting one of his activities, such as athletics. He continued in imagery, reducing his work activity and then diminishing his social life. After each imagery scene, the client reported, much to his own surprise, feelings of guilt. Further analysis revealed an irrational notion of self-worth based on accomplishing all that he thought he should do; thus, the underlying emotion of guilt was successfully avoided by maintaining an extremely active life.

A similar problem is often encountered with clients who report an inability to control addictive behaviors such as drug abuse, smoking, drinking, and overeating. They may not acknowledge any emotional problems which increase the frequency of their addictive behaviors, although they do sense guilt over having done them. With such clients, the therapist may ask them to imagine that they are sitting in front of the food or cigarettes and are denying themselves these pleasures. Clients usually report a very uncomfortable feeling akin to intense agitation, heightened arousal, muscle tension, or jitteriness. This emotional Consequence, a result of their irrational belief that they *need* to have what they desire, may have remained out of their awareness since they were so successful at avoiding the unpleasant feeling by quickly devouring that which they desired. Such an imagery exercise may help clients get in touch with their C's.

EMOTION IN THE SESSION

Whether or not patients are able to identify emotional reactions in relation to their life events, the therapist will want to attend to affective cues within the therapy session. Body position, tensed muscles, clenched teeth, breathing changes, perspiration, giggling, and so forth may be scanned so that emotional factors may be dealt with.

When you see these signs of affect, you may begin to do an ABC analysis. Don't make the mistake of avoiding working with emotions expressed in the session. Therapy does not always have to deal with problems of past or recent history. For example:

T: Sally, I notice that your eyes are starting to swell up and you look as if you're ready to burst into tears.

C: Oh, you're right! (Sobs)

T: Sally, you really feel bad now. I wonder if you could tell what you're feeling upset about right now?

C: Well, it's so hard. My whole life is ruined. I have nothing to live for.

T: Well, why don't we talk about that now rather than the other problems you had brought up—for as long as you're believing that, you're going to feel upset and cry.

Deciding to Change the C

Once clients have acknowledged and correctly identified the distressing emotion, they have a decision to make: Do they want to keep or change this emotion? For example, they have the right to keep or give up their anger, and the pros and cons of each choice may be an interesting topic for discussion. Anger, after all, has its advantages, since acting aggressively often moves people to give you what you want. On the other hand, intense rage may be socially detrimental and physiologically destructive to the individual.

Consider the example of anger presented by a young mother. In many ways her anger worked for her; for instance, when she yelled at her son about his messy room, he quickly tidied up. The anger display also appeared to be intrinsically reinforcing; after she had a temper tantrum, she felt a pleasant state of fatigue and relaxation akin to the aftereffects of exercise. Quite simply, it felt good when she stopped. In addition, the woman was providing her own cognitive reinforcement for her abreactive display (e.g., "I did the right thing by getting angry!"). Thus, interpersonal, kinesthetic, and cognitive factors were operating to help maintain the angry feelings and behavior. To help overcome these factors, the therapist could suggest that (1) the woman consider the long-range consequences of her behavior; certainly her anger displays did not endear her to her son; (2) she was providing a poor model for her son; (3) there were more helpful ways of achieving release of tension, such as relaxation exercises; (4) there were more effective ways of controlling her son's behavior, and (5) her cognitive statements were misplaced and stemmed from an exaggerated and unflattering sense of righteousness.

A more subtle source of gain may also sometimes be operating, in which a debilitating emotion is maintained in order to avoid a more distressing one. Consider, for example, the case of a mother who lost custody of her children to the father, an event which precipitated intense and prolonged depression, which the patient seemed unwilling to surrender. What would it mean to this woman to give up grieving? Apparently she believed that it would prove her to be an uncaring and uncommitted mother, a concept which induced an even more intense feeling of guilt. Once this irrational belief was successfully disputed, however, the patient was able to give herself permission to work at relieving her depression.

Patients may, at least on some days, decide to stay upset rather than do the hard RET work of disputing. In essence, they may be saying either (1) "That's the way I am, and I can't change" or (2) "It's more rewarding (or easier) for me to be upset." Once identified, either of these hypotheses may be challenged, perhaps by simply requesting that the patients do the experiment which will allow them to test their hunch—"Is it in fact true that you cannot change or that it's easier to be upset?"

The point to keep in mind is that there may be many reasons why the patient is reluctant to change the C, some of which the therapist may be able to affect. If the client does not want to change the C, however, rational-emotive therapy usually cannot proceed.

Teaching Transcript

In the following therapy transcript, additional therapeutic problems are addressed. The therapist is confronted with a client who describes experiencing a *number of unpleasant emotions*, and the therapeutic job is to label them, rate their severity, and rank-order them for investigation. Note the therapist's use of a *numerical rating scale* to accomplish these goals. Such a scale is often known as a SUDS scale, which stands for Subjective Units of Disturbance (Wolpe, 1973). We highly recommend the use of these informal ratings, for they allow the patient as well as the therapist to be more keenly aware of changes in the affective state both within and between sessions.

Transcript segment

T: Your wife, Mary, called and said you were feeling particularly depressed and suicidal, and she was very concerned about you. How are you feeling today?

C: I have very confused moments. The reason I had originally felt suicidal—I don't even know how to express the feeling that I had, because I know if I really wanted to commit suicide I would have accomplished it.

Note that the client really hasn't answered the therapist's question.

T: You know how to do it?

C: It was very simple. I was just taking the privilege of indulging myself in self-pity obviously, by taking eight pills instead of twenty-five.

T: So you don't seriously think you were trying—

C: Well, I feel this way, if it happened, if the eight pills had done the job, that would have been OK, and if they didn't, fine.

T: But you weren't going to insure that they did by taking twenty-five or thirty?

C: Exactly. That's how I felt.

T: Have you had any previous suicide attempts?

The therapist is assessing suicidal thoughts and behaviors before doing anything else.

C: No.

T: Have you had any previous plans to commit suicide?

C: Well, after my first divorce I was pretty uptight and I had thought about. Twice, as a matter of fact.

T: Did you have a plan to commit suicide those times?

C: No, no plan.

T: You never said: "I'm going to do it by slicing my throat, or jumping off a bridge, or leaping out of a cable car?"

C: No. It was just like, frankly, I would be driving my car, the self-pity would come on and I'd say "I'm going to crash into the wall." I'd head toward the wall and then pull away.

T: So presently you're not having that many suicidal thoughts today?

C: No.

T: How about your feelings? How are you feeling today?

Here the therapist returns to feelings after he was reasonably sure that suicide was not imminent.

C: Extremely anxious.
T: Anxious?
C: Yes.
T: Usually, most people who attempt suicide become depressed, but you're anxious?

Notice that the therapist is working from a conceptual schema and checking the patient's response against it.

C: Yeah, I'm pretty anxious.
T: How anxious do you feel?
C: Well, when I become nervous my back goes out.
T: You get muscle pains?
C: That's why I'm wearing my girdle now. It went out Sunday night, and I didn't do anything physical. I just bent over and it just went. So I know that's an indication that something's not right.
T: Have you been to a physician about your back problems?
C: Yes. I slipped a disc about fifteen years ago. It's been a chronic thing. Many times I think it's due to muscular strain because I do work physically. And sometimes this has nothing to do with any—
T: Well, it could be just muscular tension. So, you do tend to get muscular tension and get real tight?
C: Well, I wasn't aware of it, but it's really become more of a chronic situation. My children live in Canada and that's when it really started to become chronic, when they moved to Canada. Mary brought it to my attention.
T: How long ago was that?
C: Four years ago.
T: So for the last four years your anxiety has been getting worse?
C: Only when I know they're coming in.
T: When they're coming you get more anxious. How frequently does that happen?

The therapist is acknowledging and accepting the client's feelings while gathering additional information about the client's life situation.

C: Well, they're supposed to come in twice a year. This year it's been only once and they'll be coming in in three weeks. It's starting to build—the anxiety's started.
T: So, as your children come closer you get more anxious. If you had

to rate your anxiety on a 100-point scale, zero being completely relaxed, lying on some deserted beach somewhere, and 100 being a sheer state of panic, where would you rate your anxiety right now?

The therapist is using the SUDS rating to assess the level of emotional distress.

C: Oh, at a pretty good 75, 80.
T: So that's up there.
C: It's right up at the top.
T: Now, can I ask you something else? What is it about your children coming that frightens you?
C: Well, let me say, anytime anybody mentions my children to me I sort of swell up. (Client gets tears in his eyes.)

Note that the therapist will deal with this in-session emotion.

T: So, that sounds like you're feeling sad. So there is a little sadness along with your anxiety.
C: Maybe it's because what I do is I fear and I visualize what I'm going to feel when I see them—also when they leave.
T: So, in other words, what you're doing right now is you are experiencing or imagining your feelings when they come off the plane or when they go on the plane and you feel sadness then—and you're feeling anxious about feeling sadness?

Note that the therapist hypothesizes that one C has become another A; he asks for feedback about this hypothesis.

C: Right.
T: Which one of the problems do you think is more important, then, the anxiety or the sadness?
C: That's a very interesting question.
T: Both emotions are there.
C: What I'm trying to find out myself is if it's totally a self-pity type of feeling I have. I don't know. I've been trying to analyze that for a four-year period.
T: Let me ask you this: do you have any anxiety about other issues besides your children?
C: Yes. What brought about the suicide—let's call it that for the moment—
T: The attempt.
C: —may have been due to many other things. That is, like anything I

have to do I have to work very hard at; nothing comes too easily for me.

T: Even killing yourself! You can't even do that well, right?

Note the therapist's attempt at humor and how well it is received by the client.

C: I could have if I really wanted to. That was maybe part of many of my problems. But I was married eighteen years the first time. And for literally seventeen of the eighteen years, I felt I had a very happy marriage. I was very content and we, my ex-wife and I, became very friendly with another couple and before I knew it, my best friend and my wife took off. I had found out the hard way— detective, the whole thing. And I felt after I had overcome the initial shock that I would never trust another woman again. I was very secure and all of a sudden not only did I lose my wife, I lost a friend, I lost my children—it was a three-way disaster.

T: Can we stop?

C: Yes.

T: When you think about your children and you feel the sadness when they come, does it also remind you of the sadness you felt at that particular time?

C: No.

T: Does it remind you of how vulnerable you are?

The therapist is working from a hypothesis that the client, in the face of serious problems, has an irrational belief that he cannot cope.

C: Oh yeah, because in a way I blame myself for the situation of losing my children. I am not happy about losing my ex-wife because I loved Carol very much. There is no priority. It's just that I lost my children and there are no feelings going back to that point.

T: You agree with me that when you think about your children coming, you remember the vulnerability you had. Now is it vulnerability toward the children or vulnerability of being deserted by your wife—that kind of feeling?

The therapist has heard the word "blame" above in the client's remark, but is holding that concept for a later intervention.

C: No. Just the sadness that it's just a temporary thing I have with my kids and I feel myself becoming distant on both sides. Their distance and my distance. It's such a brief period that we see each other.

T: So what you're sad about is that you don't see your children a lot.

C: Right.

T: Let me stop and redefine your words. You said that you feel sad. I agree that you do, but again, if you used a system of 0 to 100 to describe how sad you were, how many points would that be? Zero would be completely happy, peaceful, and doing great—and 100 is at the brink of stabbing yourself in the heart because life is utterly hopeless. What do you feel?

C: Well, let's bring a little guilt in there—

T: I just want you to give me a rating.

C: Oh. You want the rating. I find it very hard—

T: Are you having a lot of sadness, like about 100? Or about 10?

C: No, I guess about 100.

The therapist is not letting the client deflect the conversation. He is finishing the work on sadness about the children and, while he has heard the comment about guilt, he is saving it for a later point in the session.

T: I guess technically, it may be important for us to discriminate—anything above 25 points may be considered sad, and maybe what you're feeling really isn't sadness but is really depression. Because I think any man would feel sad losing his children the way you did—and sadness now. But they would not be as debilitated as you are. So that the sad feelings you're probably never going to get rid of. You're going to feel sad about not having your children . . . at least I hope so. You're not going to be cold-hearted, and I don't think I could help you to be that way; even if I could, I don't think I'd want to. But the point is, your problem isn't sadness—it's depression. You're really depressed about this. And I think it's important that maybe we use different words, rather than just sad. Now, what is the guilt factor?

The therapist has discriminated and helped the patient correctly label his emotions. Not only the high SUDS level, but the guilt and self-denigration and the suicide attempt, are clues that his problem is depression, not merely sadness.

C: Whatever my ex-wife needed—it was mostly in the financial area—I overindulged her. Our life-style went far beyond my financial means because I felt this was what she needed. And I work hard, many hours, and I go home and go to sleep. Get up and go to work, go home and go to sleep. That was a round robin. Except the weekend. I used to look forward to the weekends like it was a vacation of two months coming up instead of only a few days—just so I could spend time with our friends and enjoy my life. The guilt comes in where I wasn't smart enough to realize that there is more than just working.

T: And because you didn't realize that, what happened?

C: She found the fun part of her world with my friend.

T: Because you weren't there, she went somewhere else, and if you were smart enough to know better, you wouldn't have lost your children?

C: Exactly.

T: You're really stupid, aren't you?

This is an attempt at humor and was said with a grin.

C: No.

T: You're really beating yourself about it.

C: Well, I'm beating myself about it because I was almost falling into the same problem in my new marriage again. And I wasn't quite aware of it and I'm very confused about it. Because what I started to say before and I want to get that part out of me, what brought on this attempted suicide was my lack of confidence in living—and also friends. I don't have a true friend, even after this past weekend.

T: You don't trust them, like you don't trust women?

C: Exactly. Maybe, after this weekend, I have now found a new friend. It's about time. But Mary has always made me feel fidelity, honesty, on a conscious level, and that I am Number 1 and no man will ever come between us. And I was very comfortable. It took a lot of work for me to believe again. And unfortunately a very ridiculous situation came up. Mary has been very depressed about not being able to find a position. This has been going on for two years now. And last week, I don't know how the conversation came up, Mary said to me, she could even go to bed with a guy if he would get her a job—the right job.

T: It's not his penis she's after, or his mind—just his money?

C: Yeah. But in the meantime, my mind has really had it. So I told Mary how I felt and that weekend became a disaster weekend. I couldn't cope with the fact that my wife would go to bed with another man at any price.

T: It appears to me, at least in RET terms, there are several Activating
     events, several emotions, going on at the same time. Some of them
     being depression, some of them being anxiety, and some of them
     being guilt. The Activating events appear to be seeing your chil-
     dren, missing your children, having left your children or causing
     that to happen, and another is a futuristic one that your wife would
     leave. From what you tell me, it appears that the thing that upset
     you the most is something that is right now. That is, you are afraid
     that your wife will leave. And any slight indication that that might
     come true really leads to an awful amount of anxiety. And it ap-
     pears that when you think about your children, possibly you think
     about your wife having left you suddenly, and if it could happen
     then, well—

*Even though this was a first session, the client had been introduced to
RET through books he had read. Note that the therapist summarizes the complexity of the client's problems and is hypothesiz-
ing that the client believes that he caused his former problems and
may do so again with his present wife.*

5 Getting at the B's

Belief systems come in two major forms, which Ellis (1962, 1971, 1973, 1979b) has called the *Rational Beliefs (RB's)* and the *Irrational Beliefs (IB's)*. Both rational and irrational beliefs are *evaluations* of reality, not descriptions or predictions of it. Thus, they are not merely sentences, such as "Something might happen," but if something does happen, they express an evaluation of it (e.g., rational: "How unfortunate"; irrational: "What a catastrophe! How horrible!"). People are able to hold both of these types of thoughts at the same time. An important task in therapy is to help clients discriminate RB's from IB's, since ultimately they will be asked to challenge their irrational notions and replace them with more rational philosophies. How, then, does one discriminate rational from irrational thoughts?

Attempts to characterize RB's have resulted in the following suggested criteria. Examine the rational statement, "It would be bad if my wife left me," against each criterion.

1. *A rational belief is true.* The belief is consistent with reality in kind and degree; it can be supported by evidence; and it is empirically verifiable. It is logical, internally consistent, and consistent with realities. Thus, a rational belief is not merely a logical belief; logic is a necessary but not sufficient ingredient in identifying a rational philosophy. Consider our example above; we could prove that unpleasant effects would result from the client's wife leaving. Presumably he would lose many pleasant things.

2. *A rational belief is not absolutistic.* Instead, it is conditional or relativistic. A rational belief is usually stated as a desire, hope, want,

wish, or preference, and thus reflects a desiring rather than a demanding philosophy. Can you see how the rational example above reflects a preference rather than a demand? The client simply implies, "I'd prefer it if my wife stayed in our marriage."

3. *A rational belief results in moderate emotion.* Thus, RB's lead to feelings which may range from mild to strong but which are not upsetting to the individual. This is an important distinction, since a common misconception about RET is that rational thinking leads to the absence of emotion. Quite the contrary; it would be quite a stretch of the imagination to assume that a zero level of emotional concern would be helpful or rational. Moderate emotional arousal serves as a motivator to problem solving (e.g., looking at the Activating event to see if it can be changed), while underarousal or overarousal may be a hindrance to this skill. Returning to our example above, when the client thinks about his wife leaving him, he probably feels sad but not clinically depressed.

4. *A rational belief helps you attain your goals.* Thus, RB's are congruent with: satisfaction in living, minimizing intrapsychic conflict, minimizing conflict with the environment, enabling affiliation and involvement with others, and growth toward a vital absorption in some personally fulfilling endeavor. More simply, perhaps, rational beliefs provide us with the freedom to pursue goals in a less fearful, noncondemning fashion and allow us to take risks which may be involved in attaining these goals. From our sample rational belief, we conclude that our client's goal is to live as happily as possible, and this cannot be done if he is clinically depressed. In addition, if the strong evaluative thoughts about his wife leaving were to result in a clinical depression, his behavior would perhaps drive his wife and others away.

Irrational beliefs, on the other hand, are characterized by different, often opposite, features:

1. *An irrational belief is not true.* It does not follow from reality; it may begin with an inaccurate premise and/or lead to inaccurate deductions; it is not supported by evidence; and it often represents an overgeneralization. IB's, therefore, tend to be extreme evaluative exaggerations of a situation and are often reflected in descriptors such as "awful," "terrible," or "horrible." A sample irrational belief might be, "I couldn't bear it if my wife left me." Such a statement obviously is not a reflection of reality.

2. *An irrational belief is a command.* As such, it represents an

absolutistic rather than probabilistic philosophy and is expressed as demands (versus wishes), shoulds (versus preferences), and needs (versus wants). Irrational beliefs are often overlearned since childhood and are frequently based on narcissistic or grandiose demands placed on the self, others, or the universe. Ellis (1979a, 1979b; Ellis and Harper, 1975) describes these as the three Major Musts:

> *I must:* (do well, get approval, etc.)
>
> *You must:* (treat me well, love me, etc.)
>
> *The world must:* (give me what I want quickly and easily, treat me fairly, etc.)

The derivatives of these thoughts generally take a form somewhat like: (a) it's awful, (b) I can't bear it, and (c) I'm a louse for behaving lousily. We occasionally even manage to disturb ourselves with completely contradictory musts—for example, demanding to make a great deal of money while simultaneously demanding to be universally loved. If you set out to make as much money as possible, you will probably step on some toes! To return to our sample IB, the client is typically saying, "Since my wife *must* not leave me, I can't bear it if she does!" as well as "Since I can't bear it if my wife leaves me, she *must* not leave me." Can you hear the command in these statements?

3. *An irrational belief leads to disturbed emotions.* Apathy or anxiety may be debilitating at worst and nonproductive at best. If a client has not been functioning well in his or her recent life and thinks either (a) "*It doesn't matter* that I'm functioning poorly" or (b) "*Isn't it awful* that I'm functioning so poorly," the client will most likely experience one of the two nonhelpful emotional extremes, apathy or anxiety. Appropriate concern, however, would be generated by a more rational thought, such as: "It matters, and I'm going to work on functioning better, but in the meantime, it's not awful or the end of the world that I'm functioning poorly."

4. *An irrational belief does not help you attain your goals.* When one is tied up in absolutes and shackled by upsetting emotions, one is hardly in the best position to work at the ongoing business in life of maximizing pleasure and minimizing discomfort. The client in the example above illustrates this problem. He will not be able to attain his

goal of a happy life if he is continually worried about his wife leaving him.

WORDS AND MEANINGS

Ellis (1979a, 1979b) has suggested that in discriminating irrational beliefs, we look for the *should* and look for the *must*. Although these key words may indeed be clues to a demanding philosophy, they are often used innocuously. A common error made by new RET therapists is assuming that all utterances of words such as "should," "ought," "must," or "have to" represent a demand concept. These words have many meanings in our language, one of which is *predictive*. The sentence "It should rain tonight" means "I expect it to rain tonight because of certain information I have." A second meaning is *advisory*, as in the sentence "You should see the movie I saw last night," which means "I liked the movie and I think you will too." Another meaning is *conditional*, which reflects an "if-then" proposition. "I should have the vacuum repaired" probably means "If I'm going to clean the rugs, I should have the vacuum repaired." The troublesome definition represents a *moral imperative*, implying that an event must occur. Each of the examples above could have absolutistic meanings, and the therapist can make the discrimination by attending to the context of the client's statement and his or her emotional state. As a caveat, it would be wise for the therapist who hears a client's "should" to rephrase the sentence and feed it back, to assure that it represents demandingness. Otherwise, time may be lost in stamping out irrelevant shoulds, and the therapist may succeed in merely developing a new unexamined taboo ("I should not say 'should'").

If, as we have pointed out, it is self-defeating to hold irrational ideas, why do we do so? A number of factors may come into play. First, this tendency is certainly reinforced by common cultural stereotypes which are reflected in our language, our stories, and our songs. A recent review of popular music, for example, found that about 82 percent of country-western and rock songs expressed irrational philosophies (Protinsky and Popp, 1978). Second, there may be a kind of self-reinforcing thrill achieved when we are irrational. Think of the boy who has tearful

As an exercise, go through the following sentences and see how many you can correctly identify as rational or irrational. Answers are given on page 285.

I wish I had succeeded at X; it would have made things a lot easier.

What a shame that things didn't work out well.

Damn, I wish it weren't raining!

What a disappointment it was, not getting that job.

I wish we lived closer to school so I wouldn't have to walk so far.

I get so uncomfortable when my husband nags at me.

It certainly is annoying to listen to that music.

If you want to pass that test, you should study hard.

These exercises really are a bother.

hysterics because he didn't make the team or the girl who didn't get invited to the dance. Distortion and exaggeration can be exciting, and, of course, may also get us attention or sympathy from others in our environment. Perhaps the most basic reason people are irrational, however, is stated by Ellis (1976), who suggests that almost everyone thinks irrationally some of the time; he asserts that it is the human condition. Strange as it may seem, this third explanation for irrationality may be clinically quite comforting. Such a suggestion appears to function well because it changes the attribution and allows clients to stop blaming themselves for their irrational beliefs.

THE MAJOR IB'S

Ellis (1976) has codified the irrational notions heard in therapy with thousands of his clients into several major categories. Keep in mind, however, that the following list is a typology of broad classes; they may not be expressed in pure form by any given client. A significant job of the therapist, therefore, is to locate the client's *idiosyncratic* irrational beliefs, which may or may not be subsumed into one of the following classes. To aid in training your ear, we have included sample phrases or sentence fragments in which the pertinent irrational belief is embedded. Following the discussion of each irrational belief we include an illustration of its rational counterpart. We encourage you to test your understanding by trying to anticipate, in writing, the RB's.

1. I must be loved and approved of by every significant person in my life, and if I'm not, it's awful.

I can't stand being called a castrating female.

Nobody likes me.

I'm afraid to ask her for a date.

I couldn't stand it if he were mad at me!

I'd be a fool if I did that.

I couldn't do that in public.

I would do anything for this person.

This irrational belief is among the most pervasive and troublesom᷈ in therapy. It represents a fear of rejection or disapproval by others. Ellis (1974b; 1977a) occasionally refers to the problem as "Love Slobbism," and it may be particularly evident in female patients as a result of our culture's sex-role socialization messages. A woman without a partner often views herself as an unfinished product, an incomplete entity. As Janet Wolfe (1975) has pointed out, women holding such a concept often engage in many self-defeating behaviors. They may not assertively ask for what they want, or may passively go along with what they don't want in sex-love relationships for fear that if they speak up, their partner might think them inadequate and reject them.

(RB: It would be desirable and productive to concentrate on self-respect, on winning approval for practical purposes, and on loving instead of being loved.)

2. When other people behave badly or unfairly, they should be blamed, reprimanded, and punished; they are bad or rotten individuals.

It's all your fault.

He shouldn't have done that to me.

My parents should have been fair. Then I wouldn't be in this trouble.

She's no good.
You male chauvinist pig!
He's stupid.
He deserved it.
I'd like to see him pay.
I'll get back at him.
Of course, he should be punished.

By listing this belief as irrational, we do not mean to imply that *punishment* is in some way irrational or ineffective. While we believe that imposing penalties can be an important way to influence others' behaviors, we do not believe that any human being morally *deserves* punishment. The elements of irrationality in this belief are the concepts (a) that the *person* is to be condemned, (b) that the person *should* or must be punished, and (c) that a person can be rated as bad. Behaviors, not people, are legitimately rated; similarly, punishment is effective in changing behaviors, not in condemning people.

(RB: Certain acts are inappropriate or antisocial, and those who perform them are behaving stupidly or neurotically and would be better helped to change.)

3. It's awful when things are not the way I'd like them to be.

I won't be treated unfairly.
I can't go on without it.
I can't imaging not having it.
But if I don't get into graduate school . . . oh, my God!
She never has sex with me.
I can't stand being fat.
He's always given me what I wanted in the past.
All the other kids have . . .
If he does that one more time, I'll scream.
I spend all my time picking up after you. I have no time for me.

The patients' statements are a good illustration of unfinished speech. In none of the examples above does the client directly state an evaluation of the situation described; the evaluation is implied in the context of the speech or the tone of voice in which the comment is made. For example, in the statement "She never has sex with me," there may be an unspoken conclusion ". . . and she should; since she doesn't, it's awful." It is useful to encourage the patient to finish the thought and realize that he has, in fact, made an exaggerated evaluation of the problem and its consequences.

(RB: It's too bad that things are not often the way one would like, and it would be advisable to change or control conditions so that they become more satisfactory. If change is impossible, one had better temporarily accept their existence.)

4. I should be very anxious about events that are uncertain or potentially dangerous.

It could happen.
Oh, my God.
I can't think of anything else but that.
Nobody seems to understand how serious this is.
It's on my mind all the time.
I can't just let it happen.
If you're not upset, you probably don't understand the situation.
What do you mean, "relax"?
But how can I be sure it won't happen?
Me, get on a horse?

This irrational belief is based on the demand for certainty in our lives and results in anxiety when we do not get guarantees. Patients who hold this irrational belief are giving themselves two troubles for the price of one. They will probably upset themselves not only when the unfortunate or undesirable event happens but also well in advance.

(RB: One would better face the danger or fear and render it nondangerous, and when that is impossible, accept the inevitable.)

5. I am not worthwhile unless I am thoroughly competent, adequate, and achieving at all times, or at least most of the time in at least one major area.

What an idiot I am.

I shouldn't have screamed at the children.

I'm not smart enough to apply to graduate school.

I can't face myself.

What can I do with myself now that I'm retired?

How could I get a C?

I shouldn't have come so fast.

Without him, I'm nothing.

My client didn't get better!

This irrational belief is one of the two or three most commonly heard by therapists. It is perhaps most prevalent among males in our competitive, achievement-oriented society. It is usually connected with a strong fear of failure; the person believes that if he doesn't succeed, *he* is a failure (not simply that he failed at a task). This form of self-denigration is particularly anxiety-provoking when failing is anticipated and particularly depressing when failure has been experienced.

(RB: It is more advisable to accept oneself as an imperfect creature with human limitations and fallibilities. It is better to *do* than to need to do well.)

6. There's got to be a perfect solution to this problem; I must be certain and have perfect control over things.

There's gotta be a better way.

If I keep searching, I'll find it.

I just can't make a decision.

But how can I be sure?

Isn't that risky?

How will I know what's the best way to do it?

I know what I want, but I still can't decide.

If I stay I'll be miserable, and if I go I'll be miserable.

I lack self-confidence.

Doctor, do you mean you can't tell me what to do?

There are basically two parts to this irrational notion. The first is that there is an ideal or perfect *solution* to the problem, that one must be able to find it, and if one doesn't, the results would be terrible. The second element is that whether or not there is a perfect solution, the patient believes he or she must have perfect *control* over the problem while it is evolving. This IB can also be directed at other people. The patient may become angry at others who don't provide solutions to or control over difficult conditions. One of the people the patient is most likely to be angry at is the therapist when problems aren't resolved easily and quickly or the therapist can't point out the road to a perfect ending.

(RB: Our world is one of probability and chance, and life can be enjoyed despite this.)

7. The world should be fair and just.

How could she do this to me?
Why does this always happen to me?
He shouldn't have done that.
I didn't deserve it.
But I did everything I was supposed to do.
They had no right to fire me.
How dare you.
He'll get it in the end.
You can't tell me what to do.
I don't ask for much.

This belief is irrational primarily because of its demandingness. Clients who believe this are unwilling to accept the world as it is and feel that they can and must be better constructors of the universe than whoever created it. This IB is often one of the key elements in the cognitive system of adolescent clients. The therapist will not do well to agree with the clients that it's awful and terrible that the world isn't treating them fairly, but can ask clients where they ever got the idea that the world *should* be fair. Adolescents can be very idealistic and tend to have fixed notions of how the world should be (their way!).

(RB: the world is often unfair, and good guys sometimes do die young. It is better to accept this fact and concentrate on enjoying oneself despite it.)

8. I should be comfortable and without pain at all times.

I needed this aggravation?

It's just too hard.

But I don't like it.

I might get hurt.

But I get so hungry.

I can't stand it.

What a hassle.

I'd be happy if I could just get away from it all.

Can't we park closer?

What, me go to the dentist? That hurts too much.

We've been standing in line five minutes already.

I'm afraid to get pregnant because it'll hurt to give birth.

The reader may be surprised to see the word "pain" used in the description of this irrational belief; we refer to both psychological and physical discomfort. Physical discomfort is involved in several situations unconnected with physical illness, such as inconveniences of various kinds. Belief in one's inability to stand discomfort is a form of Low Frustration Tolerance (LFT) and often leads to addictions and behavioral excesses, or at the very least to whining and complaining which is interpersonally offensive. Discomfort anxiety may also prevent patients from achieving long-range goals or long-range pleasures because they define the present discomfort as unbearable. If you are going to walk up a mountain stream in order to bathe in a waterfall, you're probably going to have to step on stones and rocks. Many people believe that they must be comfortable in whatever they do; such a notion is obviously self-defeating.

(RB: There's seldom gain without pain. I can tolerate this discomfort, although I may never like it.)

9. I may be going crazy, and that would be unbearable.

I can't even think straight anymore.

I saw a TV show last night about a man with my problems, and he ended up in the nuthouse.

I'm so afraid I won't be able to control myself.

What'll happen to me?

I'm scared I might crack up!
What if I lose control?
I think I'm losing my mind.
Anyone with my problems must be very disturbed.
I could end up like my mother . . . she killed herself.
What does this symptom mean, Doctor?
Is that normal?

Phrenophobia, the fear of going crazy, is a common concern among patients and often underlies what we have called symptom stress. Victor Raimey (1975) has referred to this problem as *psychological hypochondria*. Why are people deathly afraid? Typically, as nonprofessionals, they are grossly misinformed about psychopathology and imagine themselves becoming raving maniacs who must be locked away for prolonged stays in a "snake pit." The underlying cognitive themes usually involve both self-rating ("I'm no good") and discomfort anxiety, as above ("I couldn't stand the hassles").

(RB: Emotional distress is certainly not pleasant, but it is hardly unbearable.)

The remaining four irrational beliefs take a somewhat different form. They are less clearly evaluative but they do reflect irrationality, since they are neither empirically verifiable nor conducive to achieving one's goals.

10. It's easier to avoid than to face life's difficulties.

Well, nothing's going to help anyway.
Why bother trying?
I'll do anything to avoid that.
It's no use.
Oh, it's not such a big problem anyway.
The booze helps me forget, Doc.
I'd just rather get high.
I don't like where my life is now, but . . .
If I don't think about it, it doesn't bother me.

It won't help anyway.

I'll think about that tomorrow.

I've been meaning to do something about that but just haven't gotten around to it.

This notion is similar to belief 8 (the need for comfort) and implies an evaluative component: "Life's difficulties are so horrid that they must be avoided at all costs." This avoidance can be a significant impediment to progress in therapy, and the therapist would be wise to confront the procrastination directly and to forcefully encourage clients to vigorously challenge this IB.

(RB: The so-called easy way is invariably the harder way in the long run.)

11. I need someone stronger than myself on whom to depend or rely.

A woman needs a man.

I can't cope without her.

When things get hard, I just rely on the Lord.

I can't do it alone.

But he always knows what to do.

Nobody can cook like my mother could.

Behind every good man, there's a woman.

You can always rely on the Man Upstairs.

What'll I do if you leave?

Doc, I've been waiting all week just to tell you this.

Doctor, you can't go on vacation!

In this irrational belief we find people stating that they cannot cope or cannot solve their own problems. While many of us find it helpful to turn to others for advice and counsel, including counsel in prayer, exclusive reliance upon someone else or on a higher power simply defeats one's own efforts to solve problems and work toward one's goals in life. The key element is the word "need," for as it is said, "God helps those who help themselves."

(RB: It is better to take the risks of acting and thinking independently.)

12. Emotional misery comes from external pressure, and I have little ability to control or change my feelings.

> He made me feel like two cents.
> I'll be devastated if she leaves me.
> He made me so mad.
> When he comes in the room, I see red.
> He'll ruin my evening.
> Well, society's trained us to be that way.
> You made me love you.
> If you'd stop picking on me, I could change.
> If only I had that job I'd be happy.
> You make me sick.

Changing this belief is a cornerstone of the work of the rational-emotive therapist. Unless clients assume responsibility for their own feelings and understand that they have produced them and can therefore change them, they will continually be blaming their misery on a variety of outside factors. Belief 12 is actually a hypothesis about the effects of environmental stimuli on human behavior. Thus, according to our strict definition that beliefs are evaluative cognitions, this notion is not an irrational belief per se. It is, however, an idea that will prevent people from helping themselves and will discourage them from correcting their IB's unless it is changed.

(RB: Emotional disturbance is largely caused by the view one takes of conditions. One has enormous control over one's destructive emotions if one chooses to work at changing the bigoted and unscientific hypotheses employed to create them.)

13. My past is the cause of my present problems; because these events were strong influences on me, they will continue to be so.

> Well, I was brought up that way.
> My whole family's like that.
> I must have been conditioned to do that.
> Well, I was adopted.
> I never did well in school.

When I was a kid—
I had a rotten childhood.
All of us Italians are emotional.
Doctor, you couldn't understand it unless you were Jewish.
It really is my mother's fault; she made me this way.

This idea, again not clearly evaluative in form, is one of the most insidious and pernicious impediments to successful psychotherapy. Its very statement implies that therapy cannot work and that clients are unchangeable. The clients may cite their personal history, their genetic or ethnic background, or some significant life event as a reason that they cannot change. Of course, when they believe they cannot change, they are unlikely to try to change. If this belief is irrational, it is so because it is an impediment to the person's happiness as well as because of its absolutistic nature. It is a prediction about influences on human behavior but, we believe, an incorrect one.

(RB: One can learn from past experiences while not being overly attached to or prejudiced by them.)

It may be helpful for the new rational therapist to remember that all of the IB's may be reduced to one of the three core irrationalities:

1. A philosophy of self-denigration
2. An intolerance of frustration
3. Blaming and condemning others

It will be wise for the therapist to keep questioning clients until they admit one or more of these core notions. Core irrational beliefs can also be identified by patients' evaluative definitions. An event is irrationally labeled as horrible by *definition* rather than because of an objective calculation of its negative consequences.

FINDING THE B'S

Belief systems are not always easy to identify, since much of our thinking process consists of greatly overlearned cognitive habits which have become automatic. We rarely stop in our busy lives to think about our thinking. Many years ago, John Watson, the founder of behaviorism, suggested why our self-talk is covert; quite simply, talking aloud to ourselves is socially punished. The Soviet developmental psychologists Vygotsky (1962) and Luria (1969) have traced the process of submerging speech in children. At the earliest stages of verbal development, children's behavior is controlled by overt verbalizations of others. Somewhat later, children can be heard giving themselves similar behavior-control directives aloud. Ultimately, they progress in the submerging process so that the self-talk is completely internalized. In addition, with repeated practice, not only is the need to focus on the internal commands reduced but a kind of short-circuiting apparently takes place so that individual elements of the self-talk get subsumed under larger headings. This last point will perhaps be clearer if you recall learning to drive a stick shift car or watching your child learn to tie his or her shoes. In both cases, the complex task was broken down into smaller units of instruction, initially communicated by someone other than the learner, then usually verbalized aloud by the learner, then repeated subvocally, and finally integrated into a smooth whole that could proceed without conscious attention. The thinking processes that precede emotive reactions presumably follow similar, although perhaps more subtle, developmental patterns. A clinical issue may then involve helping the patients to locate and verbalize their thoughts, beliefs, attitudes, and philosophies.

Sometimes the therapist may encounter clients who are in touch with their self-talk and volunteer it easily. More common, perhaps, are patients who, when asked what they are thinking, respond with feelings—"I think I'm sad/anxious/apprehensive/etc." The therapist's task then becomes one of teaching the client to recognize, for example, that "apprehension" is not a thought but a feeling.

How do you help clients to verbalize their B's? The simplest procedure is to ask. Here are some questions you might use to elicit cognitions:

1. What was going through your mind? (or, if a client is emoting in a session, "What is going through your mind right now?")
2. What were you telling yourself?
3. Were you aware of any thoughts in your head?
4. There goes that old record in your head again; what was it playing this time?

5. What was on your mind then?
6. What were you worrying about?
7. Are you aware of what you were thinking at that moment?

If clients claim that no cognitions were present, the therapist may want to keep in mind that not only the presence of irrational beliefs but the absence of structured thought may be an indicator of psychopathology. Therapeutic work may begin by teaching clients how to tune into and monitor their thinking by the use of therapist *suggestion*. By piecing together information about the clients' situations, behaviors, and emotional reactions, therapists may infer the presence of specific IB's, which they can then model for the clients as follows:

"Well, I don't know exactly what's going through your mind, but when people feel anxious, they're often saying something like this to themselves—"

or

"In my experience, when people have a great deal of difficulty making decisions, they're often saying to themselves something like—

Of course, it will be important to validate these hunches by conferring with the patient—for example, "Does that sound familiar?" or "Could you be thinking something like that?" In subsequent sessions, when the patient brings up another anxiety statement, the therapist can refer back to this teaching—"Do you remember that explanation of anxiety we were talking about last week? Well, what do you think you were saying to yourself this time?" In this manner, the therapist is helping the client to recognize the thought-emotion connection.

In a similar manner, the therapist may wish to provide the irrational belief, rather than being too evocative, with clients who are particularly halting and/or ruminative. The irrational belief may be stated as a generality and followed up by a question. For example: "Many people might say to themselves, 'If she thinks I'm stupid, that would be terrible!' Are you thinking anything like that?" If the answer is yes, the hunch is validated and the point has been made. If the answer is no, the therapist may then inquire, "Well, what *were* you thinking?"

Frequently clients talk to themselves in what, syntactically, are half-sentences. In essence, they have punctuated their verbalization with a period, although the thought is not completed. For example:

C: For a long time I wasn't thinking about what I wanted to do with my life.
T: And now that you are thinking about it?
C: I've decided that I want to go back to school, but I don't think I can make it now.

In this illustration, the therapist has fed the thought back to the client as a sentence-completion task. Similarly, clients may verbalize only the rational part of their thinking, so that the therapist may want to append the unstated irrational philosophy as a hypothesis. For example:

C: I want to do well in school.
T: And therefore you *must*, right?

This sentence-completion technique is one of the most frequently used by RET therapists.

The missing thoughts can also form the end of a syllogism, as in the following case: "If he loved me, he'd marry me . . . but he hasn't found a way to marry me." The patient may stop her verbalization at this point, but then why would she be depressed? The therapeutic query at this juncture might entail asking the patient what she concludes about the situation. Most likely, she has finished this illogical syllogism covertly: "Therefore, he doesn't love me and that's *awful!*" A moment's reflection on the logic of this structure will reveal that "if-then" statements do not follow this pattern—for example, there could be many other reasons for his failure to appear at the altar—and even if her partner doesn't love her, is this really *awful?*

A related technique to get at the core irrational belief is to lead the client through a chain of thoughts by repeating a simple question. Consider the client who reports difficulty in making a decision:

T: Why would that pose a problem for you?
C: Well, I might make a mistake.
T: And why would that be a problem for you?

C: But if I made a mistake, I'd feel stupid (or guilty).
T: Well, that's how you'd feel, but what would it mean about you?
C: It would prove I was inadequate.

Similarly, a chain of time-projection questions may be useful: "OK, suppose you lost your job, then what happens?—OK, you lose your home, and then what happens?—OK, and then what happens?—etc." Note that the therapist does not challenge the client's projection but works with the assumption that the worst might happen.

T: What's the worst that could happen if you stood up to your wife?
C: She might leave me.
T: What's the worst thing that could happen if your wife *did* leave you?
C: I might not find another woman. My God!
T: But let's suppose you never did find another woman. What's the worst that could happen then?
C: I could get sick and no one would care for me.
T: Well, what would be the worst thing about that?
C: That would be the worst thing! That's so terrible I hate to even think about it.

Don't be surprised if, when you get to the bottom line, you find you are far away from the original problem; patients can be quite unaware of their core irrational philosophies.

As in the example above, the therapist continues to probe the core irrational beliefs by asking questions and, along the way, may uncover additional irrational thoughts. Patients may begin by complaining that they want their mother, their spouse, their children, their boss (etc.) to do what they want (IB 3). The therapist's next question might be: "Why is it important to you to have them do that?" The answer might reveal that the patients view themselves as "special"—perhaps as weak and dependent, as people who need others to take care of them (IB 11). If the therapist continues to ask why this is important, still more irrational beliefs may be revealed. In this example, clients may state that they believe it's awful that their family doesn't care for them since that would be proof that they are worthless. Their belief in their "worthlessness" would be the core IB.

Therapeutically, how does one intervene with such a chain? Essentially, there are two ways of proceeding: the therapist can stop at each irrational belief and dispute it or continue questioning and begin the disputation at the bottom line. We have no empirical evidence as to which procedure is better, but clinical experience suggests that the therapist may profitably go right to the core notions. In either case, unless the core IB's are tackled, the client may well develop new problems. For example, the clients who never successfully dispute the irrationality of self-rating may give up their "need" for the adoration of their love partner but may later link their ego to their job performance. It is therefore important to keep the patient's core IB at the forefront of the therapeutic plan. Thus, after beginning a session by asking, "What's your problem this week?" try to bring new presenting complaints back to the core IB: "How does this relate to what we've identified as your main problem?" This factor may make the difference between Band-aid therapy and a more elegant solution.

A key point to note in the above discussion is that behavior usually has *multiple determinants*. Too often, the new RET therapist will obtain the C (affect), find one IB to dispute, and consider the case closed. By allowing the patient to talk freely or by persistent questioning, the therapist may find that the C is a result of several IB's, often with spiral, lateral, or hierarchical connections.

The therapist needn't be dismayed to find a group of B's, or a "regular B-hive." The therapist can simply jot down the irrational notions as they emerge and then present the list to the client for discussion and evaluation. Perhaps the therapist can point out common themes, if there are any; in their absence, the therapeutic dyad may work together to hierarchically arrange the beliefs for disputational attack.

Another problem may be that the new therapist, while uncovering IB's on one aspect of the client's problems, may be ignoring IB's the client may hold if he took a different course of action. For example, suppose that Bert, a client, presents the problem of guilt over adultery or adulterous thoughts and requests that the therapist alleviate this guilt. Should the therapist advocate sexual libertarianism or stress the virtues of monogamy? Neither; it wold be better to decipher the core IB's which may be operating in this instance. Thus, the patient has two alternative paths (adultery versus monogamy), and it is not the therapist's job to pick one for him but rather to help the client identify IB's which prevent him from selecting one or the other path. For instance, one set of IB's may revolve around self-denigration and result in the client's guilt about his adulterous thoughts or actions. Alternatively, Bert has the choice of remaining monogamous. What IB's and emotions have prevented him from doing so comfortably? It is possible that he suffers from Low Frustration Tolerance, believing that he must act on his desires for an outside partner and could not tolerate the discomfort of monogamous living. The goal is to uncover such irrational notions so that the patient can engage in problem solving, such as weighing the alternatives, making a decision for himself, and learning to live with it.

GUIDES TO FINDING THE B FOR SPECIFIC EMOTIONS

At this point, you may find yourself overwhelmed with what may seem like an infinite number of connections between B's and C's. You may be reassured to find, however, that specific common thoughts generally lead to specific common emotions. The work of the rational-emotive therapist derives from this theoretical assumption. By way of illustration, we will present the irrational philosophies which underlie four major emotional dysfunctions: anxiety, depression, guilt, and anger.

Anxiety.   Anxiety is the result of future-oriented cognitions; people are rarely afraid, for prolonged periods of time, of events in the here-and-now. The therapist would do well, therefore, to ask future-oriented questions: "What do you think *might* happen?" or "What kind of trouble are you predicting?" What is usually heard in response is some form of catastrophizing or awfulizing. Fears may range from specific and isolated to pervasive and unspecific (the so-called free-floating anxiety). The two most common fears, according to Hauck (1974), are fear of rejection and fear of failure, followed closely by the super-fear, the fear of being afraid.

The cognitive steps to anxiety, therefore, are three:

1. Something bad might happen.
2. If it does, that would be awful—a catastrophe.
3. Because it might be a catastrophe, I *must* worry, stew, and think about it most of the time.

Thus, the first statement might very well be a good prediction based on valid evidence, although the therapist would do well to check this out.

The bad event that clients are predicting might be an external circumstance or their own self-condemnation because of some potential failure. Thus, they may be fearful of the future event because they believe it may prove their lack of self-worth. Assuming that patients are correct about the event occurring, however, their first distortion may appear at statement 2, a biased perception of A. In any case, the clearly irrational "should" or "must" occurs at statement 3, for unless patients cling to this belief, they will be unable to remain upset.

Depression. Beck (1976) has outlined a cognitive triad that *descriptively* identifies depression: a negative view of the self, a negative view of the world, and a negative view of the future. These are similar to and overlap the dynamic irrational beliefs which RET theory suggests are the main *causative* agents in depression:

1. A devout belief in one's personal inadequacy.
2. The "horror" of not having what one "needs."
3. And the "awfulness" of the way things are.

Hauck (1974), in his excellent book on depression, divides the problem into three types, each with its underlying irrational structures. Depression can be caused, first, by *self-blame;* the thinking pattern that leads to self-blame is generally as follows:

1. I failed, sinned, or accidentally hurt someone.
2. I should be perfect and not do bad things.
3. I am, therefore, a bad person and deserve punishment.

The second approach to depression is via *self-pity*, whose irrational core is:

1. I want my way.
2. It's awful if I don't get it.

Finally, one can become depressed by *other-pity* if one believes that:

1. I *should* be upset over other people's problems (or over world conditions).

Guilt. Guilt cognitions have two phases. First, patients believe that they are doing (or have done) something wrong. Second, they condemn themselves for doing the wrong thing. Again, the first statement may be an accurate assessment of reality according to the patient's value system. Considered alone, it is a statement of self-responsibility and may be worthwhile in changing one's future behavior. Statement 2 adds an extra, unnecessary idea. Consider the difference that would result if instead of #2, the patient had said, "Well, so I did the wrong thing. People do that from time to time, and I'll do my best not to do it again." Thus, true guilt always includes the second component of self-downing, which usually sabotages emotional or behavioral improvement.

Anger.   Anger covers a large dimension, but problem anger (hostility) is emotion which interferes with goal-directed behavior. Ellis (1977b) describes anger cognitions as a set of Jehovian demands. The first step consists of defining Rights and Wrongs, a kind of moral indignation. The second step is the absolutistic shoulds: "You should treat me differently" or "You shouldn't act that way." The third step is awfulizing: "It's horrible; I can't stand it!" And finally, we reach blaming and condemning: "You're a bastard!" and "You deserve to be punished and damned!" What is the essence of the irrationality in these notions? Angry feelings usually lead to inefficient behavior; damning and demanding amount to playing God; and damnation normally won't right a wrong or teach better behavior.

OTHER GUIDELINES

In the previous section, we described how the RET therapist uses the client's specific C as a clue in identifying the relevant irrational beliefs. Additionally, as you gather experience as a therapist, you will find that particular clinical problems are commonly associated with specific belief systems. Clues to irrational beliefs may be found in the A event which the client describes or in characteristics of the client which you note. In other words, in searching for the irrational cognitions with which patients upset themselves, you may begin with *cognitive schemas* which are derived from cumulative experience with similar cases. These schemas can serve as initial hypotheses. While it is beyond the scope of this book to suggest all of the common schemas, a few examples may be helpful to illustrate their form.

    If the client is a mother who is experiencing a great deal of anxiety or anger at her children for their misbehavior, we have frequently found that the key irrational belief underlying the problem is one of self-worth. The mother may have not only identified the children's behavior as bad but may also have overgeneralized, concluding that she is a bad mother. Thus, she may have rated and devalued herself based on the behavior of her children. In working with mothers, whether their children are infants or independent adults, the therapist may keep such a schema in mind as a hypothesis and focus the questions on issues of self-worth.

Another example of a schema derives from work with female clients in the age range from forty-five to sixty, for whom depression is a major symptom. During this time of life, women begin to experience the effects of menopause and often view their role as vital sexual creatures as coming to an end. They may not initiate a discussion of menopause or sexuality, so that the therapist's schema may open the discussion with core issues and irrational beliefs surrounding them.

The development and use of such schemas will evolve as you accumulate professional experience. You may find, in fact, that you have many such decision-making schemas already. The point we wish to stress, however, is that schemas suggest hypotheses, not facts. Not all maternal anger is based on issues of self-worth, just as not all depression of women in their middle years is related to beliefs about sexual decline. In other words, your hypotheses had better be empirically validated by data from the patient before you proceed with therapy.

A FINAL CAVEAT

The therapist would be wise to listen for an irrational idea that commonly occurs to clients in rational-emotive therapy and prevents them from honestly bringing problems to the session or telling the therapist about their self-talk. This irrational notion is that they *should* have gotten over that problem or that they're not *supposed* to feel anxiety or think irrationally. Some clients may plainly reveal such a hidden idea (e.g., "I'm ashamed to tell you what happened last week, Doctor"). In other cases, clients' shame or guilt may prevent them from getting help at all. The therapist may find it helpful to think of this problem as a generalized schema and periodically investigate whether or not it is operating with clients.

6 Disputation: General Strategies

In the preceding chapters we have discussed the A, B, and C—the diagnostic groundwork—of rational-emotive therapy. Thus far, we might conceptualize the therapist's role as one of a diagnostician, looking for and amplifying clues which set up the problem. Clarifying the A, B, and C is an assessment procedure, useful for both therapist and client. Until the therapist understands the important connections between B and C, these cannot be clearly pointed out to the client. Unless clients understand the importance of these same relationships, they will not see the relevance of changing their beliefs. *Changing the beliefs* is the real work of therapy and occurs at D, the *Disputation*.

What is a disputation? It is a debate or a challenge to the patient's irrational belief system and can be of a *cognitive, imaginal,* and/or *behavioral* nature. Each of these disputational strategies will be discussed in this chapter. Once the RB's have been discriminated from the IB's, the essence of the D is to challenge the IB's. For example, the therapist may ask, "Why must you succeed?" The client may respond, "Because I want to." This is a Rational Belief, but the continuation, "—and it's awful when I don't get what I want," is an Irrational Belief. Only the IB's, not the RB's, are disputed.

Patients are confronted with their internal irrational philosophies and asked to examine them, bit by bit, to see if they make sense and are helpful. Disputation is, then, a logical and empirical process in which the patient is helped to stop and think. Its basic goal is to help the patient internalize a new philosophy, epitomized in statements such as: "It would be too bad if I don't succeed, but I can bear it. I'm merely fallible, and that's not awful." This basic goal is known in RET as the *elegant solution*.

D, therefore, consists of two basic stages:

1. The patient is led through a sentence-by-sentence challenge of Irrational Beliefs. The therapist thereby raises doubts about the evaluations the patient has made of A.
2. The patient is helped to develop alternative, rational philosophies.

Let's turn now to an examination of the three types of disputational strategies.

COGNITIVE DISPUTATION

Cognitive disputations are attempts to change the client's erroneous beliefs through philosophical persuasion, didactic presentations, Socratic dialogues, vicarious experiences, and other modes of verbal expression. One of the most important tools in cognitive disputation is the use of questions. We pointed out previously that as a rule, it is generally good to avoid asking "why" questions; in disputation, however, "why" questions may be particularly fruitful. The answer to a "why" question requires proof or justification of a belief, and since there is no proof for irrational beliefs, the patient may see the logic for giving them up.

The following is a group of questions culled from disputations by Ellis (1962, 1971, 1974, 1979b) and from other therapists at the Institute for Rational Emotive Therapy in New York City and Los Angeles. We present them as examples to get you started. Note that by relying on such questions, the therapist is making the client do the work, and essentially asking the client to prove his or her irrational ideas to the therapist.

The first group of questions asks for evidence, logical consistency, or semantic clarity in the client's thinking, and can be used to challenge any IB:

What is the proof?
Where's the evidence?

Is that true? Why not?

Why is that so?

Can you prove it?

How do you know?

Why is that an overgeneralization?

Why is that a bad term to use?

How would you talk a friend out of such an idea?

Why is that an untrue statement?

In what way?

Is that very good proof?

Explain to me why (e.g.) you're so stupid you don't belong in college?

What behaviors can you marshal as proof?

Why does it *have* to be so?

Let's be scientists. What do the data show?

Where is that writ?

What evidence would it take to get you to give up that belief?

What would that mean about you as a person?

What's wrong with the notion that you're "special"?

How would you be destroyed if you don't X?

Why must you?

Let's assume the worst. You're doing very bad things. Now why *must* you not do them?

The second group of questions requires the client to reevaluate whether future events will occur and if so, whether they will be as unpleasant as the client believes. These questions are particularly useful for challenging "awfulizing."

What would happen if—?

What if—

If that's true, what's the worst that can happen?

So what if that happens?

How would that be so terrible?

How is a disadvantage awful?

Ask yourself, can I still find happiness?

What *good* things can happen if X occurs?

Can you be happy even if you don't get what you want?

What might happen?

How terrible would that be?

Explain to me why you'd have to be done in by that?

What is the probability of a bad consequence?

How will your world be destroyed if X?

The third group of questions does not challenge the logic of the clients' thinking but serves as persuasive devices to help clients assess the hedonic value of their belief systems:

As long as you believe that, how will you feel?

"Whatever I want, I must get." Where will that command get you?

Is it worth the risk?

Is it worth it?

In using the questioning strategy, allow the client time to mull over and fully contemplate your questions. (This suggestion implies, therefore, that you will be careful to ask only one question at a time; no barrages, please.) Do not provide answers to your own questions until you give clients a chance to reach for their own answers. Be prepared for silences after your questions. New therapists seem to find these silences aversive, especially if they mistakenly believe that they *must* be directive at all times. Silence, in this instance, can indeed be golden.

Be aware, however, that these unusual questions can lead to discomfort on the part of your client, primarily because many of the questions have no answer (e.g., "Where is the evidence for that belief?" There isn't any.). Therefore, while you are waiting for the clients' response, tune in to the nonverbal signs of discomfort that they may be exhibiting during this period. If your clients are exceptionally distressed, ask them what emotional reactions or feelings they are having and find out what irrational beliefs they are telling themselves. Perhaps they are awfulizing about not knowing the answers to your questions or because they realize that they are thinking crookedly; if so, they will not be attending to the points you are making during disputation. Uproot these irrational beliefs before you continue with the original disputation.

Clients frequently respond to disputational questions by giving you the *rational belief.* For example, when the therapist attempts to dispute the concept of awfulness (e.g., "Where's the evidence that this is so terrible?"), the response of the client will almost always be a justification of why the situation is undesirable (e.g., "Because I don't like it!"). In this example, the patient is failing to discriminate between *undesirable* and *awful.* The most common error made by new RET therapists is to be stumped by the client's reasoning. Instead, the therapist would do well to point out to clients that their retort was evidence for the rational statement but not an answer to the original question. The therapist had better repeat the question until the client comes to the appropriate conclusion that no evidence exists for the IB.

C: But it's awful if I don't get this promotion!

T: Well, just how is that so awful?

C: Because . . . then I'll be stuck in the same job and I won't get the extra money nor the prestige that goes with it.

T: Look, Jack, that's evidence for why it's unfortunate or bad that you don't get the promotion. Because it's bad, it doesn't follow that it's terrible. Now, try again. Can you show me how it's *terrible?*

C: But I've worked hard for this for a long time. I deserve it!

T: Jack, that may be true that you've worked hard. But that's only further evidence that it's unfortunate that you didn't get it. How is that *terrible?*

C: You mean all those reasons for it being bad don't make it terrible?

T: That's right, Jack! Terrible means you can't live with this or possibly be happy. It means 101 percent bad. Now, how is failing to get the promotion *that bad?*

Clients will often persist in giving similar answers far longer than the client in the above example. The therapist had better be at least as persistent as the client.

The second set of cognitive disputation strategies is *didactic,* including the use of mini-lectures, analogies, and parables. Lectures, as we suggested earlier, are best kept brief and may be most useful when new ideas are being presented to the client. As the patient becomes familiar with rational-emotive theory, the amount of time spent on lecturing can be gradually decreased. Lectures can be illustrated with stories, analogies, and parables. There is great room for creativity in devising stories to show that the client's reasoning is faulty. Some examples will be given in the sections below, in which suggested disputations for the core irrational concepts are outlined.

Another widely used form of cognitive disputation and a primary tool of the RET therapist is exaggeration or *humor*, a variation of the paradoxical intention technique. Ellis (1977d) is particularly noted for his use of these strategies, not only in front of audiences but in individual sessions as well. Thus, if the client says, "It's really awful that I failed the test!" the therapist might respond, "You're right! It's not only awful, but I don't see how you're going to survive. That's the worst news I've ever heard! This is so horrendous that I can't bear to talk about it. Let's talk about something else, quick!" Such paradoxical statements frequently point out the senselessness of the IB to the client, and very little further debate may be necessary to make the point. There is no rule that therapy must be stodgy, dull, or super-serious, despite what you may have learned in your previous training. Once you get used to using humor judiciously, you as well as your client may enjoy your hour together more.

A fourth cognitive strategy is the use of vicarious modeling. One can frequently point out to clients many people in their environment who have similar Activating events and yet, because they do not adhere to the same IB's, do not suffer from exaggerated emotional reactions. Much can be learned by such vicarious modeling. Clients can see that others are not devastated by problems and can be reminded that lives go on despite unfortunate happenings. This knowledge can then be transferred back to themselves. The process can also serve to sensitize clients to look for data in their environment which may have been selectively screened out. Modeling is a particularly good strategy to use, therefore, when the client's A is virtually universal, such as the common problems presented by children and adolescents. Almost all children have to cope with going to bed "too early" and, even worse, having to brush their teeth beforehand! The therapist can point out that the vast majority of youngsters go through these same tortures and manage to do so unscathed and with significantly less horror.

New therapists are reluctant to use vicarious modeling when dealing with clients who have rare or highly aversive Activating events (e.g., rape, terminal illness, the death of one's child, etc.). Such clients are likely to believe that no one can appreciate how traumatic their experience was; yet coping models are available. The client may not have personally encountered such individuals, but referral to appropriate self-help groups will provide such exposure. One of the authors recently treated the mother of a child with Giles de la Tourette syndrome.* She was unfamiliar with the disorder and horrified by the child's bizarre behavior, convinced that her child was the only case in the world. Through some investigation, the therapist found an association for parents of children with Tourette's syndrome and advised the mother to attend a meeting of this group. This experience provided the woman with coping models, and at her next therapy session she concluded: "I guess it isn't so awful . . . people *can* learn to adjust to it."

IMAGINAL DISPUTATION STRATEGIES

A second disputational strategy involves the use of *imagery*. In one such procedure, after a verbal disputation, the therapist may ask clients to imagine themselves again in the troublesome situation; this may allow the therapist to see if the emotion has changed. If it has, the therapist may ask clients what they are now telling themselves as a way to rehearse more rational beliefs. If the emotion has not changed, there may be more IB's present, and the imagery exercise may allow them to emerge. If necessary, a new ABCD analysis may be conducted and the results reexamined by a repeat of the imagery exercise. As an alternative, the therapist may wish to shift to one of the following imagery techniques, known as REI, rational-emotive imagery (Maultsby, 1975; Maultsby and Ellis, 1974).

In *negative imagery*, clients close their eyes and imagine themselves in the problem situation (A) and try to experience their usual emotional turmoil (C). Wait until clients report experiencing C and then ask them to focus on the internal sentences which seem to be related to these emotional consequences. Then instruct patients to change the feel-

---

*The Tourette syndrome involves multiple motor tics in conjunction with a verbal tic which may take the form of a barking sound or long chains of obscenities.

ing from extreme to moderate (e.g., from anxiety to concern). Assure clients that this can be done, even if it's only for a fraction of a second. Instruct clients that as soon as they have accomplished this task, they are to open their eyes. At this signal from the patients, you may simply ask: "How were you able to do that?" Almost invariably the answer will reveal a cognitive shift; usually patients respond that they stopped catastrophizing (e.g., "So I'm a lousy lover; I'm still good at computers!"). Here is an example:

T: Now, I want you to close your eyes and imagine yourself back in the situation in which you felt so anxious yesterday. Can you do that?

Wait until clients indicate they have the image.

C: Yes.
T: Now, I want you to make yourself feel anxious right now, as you did yesterday. Signal me when you're feeling anxious.

Wait for the client's signal.

C: (nods)
T: OK, now tell me what thoughts are going through your head to make you feel anxious.

Wait for the client's response, which will be some form of IB.

C: I'm saying, "My God, suppose I goof up? He'll think I'm a jerk!"
T: Now, I want you to change that feeling of anxiety to one of *mere concern*. Signal me when you have felt less anxious and now feel merely concerned—perhaps motivated to do something about the situation.

Pause until the client's signal.

T: Now, what are you telling yourself so that you feel only concerned and not anxious?
C: Well, if I goof, it's not the end of the world, and if he thinks I'm a jerk, that's too bad. I *do* make mistakes—everybody does—and I'm working at improving my performance all the time. I guess I'll be doing that as long as I live!

In *positive imagery* (Maultsby, 1975; Maultsby and Ellis, 1974), clients imagine themselves in a problematic situation but picture themselves behaving differently and feeling differently. For example, speech-anxious clients imagine themselves speaking up in class or at a meeting and feeling relatively relaxed while doing so. As soon as clients report that they had that image, the therapist asks: "And what were you saying to yourself in order to do that?" Such a technique is useful because it allows clients to practice a positive plan and develop a set of coping skills. For example:

T: OK, Mary, now I know you've been having trouble when you think about giving that speech to the PTA this week. I know you've been feeling very anxious about that.

C: Yes, I'm really scared.

T: What I'd like you to do now is to close your eyes and picture yourself up there at the podium addressing the group of parents in the audience. But I want you to picture yourself doing that and feeling relatively *calm* while you're doing it. You're speaking slowly and clearly, and feeling not too anxious. You read your speech in a nice loud voice, glancing up frequently to look at members of the group. Tell me when you get that picture clear in your head.

Pause and wait for feedback from the client.

C: (nods)

T: Now, what would you have to say to yourself in order to do what you pictured?

C: Well, I have my ideas down on paper. I know what I want to say. The parents are there to hear my ideas, not to judge *me*. I can't really expect them all to like all of my ideas, and if some of them disagree with me, that's OK. It'll make for a lively discussion. Anyway, they'd probably be nervous up here too, so I'm sure they won't mind if my hands shake a little. I won't think about that; I'll just concentrate on getting my point across.

Tosi and Reardon (1976) recommend inducing deep relaxation or hypnosis and then guiding the patient through an ABC; for example, the patient imagines approaching a feared A, saying rational statements, and experiencing an appropriate emotional Consequence. Such a procedure employs a "mastery" image which may be appropriate for children but less helpful to adults than a "coping" image (Meichenbaum, 1977). In the latter procedure, for example, patients imagine approaching an A, saying to themselves the typical irrational messages they usually employ; *then* imagine themselves disputing and replacing the self-statements with rational statements, such as, "This really isn't true . . . be calm . . . I can cope with this anxiety . . . things are not as terrible as I am thinking they are"; and finally imagine a reduction in emotion. Such an approach may be more helpful because patients often do fail to feel less anxious the first few times they *actually* approach a feared A, and they desire a tool to cope with the anxiety they very well may feel. Even the most skilled practitioners of RET occasionally experience debilitating emotions, such as anxiety or anger, and use their skills to *remove* this distress once it occurs. Thus, RET can be employed not only as a preventive device but as a restorative device as well.

A related imagery technique employed by cognitive therapists is the *blow-up* procedure, in which the patient not only imagines future unwanted events but blows them out of proportion, beyond what might realistically happen. For example, in a film by Lazarus (see p. 283), a client with a compulsive ritual of repeatedly checking whether or not gas jets were turned off imagined not only that the kitchen and his house were set afire but that his neighborhood, the city, the country, and finally the whole globe went up in flames! By the use of such exaggeration the patient may come to think of the events as humorous, and his fears may become less fearsome when they are defused.

Some therapists prefer to use imagery techniques after initially doing relaxation training or hypnosis to induce a state of greater suggestibility; these adjuncts may be particularly useful if the client is unusually anxious. The therapist who wishes to learn such techniques is referred to *Clinical Behavior Therapy* (1976), by Goldfried and Davison, or to *Hypnotic Realities* (1976), by Eriksen, Rossi, and Rossi.

BEHAVIORAL DISPUTATION STRATEGIES

The third basic form of dispute is *behavioral*, in which the patient challenges his or her IB's by behaving the opposite way. In fact, the RET practitioner will not be confident that the patient has internalized a new philosophy until it is reflected in behavior change. Patients in therapy are engaging in verbal learning, and it is important to assure that their behavior in the real world matches their verbal behavior in session.

Behavioral disputes provide clients with experiences which run counter to their present irrational belief system; clients act against their IB's. For example, if clients believe that they cannot stand waiting for events, they are asked to practice postponing gratifications. If they believe that they cannot stand rejection, they are encouraged to seek it out. If they believe that they need something, they are exhorted to do without. If they believe their worth is based on doing well, they are asked purposely to do poorly. Since behavioral disputes are typically performed outside of the therapist's office, they are usually given as homework assignments. This topic will, therefore, be discussed in greater detail in Chapter 11.

IMPORTANT THINGS TO KNOW ABOUT DISPUTING

An important prerequisite for successful disputation is the *therapist's* ability to think rationally about the client's problem. How can therapists dispute something they really believe *is* terrible? First, therapists had better ask themselves, "How terrible is it really?" If they are not convinced, how on earth will they convince the client? One female therapist, for example, found herself overwhelmed by a client's fears of sexual rejection after a mastectomy. Only after the therapist had philosophically deescalated the loss of a breast (as she said, "My sexuality is not located in my nipple!") was she able to calmly help her client to the same conclusion.

When you are ready to dispute, make sure you are disputing the *right thing*—the philosophical concept, not the metaphor in which it is expressed. For example, if Rob, a client says, "I failed—what a horse's ass I am!" it is easy to point out that he is mistaken since he clearly does not possess the characteristics of an equine buttocks. The philosophical point will have been missed, however, since the client's misconception about human worth being dependent on accomplishment is still intact.

Once you have obtained a core IB, realize that it will take a significant amount of *time to dispute it*. Since the essence of RET is to change irrational beliefs, the D is obviously the most critical part. Don't be afraid to repeat a disputation over the course of many sessions if it appears to be necessary. There are several ways to assure plentiful time for disputation. One way to increase your disputing time is to avoid taking on a new problem in a subsequent session if you have not finished disputing an older problem from a previous session. You can begin your next session by asking the client if he or she recalls the problem, outlining the A's, B's, and C's quickly and beginning immediately with disputation. A second strategy is to take the new problems brought in by the client and show how they relate to his or her core IB's, and then proceed with the disputation.

Remember, before beginning a disputation, to clarify whether or not the patient has a problem about the problem, or what we referred to earlier as *symptom stress*. For example, is the patient depressed or anxious about being depressed? If so, what is the better level on which to work, the symptom or the upset about the symptom? In almost all cases, we recommend the latter, for as long as clients remain distraught about their emotional reactions, they will be in a poor position to work on them. This meta-problem may be particularly prominent in patients with perfectionistic tendencies (e.g., "I shouldn't have these kinds of problems!) or with Low Frustration Tolerance (e.g., "I can't stand this anxiety!"). Suggestions for handling these meta-problems will be discussed below.

Whenever possible, it is wise to work first with the patient's *motivation* before beginning a disputational strategy. Point out to clients the benefits of changing their beliefs—especially that of feeling less emotional distress. Such a strategy depends, of course, on assuring that the client does want to change the C. For example, to the patient with an anger problem, the therapist may first inquire, "Can you see any advantages to being less angry?" Once these are listed, the therapist may then ask, "Can you think of any ways to feel less angry?" Once motivation is established, the client may be more receptive to a cognitive or behavioral intervention.

Thus, among the disputational techniques to help the patient challenge distress-producing B's are those which first point out the lack of value of the distress. Again taking anger as an example, the therapist might state something like the following:

"Let's first take a look at whether your anger is working for you or against you. What does rage do? It sets the stage for a fight! Also, it isn't good for you; it sets your juices flowing, makes you feel more irritated, and so forth. Now concern or annoyance, on the other hand, serve as sensible cues for you to say, 'How can I change this? What can I do help the situation? Perhaps if I explain to him . . .?' See, now we're talking about *strategies*. And if a strategy doesn't work, what would you do? You'd go back to the drawing board and try another. You see, you can do that kind of problem solving once you're not in a rage.''

If your clients are unsure about whether or not they want to change their behavior or emotion, try to determine other motivations that may be serving to *maintain the pathology*. A good technique to help the patient become aware of the reinforcers operating to perpetuate the problem is the following sentence-completion item from Lazarus (1972): ''The *good* thing about (e.g.) procrastination is—.'' Repeat this phrase until the patient has exhausted all suggestions. If clients can't think of anything to say, urge them to say something anyway, the first thing that comes to mind. Stress that they need not believe what they say, nor does it have to be true of them. The therapist may even suggest a line to complete the incomplete sentence as a model to get the client started. The therapist would do well to listen for a pattern in the client's responses, for not only may the client's statements indicate reasons to keep the distress, but new irrational beliefs may be revealed as well.

Disputation is hard work, for what you are trying to do is shift the patient's position on major philosophic issues. To accomplish this may require many trials and a great deal of *persistence* on the part of the therapist. Like any good persuader, therapists had better believe in what they are saying, and demonstrate this belief by their persistence and enthusiasm for their position—rationality.

Persistence, however, doesn't mean a continual hard sell; some disputations are soft and subtle and can take place even when the therapist is being supportive or reflective. If you are in the early stages of therapy, attempting to build rapport, you may wish to be supportive but at the same time not reinforce irrational beliefs. For example, if your client says, ''I need X,'' you can reflect by saying, ''I know that X is something you want very badly.'' The therapist is thus modeling a more rational statement while conveying understanding of the client's plight.

Practitioners of cognitive therapy frequently assume that *generalization* of behavior change will automatically take place. While we believe that generalization is one of the advantages of cognitive therapy, we do not assume that it takes place without effort. As with behavior therapies, generalization often had better be built into the therapeutic program. Thus, it may be desirable to dispute the same irrational notion across many situations, even though the irrational beliefs, the disputation, and the resulting rational beliefs may be the same in each example.

A prototype of the generalization problem is the male client with sexual difficulties, for whom a hierarchy of anxiety-arousing situations has been constructed. The client may have progressed through several sexual exercises, such as sensate focus or masturbation training, during which he successfully counteracted his irrational beliefs about failure and performance. At the top of the hierarchy, when he is instructed to resume having intercourse with his partner, he may completely reinterpret the situation and resume his irrational catastrophizing. He then might be saying to himself, "This is the Real Thing; now if I fail, it will indeed be terrible!" Thus, although you may have helped him counteract his irrational beliefs at lower points in the hierarchy, you cannot assume that it will generalize to the next step. Be sure to specifically question the patient about his cognitions during the various performance stages.

In addition, it is not to be assumed that if clients are thinking rationally in one problem area, they will be doing so in other problem areas. For example, Rose, a client, may present several problems: anxiety in social situations, guilt about sexual performance, anger at her boss, and so on. Generally, it is wise to work on one problem at a time. If the therapist chooses to work on the anxiety in social situations, and successfully exorcises all of the patient's irrational beliefs in this area, there is no guarantee that the client will automatically begin thinking rationally about sexual guilt or her anger at her boss. These other problem areas will probably require separate work.

One strategy to maximize generalization benefits is to help clients believe that they are responsible for their own success. A number of studies in the behavioral literature have indicated that internal rather than external attribution for success at an endeavor is an important cognitive factor in generalization (Meichenbaum, 1977). If clients believe that their success was attributable to internal factors, they are more likely to believe that they have control over future problems and to implement what they have learned in therapy to new problems.

A final suggestion before we turn to more examples of disputation is to use as many disputational strategies with each client as possible. The more modalities you utilize (cognitive, experiential, imaginal), the more effective the disputation may be and the more long-lasting its effects (Lazarus, 1972).

An Outline for Disputation

Disputation, to the new therapist, may seem bewildering; learning this complex set of skills can seem like a monumental undertaking. In fact, however, if you listen to the work of experienced rational-emotive therapists, an outline of typical disputation maneuvers emerges. This outline has not previously appeared in the RET literature and is something that new therapists have had to pick up subtly by modeling and matching-to-sample. We will present what seem to be common stages in a disputation, but it should be noted that neither the steps nor their sequence are fixed. These are, therefore, suggested proceedings but not offered as dogma to be rigidly followed.

Once you have identified the A, B, and C:

1. Point out to clients that as long as they hold onto their irrational beliefs, they will be upset. This step is one device for establishing motivation for the client to change.
2. Provide a rational belief and ask how clients imagine they would feel if they believed it. In this stage, you not only model more helpful ideas but your prospective examination again sets a motivational tone.
3. Once clients acknowledge that they would feel better, use this feedback to encourage them to give up the irrational belief.
4. Then proceed to ask for evidence for the IB. In this stage, all of the various cognitive disputational strategies described earlier can be employed, although often you simply repeat your request for evidence or proof until the point is made.
5. Once clients admit that there is no evidence, ask them how they feel. This is done to point out the change in affect as a reinforcer for cognitive change.
6. If the clients are feeling better, check their understanding by questioning whether they can identify what caused the change in

the C. This is an important step; clients will sometimes surprise you by saying that they feel better because they "got it off their chests" or because they "know you understand them." Don't leave such misattributions unattended.

7. Finally, acknowledge that the clients have changed their thinking, but like a good scientist who entertains multiple hypotheses, point out that cognitive change factors could include changing from an IB to an RB, using distraction, or changing the perception of A.

Perhaps a transcript of portions of a sample session conducted by Ellis will make these stages more clear. Before the relevant therapist comment, we will list the number that identifies the stage at which the therapist is working or will verbally describe the game plan. This transcript is adapted from a public demonstration in which a member of the group was asked to work with Ellis; not surprisingly, the first problem dealt with was the individual's nervousness at being on display.

Getting at the B

T: What do you think you're telling yourself to make yourself nervous?
C: I'm an idiot for being up here!
T: You're an idiot *because*—
C: I might reveal sensitive areas of myself and I would feel uncomfortable.

Clarifying which IB is more prominent

T: And you *should* feel comfortable? Is that what you're saying? Or you should not reveal it at all?
C: Not at all.
T: Because if you reveal it, what? What are you predicting would happen if you reveal it?
C: An outburst of emotion—I would feel embarrassed.
T: So you might act foolishly in front of these people, right?
C: Yes.
T: Well, if you did, why would that be upsetting? Anxiety-provoking, if you did?
C: Can you restate the question?

Client's confusion is probably an index of his anxiety level

T: Yes. You're saying, "I may act foolishly in front of this audience." But you'd never get anxious just from that statement. That's just an observation or prediction. But how are you *evaluating* yourself if you *do* act foolishly?

C: I don't understand.

Stages 2 and 3

T: Well, just that statement alone doesn't cause an emotion. Something follows. You might be saying, "I might act foolishly, and isn't that great! I might act foolishly, and that would be good practice at acting foolishly!" And then you wouldn't be anxious, right?

C: Right.

T: But you're saying, "I might act foolishly, and isn't that WHAT?" You're not saying "It's great!"

C: I need to not act out of character.

T: "And if I act out of character—what?"

C: I might act fearful.

The evaluative component of B is still missing

T: "And if I act fearful, what?" You see, you're still not giving me the evaluation. "I would like it? dislike it? be enthusiastic?" What's your evaluation of acting foolishly?

C: It would make me feel unstable.

Therapist clarifies that "unstable" is not an emotion but a self-evaluative belief

T: So, "I would be an unstable person if I act foolishly up here?" Or, "They would think me an unstable person?"

C: Yes.

Assuming the worst

T: Well, let's suppose they do! Let's suppose they say, "Ummmm, shit, he's unstable." Now, you don't know that they'd say that! They may say, "Oh boy, he's got the guts to go up there and I'm scared shitless!" But let's suppose they say you're *un*stable. What's the horror of that?

C: That would support what I already think.

T: "That I *am* unstable." Well, how are you evaluating your so-called instability?

C: As a negative.

T: "I don't like this characteristic?" But then you'd only feel concerned. You wouldn't feel embarrassed or ashamed. You'd just say, "Well, I have a negative trait called instability." Do you see that you're saying something *stronger* than that to make yourself anxious?

C: Could it be rejection possibly?

T: Yes. "Because if I'm *rejected*—?"

C: Then I'm different from them.

T: "And if I'm different from them?" What are you concluding from that?

C: I'd be lonely.

Rephrasing C as an A to show A-C connection

T: "I would be quite alone." And how do you feel about being quite alone?

C: Depressed.

Ellis summarizes the A-B complex

T: Yes. So if I hear you right, you're saying, "If I act foolishly up here, it would prove I'm different. Other people would know I'm different. They would probably boycott me to some degree, and I couldn't bear that—that would be awful." Is that right?

C: Yes.

Stage 4

T: All right. But even if that occurred—and we don't know it would occur . . . why would that be horrible? That they thought you were boycottable and you were alone? Why would that be awful?

C: The evidence is in my past experience. By being different, I *was* alienated.

T: But why was that *horrible*? Let's assume that occurred. You were alienated and left alone; why was that horrible?

C: I feel like I need someone to share things with.
T: Prove it! Prove that you *need* someone.
C: (Pause) There is no evidence.

Stage 1

T: But if you *believe* it, how will you feel?
C: Terrible.

Stage 5

T: That's right! You've defined these things as terrible, and if you gave up those definitions, you'd feel all right. How do you feel right now about being up here?
C: A little looser.

Stage 6

T: Do you realize why you're feeling a little looser? Do you know why that is so?
C: I have more of an I-don't-give-a-shit attitude.

Stage 7

T: All right. That's good. And also, you've gotten distracted some-what. Instead of focusing on them, you're focusing on what we're talking about. Now, what other problem would you like to discuss?

7 Disputation: Specific Suggestions

Disputing Core Irrational Concepts

The reader will recall that in Chapter 5, thirteen irrational beliefs were discussed. We acknowledged that this list does not encompass all IB's, nor will your clients' idiosyncratic problems fall neatly into one or more of these categories. We originally intended to organize the present chapter around this list of IB's, as Ellis has in his books, but our experiences in learning and teaching RET to new therapists suggested some disadvantages to doing so. Beginning therapists report feeling overwhelmed by having to remember all the IB's and the disputes to them. They find the task beyond the limits of their memory, particularly when working under pressure with a client.

In searching for an alternative way to present disputational strategies, we thought it better to teach how to challenge the core elements of irrational thought rather than each of the specific IB's. When we asked ourselves what was irrational about each of the evaluative IB's, we discovered that each contained one or more of the same four basic ingredients:

1. *Should statements*, reflecting the belief that there are universal musts.

2. *Awfulizing statements*, reflecting the belief that there are terrible and catastrophic things in the world.

3. *Need statements*, reflecting the belief that the client must have certain things in order to exist or be happy.

4. *Human worth statements*, reflecting the belief that people can be rated.

For example, consider Irrational Belief 1, which focuses on the dire need for love; notice how this IB may contain any of the four key elements:

    a. Other people should love me.
    b. It's awful when they don't.
    c. I need love and affection to survive or be happy.
    d. I'm a worthless person if I'm not loved.

Now, listen to the core elements in Irrational Belief 2, which is an anger-provoking philosophy:

    a. X shouldn't act that way; he has no right.
    b. It's awful that X acts that way.
    c. I need to have people do what I want.
    d. X is a bastard for not doing what I want.

Finally, here are the same elements in Irrational Belief 5, which deals with achievement in life:

    a. I shouldn't have done so poorly.
    b. It's awful that I failed.
    c. I need to do well.
    d. I'm no good—a worm—if I fail.

Let's examine each core irrationality in turn and some ways to combat them.

Shoulds

Listen for the following words in the client's speech:

must

have to

got to

ought to

should

These can be heard in *I* statements (I have to . . .), *you* statements (You've got to . . . or He should . . .), or *the world* statements (It's got to . . .). Shoulds are often stated about past events in problems of depression, anger, and guilt (e.g., "He shouldn't have done that") but refer to present or future events as well in cases of anxiety (e.g., "I mustn't make a mistake").

Should statements are internally illogical and expose a philosophy of demand rather than preference. The irrational component, therefore, is the client's insistence that events or people's behavior be different. The client upsets himself by the logical fallacy that "because I want X, it must be so," or as Ellis has put it, "My will be done!" It is as if the client believes that he can indeed control the universe, and it is perversely thwarting his efforts. These demands produce what Karen Horney (1945) called the "tyranny of the shoulds."

Many people, perhaps including the reader, believe that there *are* indeed "shoulds" about human conduct. After all, what about the Ten Commandments, not to mention the code of Hammurabi, right? RET philosophy does not necessarily question the advisability of following such codes of conduct, but it does acknowledge that these are laws devised by humans; because they are desirable codes, it does not logically follow that we must abide by them. Obviously all of us break these codes at times ("Let him who is without sin cast the first stone"). If these rules were part of "human nature," they would not have been written down by moral philosophers but rather by ethologists. Thus, people would automatically exhibit moral behaviors because they must do so by their very nature, and to do so would not be "noble." Most religious systems, while advocating a code of ethics, recognize an individual's choice in living up to it. Rational-emotive theory distinguishes between the advisability of a particular behavior and the individual's right of choice; he or she can decide not to do what is desirable and advisable. The rational individual can appreciate that even the Ten Commandments are best interpreted as conditional shoulds, not absolutes. Depending on your frame of reference, *if* you want to be happy in heaven or have an easier time of it here on earth, *then you should* honor your father and mother.

Recall our discrimination between absolutistic shoulds and innocuous shoulds (p. 75). Clients confuse the two in their everyday problems (e.g., "I have to go to work," "I have to take my medicine," or "I have to call my mother"). It can be pointed out to clients that human beings rarely act without deciding to do so. Words such as "must," "have to," and "got to" imply that we are in some way being forced to behave in a certain way which, in actuality, we choose to do. By using these terms, we place ourselves in a victim role and allow ourselves to indulge in self-pity. Instead we could substitute more correct phrases, such as "I want to" or "I choose to." For example, if the client says "I have to go to work," the therapist can retort:

> "Oh, no, you don't. You could go fishing or to the ball game, or stay in bed if you really wanted to. If you do go to work, you're going because you *choose* to, regardless of what you tell yourself. It's just that you're not willing to take the consequences of not going to your job. You see, you almost always have a choice. Even if someone holds a gun to your head, you can always choose to die!"

When the RET therapist hears an irrational should, he or she is quick to confront the client by asking questions such as the following:

Why is that "should" a nutty thing to say to yourself?

What law is there that says it *should* be?

Explain that to me—why *should* he?

How does your wanting it prove it *must* be?

I SHOULD

Should statements about oneself usually imply a demand for personal perfection; clients with this belief are remarkably intolerant of their human fallibility. The primary dispute in this case is to teach the client that fallibility is a universal characteristic of the human species. Technically, we do not make mistakes, merely choices. It is only with the information available in hindsight that we can characterize a choice as a mistake if the consequences do not work out well. While improvement is something for which one can strive, perfection has yet to be achieved by anyone. After all, most pencils have erasers for good reason!

When clients are distraught about having exposed their humanness by failing at some endeavor, the therapist may intervene with statements such as the following:

T: You shouldn't have acted that way and messed up? Well, why should you have succeeded? It would have been nice or advantageous; that we could prove. But there is not reason why you *should* succeed. True, it would have been preferable; but why must you always act well? There's no law of the universe that says you must.

It is highly advisable for the therapist to act as a contrast model in this disputation, as in the following dialogue:

T: Isn't it OK to make mistakes or bad choices? Hell, I've made hundreds of bad decisions! Now, when you do that, don't you call yourself a shit?
C: Yes.
T: If *I* did that, would I be a shit?
C: No!
T: So there's two sets of rules in the world? What made these rules?
C: I guess I did.
T: If you made the first one, can you legislate another set of rules to be fair to *you*, so that you can get to live under the same set of rules as the rest of the world?

The key ingredient in this aspect of the disputation is to point out to the patients that they are being what Ellis calls "Profound Musturbators." We are, to be sure, given certain standards of behavior by our culture; "musturbation," however, entails escalating these standards into a MUST. Consider the following therapy excerpt:

T: That's a self-demand. Why *must* you be a loving person? Why *must* you be a success in intimacy?
C: Because I want to!
T: And I must be everything I want to? You see, you're taking a good value and turning it into a crazy demand. "Because it might prove better, I must do it." Wouldn't it be nice to feel better and not suffer from such crazy ideas?

Similarly, in another case of a young woman who was enmeshed in value conflict about having an extramarital affair:

T: What did you tell yourself to make you feel guilty?

C: I'm doing something immoral.

T: Granted. You've been doing wrong by *your* standards—but you also feel guilty. Why should you feel guilty about doing wrong? Many people do wrong and don't feel guilty.

C: Because my husband and I have such a good relationship. I shouldn't do it.

T: No, I'd *better* not do it. There are no shoulds in the universe. You have three choices here: you can change your values, change your behavior, or change your evaluation. And they're not mutually exclusive. In other words, you don't have to walk around feeling so guilty.

It is also important to point out to clients that there are good reasons to give up their musturbation; it not only promotes emotional turmoil but it makes them behaviorally less efficient. Let's listen to three different therapists dealing with these issues:

T_1:   There are no MUSTS in the universe. Suppose you are saying "I have to be rational! I have to be rational! I have to be rational?" That would be *irrational*, and how do you think you'd be feeling?

T_2:   You're saying that you've done something wrong and should be condemned for it. Well, we'll go back to the first part later, but for the moment, let's assume that it's true. Why would you have to condemn yourself, put yourself down, for that reason? What does guilt do to change the situation? All it does is make you entrench and fight, rather than to do problem solving and see how you can fix the situation.

T_3:   If you're driving poorly and you say to yourself, "What a shit I am for driving so poorly?" how does that help you to drive better?

Another aspect of the search for perfection entails the patients' demands for the Perfect Solutions to their problems. Patients often come to therapy stuck on the horns of a dilemma, or to put it more psychologically, caught in approach-approach or avoidance-avoidance conflicts. They expect a perfect, problem-free decision from themselves, and when they fail to come up with one, they turn to the therapist. It may be unwise for the therapist to suggest a choice, for that may perpetuate the notion that human beings can generate perfect solutions. In addition, the patient will not have learned some important skills: (1) decision-making techniques (e.g., weighing pros and cons and constructing a "hedonic calculus"); (2) understanding the reasons for being stuck at the decision point (e.g., "I might choose wrongly and that would be awful"); and (3) learning to cope with imperfect solutions.

The last problem often comes up with clients who report being unhappy about a love relationship in which they feel trapped. For example, a wife reported that she was desperately unhappy in her marriage and wanted to leave her husband but was blocked by a number of factors:

> She might later discover she regretted her action.
> She might hurt his feelings.
> She might not make it on her own emotionally.
> She might never find another partner, etc.

In addition, she believed that it was wrong to leave a marriage ("Didn't the vows say 'until death do you part'?"), so that there was a value conflict as well.

Obviously there are many ideas to challenge in this woman's plight. The therapist could teach her, first, that she is not totally responsible for the feelings of others, for if she hung onto that belief, then the only way out of her dilemma would be to devote her life to keeping her husband 100 percent happy. In considering the moral connotations of her behavior, the therapist might point out that right and wrong are not useful as indices of behavior; what *are* useful are the consequences. Ellis' parable of the two Zen Buddhists might be helpful here:

> Two Zen Buddhists were out walking. One was an old master about ninety years of age and the other was a young novice. They came to a swollen stream which had flooded its banks. Beside the stream stood a beautiful, luscious young woman who said, "Look, Masters, the stream is flooded. Would you help me across?" The young monk shrank away in horror because he would have to pick her up to carry her across, but the old one calmly picked her up and carried her over the stream. When they were over, he set her down and the two monks went on. The young man couldn't get over this incident, however, and finally said to the older, "Master! You know we're sworn to abstinence. We're not allowed to touch a beautiful young woman like that. How could you take that luscious young woman

in your arms and let her put her hands around your neck, her breasts next to yours, and carry her across the stream like that?'' And the old man said, "My son, *you're* still carrying her!''

Thus, as with the old monk, one can choose to do something "wrong" and not feel guilty (or not do something wrong, as with the young monk, and even so plague oneself by it). Does the client want to stick to her values and be miserable, or does she want to be happy even if it means changing her values? Another technique that the therapist may employ is distancing. The client may be asked: "How would you advise your best friend if she had the same problem? Would you suggest that she remain in the marriage and make herself miserable?''

Ultimately, however, the client had better confront the fact that she seems to be demanding that her decision be a perfect one—absolutely correct and without any negative consequences. Obviously few of life's decisions will fit this bill. What she does have is three options:

1. Choosing to remain in the marriage and be miserable.
2. Choosing to remain in the marriage and work at not being miserable.
3. Leaving the marriage.

Options give no guarantees; even if the therapist had some gilt-edged Happiness Guarantees printed, they would not help. Whatever the client decides implies some risk, and the client can choose to either avoid risks or accept them as creative challenges. So, there are no perfect solutions.

OTHER PEOPLE SHOULD

The second direction in which should statements focus is in demands for perfection in other people's behavior. There are three aspects to this dispute: (1) other people have free will, and we do not have perfect control over them; (2) there are often negative consequences attached to attempts to control other people's behavior; and (3) there are negative emotional consequences for insisting that others behave as we would like.

The client usually adds two additional points as well, such as, "How *can* they act that way?" and "*Why* do they act that way?" The answer to the client's first question, although it might sound glib, is quite simple. How can they act that way? Easily! Why do they act that way? This question can lead to an interesting discussion of why others act wrongly. Among the possible answers are that others are ignorant, misguided, crazy, suffering from an incapacity, or simply that wrong behavior pays off in some way (perhaps it helps to upset the client, which may be perversely reinforcing to someone else). We might summarize these reasons as stupidity, ignorance, disturbance, or utility. An understanding of this reasoning may be an important step in building the client's tolerance for accepting the behavior of others.

When the client is demanding that another person act differently, the therapist might respond:

T: Where is the evidence that X *shouldn't* act that way? There is none. In fact, he did act that way. To demand that people must not act in a certain way is silly, because once they have done something, they must do what they have done.

It makes much more sense for the client to search for evidence that X should, in fact, act as he or she does:

T: What's the point of being angry when someone acts the way they act? When a dog acts like a dog, we're not surprised. When a cat acts like a cat, we're not surprised. Why are you surprised when your husband acts like your husband? He has a track record. That doesn't mean he can't change. But why should we be surprised when he shows us his usual behavior, especially when he doesn't seem interested or motivated to change. We can ask for change in another's behavior, but it's silly to demand it.

Here is an example of Ellis disputing the same should:

C: He shouldn't do that!
T: Why is that a nutty thing to say to yourself?
C: But he was *wrong*!
T: Let's assume that he's wrong. Why is it still incorrect for you to say that?
C: I don't know.
T: Because you don't run the fucking universe. He has a *right* to be wrong; every human does!

As pointed out earlier, there seem to be no absolute rights and wrongs, merely situationally determined choices. In addition, RET holds that whether a decision is right or wrong is independent of the client's right to choose; one can even choose to do a wrong act.

The therapist can also point out to the client that the very attempt to control the behavior of others may produce further difficulties:

T: What does it mean to control other people? Usually we use negative means, such as punitive responses, whining, passive resistance, tantrums, and so forth. But no matter how it's done, we know one thing about human behavior: anyone who is at the mercy of another person will tend to hate that other person. So the more you try to control your husband into loving you, the less likely you are to get what you want from him.

In fact, the only certain control the client has is over himself:

C: But he's so unfair!
T: OK, it's not fair. That's correct. Where is it writ that it should be? You're saying: "she must—she must—she must." Now, let me ask you, what control do you have over her? And what good does it do you to sit here and eat yourself up alive? Let's agree. It isn't fair. Now, you only have control over one person. What do *you* want to do about it?

Finally, the therapist will point out that as long as the client holds onto a demanding philosophy, the emotional upset will probably remain.

T: You have a right to ask for change. But you might not get what you want. Your job is to stop evaluating yourself based upon your ability to control others' behavior.

THE WORLD SHOULD

Clients also demand that they control inanimate objects, social institutions, and the fates themselves. How often have you heard clients wailing such things as: "It shouldn't happen to me—it's not fair!" The primary dispute is that the world doesn't have to be the way the client wants, and in fact, the world and the universe are the way they are for complex, often unknowable reasons and need not be any different. An analogy frequently used to make this point is the following:

T: Let's suppose that I am sitting in my office on a hot, sunny summer day, and I start fantasizing about how much I'd rather be skiing than working today. If I walked to the window and started shaking my fists and demanding that it be cold and snowy outside, you would look at me as if I were a little crazy. You might tell me that it's foolish to demand it be snowing and cold outside. Well, you'd be right; it *is* silly to demand that the universe be the way I want. Obviously, the physical, astronomical and meteorological factors that have caused it to be sunny and warm outside have occurred, and my demandingness and temper tantrums can obviously not change these things. Is this similar to what you're doing about your problem? Aren't you making such demands too?

This analogy can obviously be used to dispute all types of should statements; for example:

T: If it's silly to demand perfect control of the weather, it's equally silly to demand perfect control of other people and even yourself.

If the client is demanding control of something about the self, he or she may object:

C: I see what you mean about external events, but I should be able to control myself.

T: Well, but you do have *some* control. Your mistake is insisting on *total* control, when, in fact, you are a fallible human being. So, it really *is* like trying to control the weather, do you see?

Awfulizing

Disputing this irrational concept essentially entails attacking the notion of "awfulness," which implies that events are at least, if not more than, 100 percent bad. Since people rather loosely use words such as "awful," "terrible," and "horrible," Ellis first gets his clients to agree with this definition: "awful" means many things: 100 percent bad, the worst thing that could ever happen to you, the equivalent of being tortured to death *slowly*. In essence, it implies 101 percent bad, an exaggerated badness. More correctly, therefore, no event is awful, although it might very well be a royal pain in the neck.

When therapists question whether an event described by the client is truly awful, many clients defend their evaluation as follows:

T: OK, let's suppose that you got rejected and you were alone. Why would that be awful?

C: Because of the depressed feelings in my gut; I'd feel terrible.

T: But you have that backwards! The bad feeling *comes* from *defining* it as awful. Suppose you just defined it as a pain in the ass: "Isn't it too bad that she doesn't like me?" Do you think you'd still have that depressed feeling in your gut?

C: No.

T: See, if you gave up the awfulizing, you'd give up the depressed feeling. You'd still feel sorry and regretful, but not depressed. Now, *where's the evidence* that it would be awful, horrible, and terrible if you were rejected and left alone?

One way to convince a client that X isn't awful is by comparison: "Can you imagine anything worse?" or "If this is so unbearable, would you commit suicide over it?" A more concrete anti-awfulizing exercise would be to help the client construct an "Awfulness Scale" from 1 to 100. Thus, if 100 is the worst possible event imaginable (e.g., dying of cancer after having one's arms and legs amputated), where would the client place a particular problem? It may become clear that, for example, having a spouse in a bad temper is most accurately placed at about 20 to 30.

In working with children, Ray DiGiuseppe and Ginger Waters often use a similar device, the Catastrophe List. On a blackboard or large sheet of paper, have the children list all the catastrophes they can think of (given the recent spate of catastrophe films and TV shows, this is easily accomplished). After listing towering infernos, tidal waves, invasions from outer space, earthquakes and atomic blasts, the therapist "remembers" one more, the child's complaint (e.g., "Tommy sat in my seat"). It will probably not be necessary to point out that one item does not belong on the list. This exercise is used quite successfully with adults as well.

Clients may also do their own anti-awfulizing if the therapist guides them through the following questions: "What are the real and probable consequences of the bad situation?" "How long will they last?" "How will you be able to bear them?" "Let's work out the details of your plan." Inviting clients into the system in this way is much more preferable than an anti-awfulizing speech. Such a device not only serves to deescalate catastrophes but enables clients to show themselves the reality of the situation and to work out coping strategies to deal with it.

In a recent woman's group, one of the members asked: "What does RET tell you to do about really bad events? Are you supposed to feel good about bad things?" This is a common question asked not only by lay people but by professionals as well. Clearly, the answer is "No!" Unlike "positive thinking," RET does not take the position that every cloud has a silver lining; some are storm clouds through and through. We may not have a choice between a good and a bad event, but merely between two bad alternatives. How, then, can RET be of help? By helping the patient to not make a bad event worse by catastrophizing.

Suppose that an A event is truly bad (e.g., a spinal cord injury, loss of a limb, death of a child); what can the RET therapist do? First of all, acknowledge that the A is a really painful event, that most people would indeed feel bad about such things, and allow for a normal grieving process. However, after a few weeks or months, it will be time to get on with the business of developing attitudes or philosophies which can help the patient cope with bad, but unchangeable A's.

The therapist will try to convince clients that holding onto misery is not in their best interests. Again, clients may not have the choice of something bad versus something good, but only between two bad things. By adding their needless misery, both of these things can become worse. Here is a concrete example: The patient was a young man, paralyzed with a spinal cord injury, who in addition developed decubitous ulcers and muscle spasms. Nothing could be done to repair the spinal cord injury, but by becoming overly upset about his condition, the boy significantly increased the problem of spasms. In such a case, giving up his depression about his injury could directly affect the patient's well-being. He had enough bad things to deal with and certainly did not need to add depression.

Perhaps there is a relationship between helping the client to accept a problem, such as a physical disability, and acceptance of death. As Kübler-Ross (1969) has suggested, acceptance is not a simple process but rather a series of stages. There are many feelings to be dealt with (e.g., anger and fear), and denial may be very strong. The concept of stages of acceptance is a hypothetical conceptual schema; not all patients will go through all of them, nor in any fixed order. However, RET may be useful in speeding up the process of moving from one stage to the next, as a kind of short-circuiting device.

Most therapists tend to awfulize about the plight of a client who has a serious disability or terminal illness. These conditions are not, in themselves, reasons for emotional turbulence, however. In fact, recent research indicates that *most* people with terminal illnesses are not chronically upset but instead mobilize quite adept coping mechanisms (Sobel, 1978). The therapist, therefore, needn't assume that distress is a normal reaction.

In addition to acknowledging the reality and painfulness of a bad A event, the therapist can focus on patients' *abilities* in addition to, instead of, their disabilities. Although this refocusing may not be wise as an initial maneuver, as therapy progresses it will be important to discuss with clients, "What can you do with what you *do* have?" The patients, after all, may be irrationally concluding that because they have bad problems, their life is over and no possibility of enjoyment remains. The useful principle here is *containment* of the disability to its specific areas rather than allowing overgeneralization of it.

In this regard, the RET therapist would do something which other therapists might not: acknowledge a very bad situation but have the temerity to point out that it cannot be awful since it could always be worse. If patients are terminally ill, they might be reminded that they could always die *more* slowly and in *more* pain. If they've lost a loved one to death, they could have lost their lover *and* best friend. There are always worse catastrophes that could happen. While this information may not be very consoling, it may help patients get a more realistic perception of reality.

In addition to philosophic disputes, there are pragmatic reasons to give up awfulizing. First, the high anxiety levels associated with catastrophizing are impediments to problem solving. By decreasing anxiety, clients increase their ability to deal with bad events. If clients are awfulizing about an impending problem, the therapist might point out that worrying only makes it worse, since they are living through the problem twice, in the here-and-now as well as when it occurs. If the discomfort is inevitable, the patients might as well enjoy themselves until it occurs.

Awfulizing philosophies are usually associated with states of high anxiety, a common result of which is avoidance behavior. The problem with avoidance is that although it is temporarily effective in reducing anxiety, this very function promotes more avoidance via negative reinforcement. As a recent behavior therapy text suggests, fears can easily generalize.

> If, for example, one had an irrational fear of stepping on dandelions, one might easily avoid the problem by walking around a single dandelion, with little cost to one's freedom. However, one small, neglected dandelion rapidly multiplies into many problems, and soon a fearful person will find himself severely constricted, every pathway in the field blocked with multiple dandelions. (Walen, Hauserman, & Lavin, 1977)

Don't be fooled by avoidance behaviors; sometimes patients will avoid *positive* events in order to ward off imagined future distress. A common example of this paradox is seen in patients who avoid intimacy even though they highly desire it. They refuse to get into love relationships for fear that, at some future time, the relationship might end. Since they've defined the ending as awful, they have chosen to deprive themselves of present possible pleasures. Catastrophizing, in this case, results in considerable cost to the patient.

An important behavioral dispute used by RET therapists to combat awfulizing is to have patients face their problems head-on, thereby disconfirming their hypothesis that the events were unbearably bad. Ellis has referred to such behavioral disputes as "risk-taking" experiences.

Ellis anticipated a research-based trend in behavior therapy by his insistence on the desirability of encouraging patients to be risk takers. By taking risks, by forcing themselves to do the very things which seem "too hard" or "too scary," the patient will best be able to abandon the notion of awfulness. In fact, Ellis has gone so far as to suggest that more traditional and gentle techniques (such as systematic desensitization or relaxation training) are sometimes iatrogenic in the sense that they foster the patient's avoidance of discomfort and strengthen LFT cognitions. In essence, he asserts, we continue to coddle patients and thereby help them to remain emotional babies. The best and most efficient way to overcome fears and avoidance habits is often to "close your eyes and force yourself to jump in with both feet." In other words, RET recommends a flooding or implosive model of treatment, starting at the top rather than the bottom of a fear hierarchy. Recent research (Marks et al., 1971; Rachman et al., 1973) supports this contention, and the shift from imaginal to in vivo desensitization and from progressive to flooding techniques illustrates that the *Zeitgeist* is moving in the direction pointed by RET. We refer the reader at this point to Chapter 11, in which risk-taking homework exercises are described in greater detail.

Human Worth

In his original writings on this topic, Ellis dealt with patients' statements of human denigration ("I'm a worthless slob" or "He's no good") by analyzing the philosophy of human worth in the following way. Logically or scientifically there is no way to conclusively prove that any human being has more worth to the universe than any other. Since there is no way to determine differences in human worth, one is left with the null hypothesis that all people have equal worth. A problem still remained with the formulation, however, since the assumption of a quality called "worth" implies the possibility of its opposite, "worthless." Ellis later refined his theory to eliminate the whole notion of worth, replacing it with noncontingent *self-acceptance*.

Beliefs about *self*-worth appear to be among the most difficult to change. Self-acceptance may be difficult to communicate to children, who may be surrounded by adults who persist in global ratings of the child (e.g., "good girl" rather than "good behavior"). It is often still more difficult to convince adolescents that they do not need the adulation of their peers. An important concept to teach in this regard is that people's *opinions* about one's worth are not *facts*. This discrimination may be more easily pointed out by referring to nonpersonal issues. For example, therapists may point to their wristwatch and suggest that it is the most beautiful watch in the world. Does this make it so? What the therapist is teaching is the difference between an opinion and a fact. The statement, more correctly, means, "*I judge* this watch to be the most beautiful." If the client understands this concept, it may then be possible to move to more personal opinions, as in the following example:

T: Let's say that your friend thinks you're a turkey. Does that make it so? If all your friends said you were a turkey, would you be?

In other words, self-worth need not be dependent on getting the support or admiration of others, even of deities ("Jesus loves me, I'm OK"). We can skip these intervening variables and simply choose to accept ourselves.

All self-worth statements are, in fact, overgeneralizations; it is this logical fallacy which is corrected in the following dialogue:

C: I'm such a worm!
T: You're a worm? You seem to have trouble with your terminology. The label you just gave yourself suggests that some essence of you is rotten, not just your act. You've defined yourself as a rotten person. If that's true, you *have* to do rottenly and do so exclusively and forever. That would be your fate. Don't you think you are overgeneralizing?

Let's elaborate on that last point. It is important to teach patients the difference between being a louse and acting lousily. In other words, *patients are not their behavior.* One way to teach this concept is to help patients monitor their language so that they change their labels for themselves (nouns) into verbs. Thus, instead of saying, "I'm a bad mother," it is more correct to say, "I've been doing some bad mothering." The former is clearly an overgeneralization because it would be virtually impossible to find a person who committed only negative mothering acts. Even Harlow's "monster mother" monkeys were observed to fondle their infants occasionally (1958). The reason we urge clients to change their self-labels into verbs is that self-labeling statements use a linguistic structure which is always an overgeneralization. The verb "to be" in the English language implies unity between the subject and the object of a sentence. "I am a psychologist" implies unity between "I" and "psychologist"; most of us do many other things besides function as a professional. The essence of the argument is that people are far too complex to subsume under a single rubric. Their very complexity renders them unratable. Human beings are far too intricate to judge them as a totality. Thus, Ellis suggests that clients "give up their egos," not in the sense of their executive selves but of rating themselves.

An analogy often employed by RET therapists to illustrate human complexity is the following:

> Imagine that you have just received a large basket of fruit. You reach into the basket and pull out a beautiful red apple, and then a ripe juicy pear, and then a rotten orange, and then a perfect banana, and then a bunch of grapes, some of which are mushy and rotten. How would you describe the fruit? Clearly, some are good and some are not good; you'd want to throw away some of it. And how would you label the basket? You see, the basket represents you, and the variety of fruits which vary in ripeness or rottenness are like your traits. Rating yourself by a trait is like saying that the basket is bad because it contains a piece of bad fruit.

Rich Wessler has devised a schematic diagram that illustrates the absurdity of self-rating. Note the two intersecting continua below:

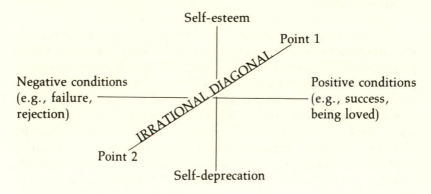

Many people make their self-esteem ratings contingent on the state of the horizontal axis. When things go well, they rate themselves highly (Point 1); when things go poorly, they give themselves a low rating (Point 2). What is wrong with this concept is the very act of the global rating itself; in essence, "wonderfulizing" is as irrational as self-deprecation. Rating is a foolish venture, for as soon as external conditions deteriorate, you'll slide down the Irrational Diagonal. The more rational concept is to stay at the zero point on the vertical axis, regardless of your position on the horizontal one. Thus, since rating oneself up implies the possibility of rating oneself down, the most elegant solution is to give up the rating altogether.

A general strategy, consistent with the concept of helping patients to do most of the hard work in therapy, is the following: Instead of trying to prove that they are not failures or worms, have them try to prove to you that they are. Not only is this strategy easier on the therapist, but it often provides the insight "self ≠ one's behavior" to the patient most meaningfully. Again, the issue is to avoid self-rating and to substitute self-acceptance or self-toleration.

T: All right, Jack, prove to me that you're a failure.
C: But I've just told you all the things I failed at.
T: That's true, Jack, but how does that make *you* a failure?
C: But I've messed up so many things!
T: I know that, Jack, but don't you see what you're doing when you call yourself a failure? You're making a prediction. To be a failure means that you have that characteristic, and you're always and only doomed to fail at whatever you try.
C: That's what is upsetting me—that I'll *always* fail.
T: But *you* can't be a failure because we don't know that you'll always fail and we have evidence that you haven't always failed in the past. You see, if you were an apple, you would always have had and will continue to have the characteristics of an apple. You couldn't change, and that's not true of failure. So you prove to me that you always have and always will fail!
C: (laughs) I guess I can't.
T: OK, so you see, failing is something you do some of the time; it's not what you are.

A difficult issue for many clients is accepting their physical attributes, and perhaps surprisingly, this problem seems to be as prevalent among men as among women. Trying to convince clients that their perception of physical reality is not so seems to be an exercise in futility. After all, when clients look into the mirror and don't like what they see, they are making an esthetic judgment. Matters of personal taste are difficult to challenge. The problem, however, is that in addition to acknowledging that the mirror image is not what they'd prefer, the clients are catastrophizing and refusing to accept themselves. Here is a sample therapy challenge to this refusal; note the therapist's acceptance of the client's perception.

T: OK, you have sunken eyes. What are you doing with that piece of information? Are you telling yourself that you must be miserable with yourself and your sunken eyes?

C: Well, I could always find someone who likes sunken eyes (laughs).

T: And what are you saying now? Again, you're looking for *external* validation of yourself. Can *you* accept you with sunken eyes?

The client initially suggested that sunken eyes would be acceptable if she found someone who liked them; this, however, would be a poor solution because it implies conditional acceptance. The therapist encourages her to continue to work at self-acceptance regardless of the approval of others.

Thus, physical appearance may be one area in which reexamining the A may sometimes be unprofitable. Acceptance of qualities which cannot be changed is important, although since some physical attributes can be corrected (e.g., with plastic surgery) the therapist may certainly encourage clients to change what can be changed.

A special subclass of this irrational concept is the problem of competition; some clients believe not only that they must be thoroughly adequate but that they must be *more* adequate than others. Their ability to feel comfortable, therefore, depends on doing better than others and involves not only self-rating but other-rating. If they stack themselves up against others and fall short, they feel not only depressed but also jealous. The social comparison process is a normal part of life and may be desirable for improving one's performance. It is problematic, however, when the patient overgeneralizes and uses the comparison in a self-derogatory way.

One suggestion to such clients is that they hardly change in any way each time they engage in comparisons; e.g., "If you're 5' 2" and then you meet someone 6' tall, does that make you shorter than you were?" or "If someone else gets a higher grade than you, how does that make you stupid?" A still more elegant solution, however, is again to work at giving up the concept of rating altogether. The therapist might point out that, after all, the basic goal in life is to *enjoy* oneself, not to *prove* oneself to the self, to others, or to the heavenly hosts.

We include at this point some sample disputations, one didactic and the other more evocative, on the general issue of self-worth:

A didactic disputation:

I'm going to suggest something rather surprising to you. Know what it is? That you're *neither* a wonderful, bright, marvelous, intelligent person, nor are you the opposite—terrible, awful, stupid, irresponsible, a dumbkopf.

You're neither of those things. You're a human. And you belong to the human race. And to be human means that you have some strengths and some weaknesses. That in some ways you're probably quite intelligent and coupled with that is a tendency to make human errors. Because that's also what it means to be alive and to be human.

And if we're going to get you better, we'd better go after your belief system. You're holding onto one now that insists on categorizing you as OK-not OK, stupid-smart. You think that you are a simple little commodity and you belong in either this box or *this* box.

And I'm suggesting to you that there's no box that could describe you. You're a complicated person; all humans are. That you *could* do an "A" paper, and from it you don't need to leap to the conclusion that therefore you're a wonderful, bright, intelligent, perfect person. 'Cause you're no such thing.

If you handed in a paper and it was not such a hot paper, you could do at least two things. You could say, "Oh my God, I'm stupid, I knew it, I knew it, I never should've handed it in. Now I see the evidence, just what I always thought, I'm no good. Donna belongs in the Stupid Box." *Or* you could say, "Well, I'm only learning how to write stories. That's what I'm here for. I'm not already perfect or I'd be the professor. And he's not perfect either or he would be a famous writer! That doesn't mean he doesn't have something to tell me, so that the next one I write I could get better at."

"SO WHAT" could be two favorite little words to tuck in your pocket to say 100 times to yourself in the next week. "Well SO WHAT if it isn't an A+? What does that mean if it isn't a perfect paper? It just means that it isn't a perfect paper and it doesn't mean another darn thing beyond that. SO WHAT, however, doesn't mean "It's not important at all," but "It's not all-important to succeed."

An evocative disputation:

T: You really believe that you're an utterly worthless person. By definition, that means that you're always doing things poorly. Can you prove to me that that's correct?

C: But I've failed at so many things.

T: Just how many?

C: I've lost my job, my wife is threatening to leave me, I don't get along with my kids—my whole life's a mess!

T: Well, let me make two points. First of all, those aren't every aspect of your life. Second, you take total responsibility for all of those events, rather than only partial responsibility.

C: But even if I'm not totally responsible, I'm still a failure.

T: No. You've failed at those things. There are other things you haven't failed at.

C: Like what?

T: You still manage to get up every morning, you keep up your appearance, you manage your finances well considering your economic plight—there's lots of things that you do well.

C: But they don't count!

T: They don't count to you right now because you're overconcerned with negative issues, but they certainly *do* count. There are lots of people who don't do those things well. Are *they* failures?

C: No—but—

T: You know, Jack, you are one of the most conceited people I've ever met!

C: What do you mean? I've just been telling you how lousy I am!

T: The fact that you hold two different standards tells me how conceited you are. You hold much higher standards for yourself than for anyone else, which implies that you think you're much better than others. It's OK for those lowly slobs to have problems, but not a terrific person like you. Isn't that contradictory to your notion that you're worthless?

C: Hmmmmm.

T: How about instead of rating yourself as worthless, you just accept these failings that you have and try your best to improve them as much as you can?

C: That sounds sensible.

T: Let's take one of those problem areas and see how we could improve things. . . .

Needs

Need statements are similar to shoulds, for one is failing to discriminate between what one would *prefer* to have and what one *must* have in order to live or be happy. The primary disputational strategy in dealing with need statements is to show clients how to take their own language seriously and literally. There are relatively few things that we truly *need* in this world; a little food, liquid, air, and shelter are biologically necessary for survival. No one knows what commodities are necessary for psychological adjustment, although patients who are having relationship difficulties are quick to claim that "all you need is love." In the literature of psychology there is some evidence that children and young animals prosper better with some love and affection, but we have no evidence that a single adult has ever died without it. Love is highly desirable, both to give and to get, but we do not *literally* need it. As long as clients believe that they need it and talk as if they need it, they will start to behave as if they need it, and that's where the trouble begins. A first step, therefore, is to help clean up the client's language.

Discriminating wants from needs is a distinction our society does not teach but is one which can be learned even by young children. In the following therapy excerpt, the client is a seven-year-old girl who is having trouble making friends at school:

T: Do you need to play with them?
C: What does "need" mean?
T: A need means this: what are some of the things that you need? You need water. What happens if you don't have water?
C: You die.
T: That's right. You need air. What happens if you don't have air? Same thing.
C: You can die.
T: That's right. What happens if you don't have food?
C: Die.
T: That's right. Can we say that you need food?
C: Yeah.
T: And water?
C: Yeah.
T: And air?

C: Yeah.

T: That's right. Do you *need* television?

C: No.

T: But sometimes you say you need to watch TV, don't you?

C: Yeah, 'cause I like to.

T: Yeah, you like to and you want to, but that's not a need, is it?

C: No.

T: No, it's not. Do you need candy canes and ice cream?

C: No.

T: You don't need them. but you want them, don't you?

C: Yeah.

T: But you don't need them, do you?

C: No.

T: OK, do you need a new bike?

C: No, I got one already.

T: But what if your bike got broken, then would you need a new bike?

C: Yeah.

T: No, you would *want* a new bike, but you wouldn't need it. I mean, you wouldn't die without it, would you?

C: No.

T: You could keep on living without a new bike?

C: Yeah.

T: It may not be as much fun as having a new bike, but you could live, right? Do you need a new pair of sneakers if your old ones have a hole in them?

C: No.

T: So do you see the difference between a *want* and a *need?* What's the difference? You try to explain it to me.

C: A need is what you need to help you to live.

T: A need is something you've got to have to live.

C: And a want is that you want to have it.

T: That's right. You'd *like* it, it's enjoyable. Now, how about: Lisa wants the kids in school to like her. Is that a want or a need?

C: Want.

T: It's a want, right?

C: Right.

T: So we talked a little bit about wants and needs. Now, what happens if you tell yourself "Oh, I *need* to have so-and-so play with me in school—I need to have her like me." How do you think you're going to feel if she doesn't like you?

C: Sad.

T: Sad. Like sad a whole lot or sad a little bit?
C: A lot.
T: A lot. How about if you said, "I need to have Kate like me. I *need* to be her friend."
C: I *want* to be her friend.
T: "I want to be her friend." Oh, but isn't there a difference? If you said, "I *need* to be her friend" and she wasn't, how would you feel?
C: And she wouldn't?
T: And she wouldn't. And you said, "I *gotta* have her friendship—I need it to live!—and she won't be my friend."
C: Sad.
T: You'd be very upset. So what if you said to yourself instead, "I would like to have Kate like me. I want to be her friend, but if she's not gonna be my friend, I can live without it." Would you be sad a little bit or sad a lot?
C: Sad a little.

Low Frustration Tolerance

Ellis has recently developed a new conceptualization of a core irrationality which focuses on the need for comfort. Keep an ear open for these common phrases which indicate *discomfort anxiety* (Ellis, 1978a):

I can't bear it
I can't live with (or without) it
I can't stand it
I can't tolerate it, etc.

People seem to believe that they cannot tolerate pain, discomfort, or adversity; their willingness to bear discomfort is not necessarily directly correlated with the nastiness of the aversive event. Usually, in fact, they report that they "cannot stand" what they do not like; we referred to this problem earlier as Low Frustration Tolerance, or simply LFT.

There are two ways to combat LFT: linguistically and experientially. Linguistically, the therapist challenges patients to prove that they cannot bear something. Obviously such proof does not exist. Saying that they can't stand it is silly, because they can stand it (although they may never like it) and even be happy despite it. The philosophy is actually a demand similar to the should statements above. Clients insist that they must not be inconvenienced, discomforted, or frustrated, and if they are, it is awful. The following dialogue illustrates a challenge to these notions:

C: I can't stand it when my mother acts that way—neurotically.
T: (with exaggerated intonation) "I should have a happy adulthood. I'm so richly deserving, I should have a happy time." But she may *never* change. What are you going to do about that?
C: Nothing.
T: Could you say to yourself, "Isn't it interesting that she's doing her number?" You could readjust your thinking so you're not making nutty demands. You see, it's akin to standing at the window *demanding* that it not be raining. If environmental events are impossible to control, the same goes for people's behavior. Getting angry isn't going to make it different. It might be best to just accept the reality.

Experiential disputes of LFT provide clients with homework assignments in which they practice experiencing those events they had previously defined as unbearable. This practice can take the form of a generalized exercise such as one used by Bill Knaus:

T: Focus on an itch you are experiencing somewhere on your body right now and refrain from scratching it for thirty seconds—and now another thirty seconds—

Or use one specifically tailored to the client's presenting problem. For example, if clients become angry in certain situations, they may be asked to behaviorally dispute by staying in the very situation that provoked anger and practicing "standing it," or purposefully exposing themselves to the obnoxious individual at whom they were angry. Rational-emotive imagery may also be useful, as in the following therapist suggestion:

T: Let's go through the scene. OK, imagine yourself at your mother's front door. At the first sign of emotion, ask yourself what's going through your mind?
C: I'd better just pretend not to be angry.

T: Well, instead of just sitting on your feelings, denying them, ask
     yourself: what would it take you to get yourself *truly* calm?

Thus, the patient can accomplish both a rehearsal desensitization and a
repertoire of rational cognitive coping statements.

A philosophy of LFT may prevent the client from reaching many
life goals, primarily because he or she refrains from putting in the hard
work necessary to achieve these goals. The therapist can point out that
"there's seldom gain without pain" and that learning that they *can*
stand discomfort could help such clients learn to face adversities more
easily, take greater risks, and work harder to maximize their pro-
ductivity and accomplishments. Thus, reducing LFT and attacking the
need for comfort may help one write that new book, leave a spouse, start
a new business, or whatever the client's personal goals may be.

8 Disputation: Problems and Solutions

Trouble-Shooting Disputational Problems

Having outlined some disputational strategies, we realize that you may hit some snags in getting your points across. In this section, we will try to anticipate some common problems that new therapists encounter in disputation and offer suggestions to deal with them. Most of these problems revolve around clients who either don't understand or don't believe disputational arguments. Thus, after you have disputed an irrational concept, check to see whether or not your client has understood the process.

Ask yourself, "Is the patient just saying the right words but not really believing them? Is the client placating me to get my approval?" How can you determine whether the patient is merely "parroting"? We suggest four strategies:

1. If patients come to the session in obvious emotional distress, or if you can create some emotional reaction by reenacting troublesome situations with Rational Barbs or imagery exercises, you can validate their understanding by looking for signs of tension reduction. Examine whether or not the clients can calm themselves down in the session. An excellent way to determine this is to employ numerical ratings of distress. As described in Chapter 4, we recommend that therapists use a SUDS scale to evaluate the client's level of stress at the beginning of a session; a decrease in the SUDS rating may be good proof to you and to your client that the disputation is effective.

2. Sometimes you will not be able to make this determination in a particular session; instead, the proof will emerge over time. What you will look for is *consistency* in the client's thoughts, feelings, and behavior across sessions. For example, if a male client claims that he "knows" that being rejected for a date isn't terrible but continues to avoid approaching women, the therapist will want to eventually confront this discrepancy directly by pointing out the difference between "knowing" and "believing." One may know about the theory of Marxism or Catholic dogma and yet not believe in or choose to live by either.

3. A third validation strategy is to invite significant others from the patient's life into the session; obviously this would be done only after securing the client's agreement and making sure that he or she understands the reason for this strategy. At such a meeting, the therapist may ask questions such as: "Do you see any changes in X's behavior?" or "How is X really acting?" Inconsistencies between reports from others and the patient's self-report may enable the therapist to confront the client as follows: "You see, Jack, it looks like you don't *really* believe it. We'd better get to work harder!"

4. Since some patients remain relatively passive in therapy (often because their therapists are too active), the therapist will want to look for indicators that they can approximate a disputation by themselves. One good technique to check on patients' understanding is to have them fill out self-help forms (see p. 219) as homework between sessions. If they cannot accurately work through a self-help form, they probably haven't understood. Profitable time can be spent in the next session going over and correcting any errors on the form. A second technique to validate understanding is known as *rational role reversal* (Kassinove & Di-Giuseppe, 1975), in which the clients are asked to change roles with the therapist. Clients can thus demonstrate how they would help someone with a problem like their own. In this way, the therapist can estimate how much of the disputation the clients understand and how committed they are to giving up their irrational, disturbing ideas.

Clients' misunderstandings may not always be obvious. One way to check this out may be to listen very carefully to their choice of words and their intonation. For example, listen for "I am . . ." sentences, such as "I am incompetent." Clients may not be aware of it, but when they say "I am X" they imply unity and identity between the subject and predicate of their sentence. Help the clients to rephrase these statements more accurately (e.g., "I acted incompetently"). The feedback that clients get from their own language may continue to propagate their irrational thinking unless the therapist corrects their speech. In a similar manner, patients can be taught to avoid the feedback from words with depressive connotations such as "pain," "hurt," "mad," and "bad," by deleting the pejorative word and reversing the sentence. Thus, "I feel miserable" is less preferable than "I certainly don't feel as chipper as I'd like to."

Listen also to the client's tone of voice, looking specifically for the registration of affect. The client may say something like: "I don't have much to offer men." Said in a flat tone of voice, such a statement can be easily missed by client and therapist, and the important irrational concept behind it left undisputed. If the client is stopped, however, and asked to repeat the statement with more emotion, the therapist may help the client confront and deal with a remaining issue.

You may miss the subtle residuals of the client's irrational beliefs if your *active listening skills* are not developed. One of the problems of new therapists that impede their listening skills is their tendency to "spectator" their own performance rather than the client's. Thus, you may be monitoring yourself too closely by this focus: "Was the last intervention I made good? Now, what clever thing am I going to say next?" And so forth.

Here is a training exercise to check on your active listening skills. Take a recent therapy tape and stop it approximately every two minutes; ask yourself, "What did the client just say?" Then go back and check to see if you have accurately recorded all the fine points in the client's conversation. Remember, don't focus primarily on your behavior in the session, but on accurately hearing the client's statement.

Frequently clients do not *fully* express entire thoughts; they use linguistic shorthand. Such abbreviations can hide irrational concepts. For example, a male client was asked to stand up in front of a large group at work and spontaneously discuss a topic. When the therapist asked what he was thinking while he was being introduced, the client replied, "I thought, 'Oh my God, what will I say?'" Do you hear the beginnings of

an IB here? People usually don't beseech deities unless some catastrophizing is going on in their thinking. The very question "What will I
say?" implies that he's worried and *doesn't* know what to say. The "Oh
my God" is an additional indicator of his anxiety and of the belief that he
has to do what had been asked of him, that he's trapped in and victimized
by the situation. Thus, a great deal of hidden information is contained in
a very simple sentence.

How do you get the person to state these unspoken concepts? The
therapist can help in the translation step by step; for example, help
clients rephrase the question "What will I say?" into "I don't know what
to say." At this point, the therapist is in a better position to ask, "How
do you feel about that?" Thus, until the premise is stated, patients can't
really find out how they will react to it. Once clients identify that "I feel
anxious," the therapist has an A and a C. To get at the missing belief,
the one-word interjection "because" can be very helpful:

T: You're anxious about not knowing what to say *because*—
C: I might make a fool of myself.
T: And if I act foolishly—
C: That would be awful!

Even if you are not using a formal ABC format in speaking with
your client, you had better be using this format in your *listening*. Go over a recent therapy tape and, as you listen to the
client's story unfold, write down the A, B, and C as they
emerge, also noting key unusual words in the margin of your
paper. After you think you have uncovered the hidden B's, plan
your next disputational strategy.

When we first began doing RET, we were surprised and chagrined
when, following what we viewed as an exemplary dispute, clients re-
turned the following week reiterating their irrational concepts. It took us
a while to learn that RET is not a magic therapy; while one-trial learning
may occasionally occur, it is not the rule. Most clients have a long
reinforcement history for their IB's, and they are not going to give them
up or change them easily. Success may come only after repeating the

same disputes, filling out numerous homework sheets, and engaging in many challenges to the IB. A mistake that new therapists make is trying an RET strategy for two or three sessions, becoming discouraged when success isn't immediate, and turning to another theoretical orientation for the Magic Answer. While we acknowledge that RET may not be the necessary and sufficient therapy for each and every case, it is recommended that you give it a fair chance. If several years of psychoanalysis are required before change is to be expected, more than a few sessions of disputation are not unreasonable. The therapist may have to spend months on the same concept before the patient "sees the light." Don't be afraid of redundancy, therefore; redundancy is important in all communication but may be essential in psychotherapy.

As you progress through sessions with your clients, it is important to stress not only the rational beliefs but also the *process* of disputing. After you've spent one or two sessions challenging clients' irrational beliefs, it's easy to get into the habit of just providing them with rational alternatives. Disputing, however, is a process of *asking questions* about their irrational beliefs, not merely replacing them mechanically with rational statements. The important skill here is teaching scientific thinking, the search for evidence to support a hypothesis; merely supplying a rational replacement omits this important step. Unless clients have learned the skill of questioning themselves, they may not be able to generalize beyond their immediate problem.

Another inappropriate style that develops among new RET therapists is what we'll call the Knee-Jerk Disputer. Every time they hear a "need," "should," "must," or "terrible," these therapists are too quick to ask, "Where's the evidence?" This strategy frequently misses the target. Remember that words such as these are harmful because of the concepts for which they stand, not for their face value. These words are used frequently in everyday language as figures of speech. For example, "That was a *terrible* steak!" or "You *have* to see the new ballet" or "I *need* a cup of coffee." Thus, the Knee-Jerk Disputer may be shooting down pseudo-problems; while people may, in fact, be irrational about their need for coffee or the awfulness of their steak, these may not be the clinically significant beliefs related to their pathology. So, make sure that you have identified the relevant irrational beliefs before moving on to the D, lest you merely establish silly new taboo words. Does it make sense for the word "shit" to be OK, but "should" to be taboo?

Client Behaviors Which Block Change

Some clients pose special problems for the new therapist. Let's go over a few such types:

1. *The argumentative client.* Are you picking up antagonism in your clients? Do their voices have an edge? Do you feel you're fighting rather than disputing? Are you fatigued by your interaction? How can you handle such clients? First of all, stop fighting. If you sense that the two of you are tugging at opposite ends of a rope, let go of your end. Try to go through an entire session without trying to convince the client of anything, and see what happens. Or, play devil's advocate and agree with such clients (e.g., "You're right, Bill, you really *are* incompetent). Imposing your ideas on such clients may only serve to intensify their resistance to you. Focus instead on the strength of the client by intervening primarily with questions (e.g., "What do *you* think you could do to get over your problem, Bill?").

2. *The "yes-but" client.* Clients who counter your suggestions to them with a "yes-but" response are demonstrating another form of argumentative resistance. A "yes-but" is really equivalent to a "no." Such clients are playing helpless and often render the therapist helpless. Consider whether their resistance is attributable to your behavior; are you, in fact, off-task, or have you focused the discussion on an irrelevant issue? If not, perhaps such clients are simply unwilling to listen to you because they attribute qualities to you that they have generalized from other troublesome people in their lives. For example, they may have difficulty accepting suggestions from anyone whom they view as an authority figure. In such a case, you may consider bringing in a credible significant other from their lives to whom they may be more willing to listen—such as a spouse, sibling, or close friend—and using them as disputational models. If the message comes from them, or at least gets reinforced by them outside the session, you may increase the chance that these clients will accept the message.

Another possible explanation for clients' "yes-but" behavior is that they simply do not want to change. In such a case, a useful question to ask yourself is, "What's the payoff for the client?" In other words, what positive or negative consequences may be operating to maintain the dysfunctional beliefs or behaviors? One client of ours, for example, continually ranted, raged, and blamed her friends for not calling her as often as she'd like; every disputational sally was met with a "yes-but" reply. It occurred to us that she was stuck on her Other-Blame because it functionally served to avoid Self-Blame and self-examination. One technique to uncover such motivations is to repeatedly ask patients to fill in the end of the following sentence: "The good thing about (blaming others, in this case) is _____."

3. *The intellectualizing client.* RET may be difficult to accomplish with bright clients whose defense against self-examination is to intellectualize. They combat the therapist with reasonable arguments, can beat the therapist at deductive logic, and even sound quite rational. Why, then, do they continue to come to therapy? Because although they do not clearly recognize or verbalize it, they have *emotional* problems. The therapist would be wise to keep the focus on emotions and, instead of relying on didactic approaches, bring in other procedures such as experiential exercises or imagery techniques. Such clients are very likely to object to such gambits, however, and may refuse to do something they define as "silly." The therapist could counter this argument by pointing out: "Well, going around feeling nervous and upset is pretty silly too. Is this exercise any more silly than that?"

4. *The intellectually limited client.* It is appropriate to acknowledge that disputation toward the elegant solution may not be appropriate for all clients. Among the exceptions we would consider the following: (a) very young children, (b) clients with limited intellectual ability, (c) clients with severe brain damage, (d) clients with severe psychosis whose pathological thought processes interfere with logical thought, and (e) highly anxious clients, whose level of arousal is too intense to enable them to think clearly. With such clients the therapist will be more effective by simply *drilling* in rational coping statements such as those recommended by Meichenbaum (1977), which are discussed in the next chapter, and by using operant principles to encourage the patient to exercise these rational replacements between therapy sessions.

5. *The "it's-not-working" client.* There are some common reports by clients who are beginning to learn RET but who are impatient to experience change. Here are some sample therapist-client interactions that illustrate this problem and provide some suggestions for dealing with it:

C: I say to myself, "I don't *have* to, I want to," but it doesn't make me any calmer.

T: Well, Jim, that just indicates that you haven't really given up the *must*.

C: How do I do that?

T: By looking for your irrational beliefs and disputing them. Ask yourself, "Where's the evidence?" Be a scientist. We don't merely accept the fact that the world is round because it sounds good, but because of the data. Where is the evidence that you *must* do well in school?

Another example:

C: I know it *intellectually*, but I don't feel any different.

T: When you say you know it "intellectually," what you really mean is that you know it *some* of the time *weakly*. But *most* of the time you believe your irrational belief *strongly*. Do you dispute with yourself *convincingly*?

C: I guess I could work harder at it.

T: Right, and you won't believe it strongly until you begin to *live* it, to *act* on it. Now, what could you *do* this week to prove to yourself that you don't need Mary's love?

Another example:

C: I know that the rational beliefs make sense, but I can't feel it when I'm actually in the situation.

T: Well, you can't feel more relaxed unless you rehearse a lot *before* you get into the situation. Let's rehearse how you'll handle your anxiety right now, to set a model for you.

And finally:

C: I understand this disputation stuff, but I don't know how to do it when I'm not with you. I still get anxious and then I start obsessing.

T: Well, Mary, the trick is to use your symptom as a cue to start the chain: "I'm obsessing. Why am I obsessing? To avoid anxiety. What am I anxious about? Some beliefs I'm holding. What are my irrational beliefs? Now I'll start to dispute them." So, you see how your symptoms are tied together? Your obsessions are partly an avoidance behavior to distract you from your anxiety. Instead of distracting yourself, use them as a bell ringer to face your anxiety and uproot it, OK? Now you repeat that to me so I can see if you've got it.

The point of the examples above is that clients frequently hold to a false dichotomy, that there are intellectual versus emotional insights. The concept of an emotional insight runs counter to the most basic principle of RET, which is that thinking largely *causes* emotion. In addition, the concept itself is a non sequitur; people simply do not think or achieve insight with their visceral organs. When the client claims he or she has intellectual but not emotional insight, the therapist reinterprets this claim as either a problem of "knowing" but not "believing" the rational ideas or of inconsistency of beliefs across time. The solution in either case is clarification and harder work for the therapeutic dyad.

Now that we have covered the basics of the disputational process, hopefully you have a blueprint which will help you to build a more elaborate structure. The work of the RET therapist does not end with disputation, however. The end product in disputation is not to have the distressing Activating event disappear, but to help the client to accept it if it cannot be changed or to calmly and methodically try to change it if this is possible. Thus, much more work may be needed both in and out of session. In the next chapter, we will focus on some of these in-session behaviors.

Cautions

If your clients have experienced some control over their emotional distress, be sure to warn them not to hold perfectionistic standards in this new skill. Thus, if one client says that she thinks she can now control her anger, it would be wise to ask, "How long do you think it will be before you get angry again?" Such a question can not only pose a gentle warning but can help the client prepare for this probability. If you omit this step, the client may become discouraged the next time she does become angry and may even devalue the gains made in therapy and no longer dispute when she is in troublesome situations. The reader will recall that a major tenet in rational-emotive theory is that all people think both rationally *and* irrationally. With hard work, we can increase the proportion of time spent in rational thinking, but we can never expect to think absolutely or completely rationally.

In addition, there are often advantages to be attained by displays of strong affect, and even if clients can think rationally they need not give up these advantages. When clients discover the insights of RET, they may sometimes make absolutistic demands of their new rational beliefs and decide, for example, that they must never behave angrily again. Very often, however, as is taught in assertion training, it is advisable to escalate assertive behaviors in order to get what one wants. Ellis describes a personal incident as an example in which assertive behaviors were not effective, while threatening, acerbic remarks were instrumental in getting others to comply with his requests. When he changed offices, new slipcovers were ordered and were due to be delivered six weeks later. This date came and went, but no slipcovers appeared. One assertive phone call later, he was promised delivery. The next week the scene was repeated, and another assertive phone call failed to change the laxity of the firm's service. Weeks later, when the firm insisted that Ellis had to pick up the slipcovers himself now that they were, at long last, ready, he forcefully and deliberately suggested that he would be happy to remove the gentleman's "fornicating gonads" if they did not arrive within the hour. The slipcovers arrived. The point of the story is that Ellis was *acting angrily* but was not actually *feeling* angry. He knew that a *show* of anger would probably promptly get him what he wanted; so he feigned it without feeling it. Clients who fail to make this discrimination between thoughts and actions may frequently not get what they want, since strong language may be an important tool when dealing with "difficult customers," such as credit agencies, the phone company, and government bureaucracies.

Another distortion occasionally encountered occurs when the client uses the concept of personal responsibility for one's emotional reactions as a justification for obnoxious social behavior. In one case of marital counseling, for example, the husband refused to deal with relationship issues, would not compromise on requests for behavior change, and continued to annoy his wife. He rationalized his behavior by claiming that she was responsible for her reactions and her problems; if she was upset, she was doing it to herself. The wife, on the other hand, was evaluating his behavior quite rationally and (in the opinion of the therapist) was appropriately annoyed. While the husband correctly understood the basic principle of RET, he did not understand that rational thinkers can have negative feelings and desires to change the A. Although the husband was not causing his wife's C, he was nevertheless a component part of A and had responsibility for the marriage. RET distinguishes between not *causing* but still *contributing* to a C by being obnoxious to someone at A. In reality, this man was demanding that his wife have no objections to his behavior and was misusing rational-emotive theory to justify his position. The therapeutic response to such a misinterpretation of RET involved teaching the client that one does live in a social community and that although there is no *necessity* to behave ethically and responsibly, it is clearly *advantageous* to do so. The advisability of living within social contracts is a key element in rational-emotive philosophy.

Although the client in the above example was misusing RET principles, rational-emotive theory holds that we are not *totally* responsible for other people's emotions. The client may clearly have the responsibility for being an Activating event for another person but does not bear full responsibility for the other's emotional distress. Our behavior may not please others, but it is their evaluative self-statements which *directly* cause their misery. If the client already understands that others don't cause one's personal misery, this understanding may be the most direct route to challenge any subsequent statements that indicate the converse—that the client directly produced misery in others. For example:

C: I feel guilty because he's so upset.
T: Now, wait a minute, Gail. You can't have it both ways. If you're responsible for your bad feelings, then he is so for his. He may not like what you did, but if he's very upset, how are you totally responsible for that?

The notion of *total responsibility* is a key concept and may be more elaborately pointed out to the patient, as in the following therapy segment:

T: Are you making yourself totally responsible for someone else's problems? If it's a young child, you are partly responsible; but, for example, when your nineteen-year-old gets into drugs, your attitude had better be, "Well, so he's into drugs and will have to take the consequences." When the situation involves two adults, the nutty idea may take the form: "If I do this, then he'll be happy; if I don't, he'll be miserable. I therefore have to act the way he wants to prevent his misery." What's wrong with such·a notion?

Again, mini-experiments may help to get across the point. The following example, from Norma Hauserman, an RET therapist from Baltimore, deals with a young widow who wanted to take her small daughter to Europe for the Christmas holidays to visit a sailor she had met when an Italian ship had visited the port. Her idea met with great displeasure from her mother-in-law, who carried on in the following vein: "What a bad person you are! Your husband is not yet cold in his grave. How dare you take the child to strangers at a holiday time?" etc. The daughter-in-law was suffused with guilt, concluding that her consideration of the trip had led directly to the older woman's upset and that she was therefore a rotten person. The challenge went as follows:

T: Let's do the experiment. Tell *me* you're going on a trip and see how I respond.
C: (complies)
T: That's great! (Pause) So, your going on a trip cannot produce upset in others. It's your mother-in-law's *perception* via her irrational beliefs that makes her upset. You can't be totally responsible for her upsettedness.

Notice that the young woman's dilemma can be construed in terms of the ethical principles discussed earlier in rational-emotive philosophy. The optimum choice is one that is both pro-self and pro-social. This choice would involve both pleasing herself and pleasing her mother-in-law. There are times, however, when such choices are simply not available, as in this case. What is the client to do? She can either stay at home and please the mother-in-law or go to Italy and please herself. If she takes total responsibility for the mother-in-law's feelings, she will probably stay home, but if she realizes that her mother-in-law is contributing to her own unhappiness by upsetting herself, this may put a different light on her decision and help her to make a choice that is both ethical and rational.

We are *not* advocating that clients act in callous disregard of the feelings of other people. However, for us to make our life decisions only on the basis of how others feel and to take total responsibility for their feelings is both unrealistic and personally unsatisfying. The goal in RET is to live compatibly with others but not to be subservient to them.

Somewhat removed analogies may also be useful. The therapist may ask the patient to contemplate going up to 100 different people and telling each one, "My, you're ugly!" Does the patient imagine that each of the 100 people would feel miserable? Probably not. A variety of reactions, in fact, is more likely to ensue, including depression, pity, even mirth.

As an exercise, list the cognitions that might lead to these three different emotional consequences. Then see if you can expand the list further. (See Answer Key, p. 286.)
Depression cognitions:
Pity cognitions:
Mirthful cognitions:
Other:

CONCLUSION

We conclude our three-chapter discussion of disputation by providing a detailed transcript of a complete therapy session. In this meeting, therapist and client establish the ABC's of a problem emotion and the therapist helps the client to dispute her irrational demands.

T: Let's check up on things. We were talking last time about your mother. What's the progress report?

C: Well, the exact day after I had sat here and talked to you about not letting my Mom bully me—in the sense of just trying to ignore it and not reacting—the next morning was like a major explosion. You know, I don't even know if it pays to go into all this, the details of it, but it ended up with my mother physically attacking me, my brother coming between us, her pretending to faint right on the floor, kicking her feet and banging her hands on her head and pulling out her hair!

T: A temper tantrum?

C: Right. For two days she ignored me and then pretended that it
    didn't happen and—OK, so that's given—I'm living with my
    mother, who is really neurotic, who is going to be picking on me
    until I leave and there's no way out of that, really. I mean, that's
    given. I've tried to channel, you know, my upsets about that and
    many other things into my studying. I mean, just in the sense of
    the harder I work the faster I'll get out, the quicker I'll have money.
    I see it as just alleviating so many difficulties, though not all, but
    many of them, so if I just sit here and study and study and study I
    will work my way out of this situation.

T: Let me ask you a question. Are you saying that in a helpful or
    nonhelpful way? You see, if you're still allowing yourself to get
    overly upset about your mother's behavior and are still viewing
    your situation as a horror, then you may be working frantically.
    You may be saying, "I have to work faster, I have to work faster—
    the horror is still too close!" Is that true for you? Are you doing
    good work when you sit down to study?

C: Well—

T: Or are you working frantically?

C: I'm doing that. I go "I've got to hurry up and get out of here." I
    really am. The picking is what gets to me. It's like she can't come
    out and say "Gee, I really don't like you and I wish that you
    weren't here." Although she says that too when she gets mad, at the
    times she's not saying it, she's saying it in other ways.

T: It's not pleasant to be living with somebody that doesn't want you
    living with them. Remember, we talked about this last time—about
    the three different categories of things that she does. Sometimes
    she says "I don't like you, I wish you would get out of the house."
    Some are innuendos, and others, perhaps no one else would react
    to, but you do because you're sensitized to react to them.

C: I try to sort them out. I mean, I have been hanging around you long
    enough to know at least to try to be rational about my problems,
    but it doesn't really stop the initial flow of rage and hurt. The
    feeling comes and I start saying, "Well, even if she doesn't like me,
    even if she's showing obvious preference to my brother," things
    like that—

T: Then what? Finish the end of the sentence.

C: That doesn't mean that I am not a good person.

T: Her opinion is just her opinion.

C: But, at the same time, the anger is still there, and when I'm alone
    and when I'm riding the train and thoughts are just flowing

through my mind, the anger comes over me to the point where I, I really have very vicious fantasies about her.

T: OK, let me stop you for a minute. It sounds like you're doing one very good thing. It sounds like when she starts her routine and you find yourself reacting to it, you do a good thing—which is using your emotional reaction as a bell ringer. You say "Oops, I'm overreacting."

C: I do that. I did that after the fight. But the next morning— (proceeds to tell another story of an encounter with her mother)— and then she came flying at me. "Get out of my house. I hate you!" And then it escalated into a big fight. So I lost my temper and in that case I was human. Because I was angry. It was building up for a week.

T: OK, so you're not perfect.

C: No.

T: But let me get back to where I think one of the problems is. As I listen to you, it seems that sometimes you are quite good at this rational self-talk and sometimes it's not working. Let's problem-solve and see when it's not working and *why* it's not working. Now, you said that at the time your mother was acting crazy with you, you were able to say to yourself, "Well, her opinion is her opinion. If she thinks I'm a shit, that doesn't make me a shit." Those kinds of self-statements are very useful for counteracting a specific kind of emotion. Can you guess what emotion that would be?

The therapist is helping the client to discriminate the B's and C's for two separate emotional problems.

C: Well, I guess hurt—or putting yourself down because someone else is criticizing you.

T: Exactly. Self-put down is depression. But those cognitions, those very helpful thoughts are not going to help in *anger* because there is a different set of irrational things which are going on—different from depression. So, it's like taking the wrong medicine.

C: Do you think that it fits into this kind of therapy—the idea that anger suppressed becomes depression? Because I've heard that said.

T: I've heard it said too. Let's put it this way: I don't think that anger *expressed* is any more useful than anger *repressed*. The key to success there is not whether you say it or not say it, have your temper tantrum or not have your temper tantrum, but to uproot the anger itself from its antecedents. You uproot it from the causes of it, just like you did with your depression. You get to the head talk. You've got really good coping techniques for depression; now let's get some coping techniques for the anger, OK?

C: OK.

T: First of all, let's do a little ABC on the situation. A, mother does something, and C, you feel anger, not depression. What are some of the B's you can imagine?

C: When I feel angry?

T: Anger. Not depression.

C: OK.

T: Look for a "should" again.

C: Well, I should not be in this situation where someone is being so unjust to me.

T: OK, that's a good thought to be in touch with. Now, is that an anger-provoking thought? It sounds like a poor-me thought.

C: Yeah.

T: Poor-me's don't get you angry.

C: Well, my mother should be understanding.

T: That's usually where it falls. Anger is directed outward, not at yourself, but outward. It's "mother should." Mother shouldn't yell at me, she shouldn't say nasty things. Any others you can think of?

C: (Tells another brief story of a home incident)

T: OK, stop here. What's the irrational belief there?

C: All right. Even though they're treating me that way—they *are* treating me that way. The reality is right, my brother is definitely preferred.

T: And what's the irrational belief?

C: That it doesn't mean that I am the way they see me.

T: No, what's the irrational idea that you're saying? Do you know?

C: Somehow, because I allow myself to be treated that way, that really turns me into that kind of a person. And if I really had pride or self-respect or common sense or whatever, I could turn it around so that it wouldn't be that way.

T: That's your depression, your poor-me thoughts and bad-me thoughts. Let's leave those aside for the moment. What's the anger belief? Not only shouldn't she yell at you and say nasty things to you, but how should she treat you?

C: Well, she should treat me as an equal member of the family.

T: She *should* treat you fairly and squarely. These are some of your shoulds. We know from the theory that the shoulds are where the trouble is. Your belief is that your mother shouldn't do those things, that she should treat you fairly.

C: I also have those *shoulds* for myself. I *should* not yell at my mother. I *should* not, you know, express any kind of temper or dissatisfaction in ways that are going to make people uncomfortable. When inwardly, I really want to go in there and let her have it and say, "What is this crap, I mean, here he's been sleeping in the bed all year and you've been telling me the reason is that he's paying you money, and then you're telling him that you're giving it all back to him."

T: That would be good to say if you weren't in a rage, but were merely determined to try to change what could be changed. If you did those things assertively, you could do them better, more efficiently. But let's go back—we've got an A, a B, and a C.

C: OK.

T: We've got the anger and the anger cognitions, which are all those *shoulds*. Now let's do a D. What are some questions you want to ask yourself about this?

C: Why can't I tell her what to think? This is a big question to me. The fact that I have so much anger and that I just absolutely cannot find words to even begin to say "This is a raw deal." I don't know how to go about it, whether I approach my brother or my mother.

T: Wait. That's another issue. That's the *you* issue. We want the "them" issue. Those people out there who are treating you unfairly and your anger about that. First of all, do you agree that you would like to give up your anger? Not your determination, but your anger.

C: OK. At this point, I feel that it would really be sick not to resent it or to feel anger. It is justified at this point.

T: If you're asking, "Are you trying to get me to feel nothing or to just joyfully accept this horse shit?", I'd say "No, that's crazy." You'd be crazy to be happy about it. But I don't see that getting *angry* about it is doing you any good. For that reason, I think it would be best to get rid of the rage and bring it down to where you can say, "I don't like this and I'm going to do what I can about it. I'm going to try to change the situation." After all, what does anger do for you? It gets your stomach churning and it's not very good for your system, physiologically.

C: No; for a week I've been walking around definitely feeling all those physical things. And I try to hold it in so I just get really quiet and I don't want to talk to anybody, so they're going to get on my case, that I'm depressed.

T: OK, so let's work on the anger. It's been a while since we've done an ABCD formally, so let's sort of retrain. When you do D you go back to the nutty ideas, one by one, and you ask yourself questions.

C: Why should my mother be fair to me?

T: Right! Where's the evidence that your mother should act nicely to you?

C: I don't know. Going to school, I see so many people at home living well. They're running around with the family charge card and they're doing whatever the heck they want to do, and everybody's kissing their ass and they think it's the greatest thing.

T: I absolutely agree that this would be nice. But why *should* your mother do that?

C: Why *should* she? (pause) I think she *should!* She *should* be fair.

T: Why?

C: Just because I want her to. (laughs)

The therapist has allowed the client to repeatedly struggle with the question rather than answering it for her.

T: That's right. "She *should* do everything I want." Where's that going to get you?

C: Hmmmmm.

T: Now I'm agreeing 100 percent that it would be really nice if your mother treated you fairly. It would be pleasant, it would make your life simpler, it would be advantageous to you. Your life would be much easier if you had a set of rich, loving parents who treated you fairly. We could prove that. We could do the experiment and prove that advantage. Could we do an experiment to prove why your mother *should* do that? Why does she *have to* do that?

The therapist never disputes the desirability of the client's claim that it would be advantageous to have what she wants, merely the demand.

C: It's possible at some level—she's not that stupid—that if she realizes it, it can't make *her* feel good. I mean, how can a mother feel good about being unfair?

T: Right. So maybe it would even be nicer for *her* if she treated you fairly.

C: Right, it might be.
T: But why *must* she? Even though it would be good for you and maybe good for her. Why does she *have to* do what would be nice for you?

The same disputation is being repeated.

C: OK, so she doesn't have to.
T: I don't think you believe that.
C: One thing that helps me is to think, "Well, it's not my fault, the fact that she's doing that." And the fact that she doesn't *have* to be fair and it's not really my job to make her fair and I don't exist in this time and place to straighten my mother out and make her realize how important it is to be fair.
T: That's right. But if you don't really work hard at giving up that "she's *got to*," you're going to be, first of all, continuously disappointed in her, trying to control her. . . .
C: But in terms of acting every day, once in despair I was talking about this with my father and she has been very domineering towards him all his life and picked on him unfairly, and he told me frankly, "I have found that the best way to deal with her is to submit. That is how I cope." And this is true. An observer in my home for three days would look at this man and say he is slavish, servile, and demeans himself rather than confront her.
T: OK, let me ask you a question. Does he upset himself? Is he quiet but seething inside or is he really kind of philosophic about it?
C: For years I think he walked around exactly like I did, nursing a lot of inner hurts but not expressing them.
T: Now?
C: Now he seems to have accepted her behavior and accepted that this is the way he finds easiest to behave back. My way of dealing is—I find obsequiousness very bad. If she must act in a very domineering way, it is not given that I must act in a very obsequious way. That's unpleasant.
T: I hear you saying, "It's good that my father is not upsetting himself about her nuttiness any longer. He lays back and it rolls off him." He is not trying to train her or shape her up by confronting her.
C: Right.
T: First of all, that tells me why that's a good reason for her not to change at all. She's had years of training and reinforcement.
C: Right! Having everyone in the family submit to her.
T: So, at best, if you decide to challenge the system it's going to be a

tough job. You're going to try to retrain this woman who's had sixty-some years of reinforcement for this kind of behavior. You're going to have a tough job. That knowledge may help you make your decision about whether or not to stand up to her—is it worth it?

C: Right.

T: Another thing I hear you saying, however, is in your choice of words to describe your father's behavior—obsequious, slavish. They say he's a schlemeil—people walk all over him. That's a *perception* you're talking about.

C: Right. This has put a very great part in the kind of men I've been attracted to. I could never stand a guy who would do whatever I said. I watched my father do that for so many years and I did get that impression of him.

T: Right. But that's a perception. Now what I'm suggesting is: if you were to very *objectively* describe your father's behavior, without using words like obsequious, which are rather negative or pejorative, how would you very objectively describe what he does?

C: Hmmmm. Objectively. When my mother attacks my father without any just cause, he does not defend himself and he does not attack back.

T: What *does* he do?

C: He either remains quiet, says a very gentle now-now-dear, but then proceeds to do what she tells him to do.

T: And then the issue blows over?

C: It blows over but it's a constant thing. Not just once a day, but from the second you enter to the second you leave her presence. It's a barrage. Orders.

T: So your father lets her do that, he goes along with her requests, but he also doesn't *upset* himself. He's not stewing. So he's made his own adaptation.

C: Right.

T: There's two components to adaptation. (1) What he does inside—his emotional turmoil, and (2) is what he does on the outside, behaviorally how he responds.

The therapist is helping the client to empathically understand her father's behavior.

C: OK.

T: What I hear you saying is, maybe the emotional reaction is OK. His apparent ability to not upset himself about his crazy wife is something you'd like to acquire. Be philosophical and let her be her nutty self.

C: Right. But not follow the same behavior patterns.

T: Right.

C: Because I find that image of myself is unpleasant. I found very often what I do is just give tit for tat. When she starts digging me, I dig back.

T: Let me suggest, before we go off, maybe we can look at the behaviors as a separate issue. As a series of *strategies* we could try. Step one, however, is still the same. Let's get over the rage. Now, once you can accomplish that, you can probably problem-solve the situation better. "Let's see, I can try experiments. I can try retorting and see how that works. I can try reinforcing better behavior and see how that works. I can try doing what my father does and shutting up and doing whatever she asks and see what that does. I can try being very assertive and confronting her. I could try giving her lectures. I could try giving her books to read." You might try strategies. If a strategy doesn't work, after a reasonable try, you end the experiment and say "Well, that didn't affect her behavior, I'll try something else." All those are strategies—they're just behaviors.

C: They're good though, because they make me feel good. I could try this or that.

T: Yes, like a scientist. But a scientist is never going to be a good scientist if he's demanding that the data come out the way he wants!

The therapist is pointing out why the inelegant solution would not be appropriate.

C: Yeah.

T: As long as you're *demanding* that your mother change her behavior, you're going to be angry at her.

C: Yeah.

T: Step one is to give up the demand, give up the anger and then try strategies and do experiments. So the best thing to do is to give up the *shoulds*. If you can really believe what you said, that she doesn't have to change—she may never change. . . .

C: You're right. She's definitely not going to change!

T: She may or she may not. We can try strategies. But if you can give up the *shoulds*, the *demand* that she change, and get some of your father's philosophical ideas: "That's the way she is for now—she doesn't seem to want to change—she's not motivated to change, and me sitting back demanding that she change—"

The therapist is using the father as a rational model.

C: When you say it, I really see it! I feel what you're saying.
T: So you can imagine that if you can just remember this stuff and say it to yourself between sessions, you'd be OK. Here's a great book, *Overcoming Frustration and Anger* by Paul Hauck. Another useful book is *How to Live With—and Without—Anger* by Albert Ellis. If you could read some of these it would reinforce what we just did today.
C: I really feel better. I really do. I mean, it just went from this huge horrible thing to—well, she's just her and so what!
T: Bravo! That's fantastic! That's emotional proof that disputing can work for you.
C: Yeah.
T: What you'd better do is work hard at remembering to do it between our meetings.
C: OK.
T: That's why a good book is a handy thing to have.

9 Therapist Strategies: Advanced Variations on a Theme

Active-Directive Style

RET therapists vary quite a lot in their style of interacting with patients, but as a group they can be distinguished from therapists of other schools by their *active, directive* style. Because RET therapists work with a model of identifying and challenging self-defeating thought patterns, they are alert and watchful for specific cues to these thoughts. Key words, phrases, intonations, and nonverbal aspects of the client's behavior are the cues, and the therapist will try to not let these slip by unattended. Thus, the RET therapist will often avoid asking very general open-ended questions, allowing a prolonged rambling response by the client, followed by another question from the therapist. Instead, the RET therapist tends to ask direct, specific questions so that the interaction is more a dialogue than a client monologue, with the therapist carefully following up on words and concepts revealed in the client's responses. We envision the therapist as a kind of herding dog who is guiding the patient through an open field full of distractions and keeping the patient on course.

An easy trap for an active therapist to fall into is the Advice Trap, in which the therapist either gives patients solutions to their problems or appears to be recommending a particular solution. It is important to help clients see that they *do* have options and alternatives. Still more important, however, is to teach clients that brainstorming or problem solving is a skill that they can learn, particularly when they have seen how not to upset themselves. This concept, of course, is consistent with the goal of ultimately encouraging independence from the therapist; it will be discussed more fully in Chapter 10.

Similarly, therapists will want to˙be careful not to simply supply irrational statements heard in the client's conversation or which RET theory suggests will be present. If they do make such suggestions to the client, they will want to speak tentatively and check out the ideas with the client. Thus, the therapist might say: "It sounds like you're saying you *should* do X; have I heard you correctly?"

It is still more preferable to tease out the irrational beliefs by phrasing questions in a guided manner. For example:

NOT: Why did you get angry?
BUT: What did you tell yourself to make yourself angry?
OR: Did you get angry because you were telling yourself, "Those bastards shouldn't have done that to me"?

NOT: What is related to your problems with power struggles?
BUT: What do you tell yourself to upset yourself when you find you are in a power struggle?
OR: Are you upsetting yourself because you're telling yourself that you must win?

NOT: So you believe that he should love you?
BUT: What do you think about his not loving you?
OR: And are you saying, "It's awful that he doesn't love me"?

Thus, instead of suggesting ideas to clients (e.g., "You are demanding"), try to lead them to discover the ideas by themselves by questions such as, "What were you telling yourself?" Questions, rather than answers, put the responsibility for therapy properly on the patient.

NOT: That's not true!
BUT: How do you know that's true?
OR: What evidence do you have that that's true?
OR: What could possibly convince you that it's *not* true?

Lecture versus Socratic Dialogue

At this juncture, we want to point out that there are two different ways of presenting RET principles: (1) lecture format and (2) Socratic dialogue. The lecturer directly imparts information to clients about what they are doing to cause their own disturbance and uses explanatory devices such as parables, analogies, and metaphors to make the point. The therapist using a Socratic dialogue relies more on evocative questions to guide the client to an insight or an appropriate conclusion, as did the famous philosopher. The latter, therefore, is a slower and more methodical procedure. Both techniques have value as educational devices, but the wise practitioner knows their limitations as well.

It is advisable that a certain amount of lecturing take place in therapy, since it is the most efficient way to transmit information. Mini-lectures may be particularly appropriate in early sessions to familiarize clients with some of the basic principles of RET. You may also find lecturing useful for low socioeconomic status clients, who expect a great deal of active direction from the therapist, or for clients with lower intellectual ability or brain injury, who tend to require more structure. Lecturing is, of course, appropriate when the client's problem results from ignorance about a particular topic (e.g., the female client who labels herself frigid because she does not come to orgasm in intercourse).

The use of mini-lectures, however, requires caution. If you give a lecture, even an excellent one, what is your client doing with the information? Probably what most students do: putting it in a (mental) notebook and filing it away for the next test—in this case, the next therapy session. Be aware of this tendency and, without labeling it as such, program little tests within the session to make sure that the client is really "with you." Do not go on to the next point until you're certain that the client has understood the previous one. Also, give behavioral homework assignments to assure that the client actively utilizes the lecture material (see Chapter 11).

Socratic dialogue has its own advantages, most particularly as an aid to learning and recall. Years of psychological research on the relative effectiveness of recall versus recognition memory suggests that getting the client to *generate* appropriate cognitions (via Socratic dialogue) will produce superior retention in comparison to lecturing, which merely allows the client to *recognize* appropriate cognitions. Whereas the lecture format consists of unequally weighted sequential monologues, the Socratic method allows a true dialogue. In addition, the client expresses the content in his or her own words and will recall the material in this same modality, thus further encouraging retention.

Examine your own behavior when you attend a lecture. What are you doing? Not much, right? You are sitting silently, perhaps nodding your head in agreement and occasionally taking notes. These are quite passive activities and illustrate the advisability of not limiting your therapeutic interventions to this one modality.

Now, listen to a session in which you have done some lecturing. Try to ascertain whether or not the client understood your major points. What could you have done to test that understanding?

Contrast the following two presentations:

Lecture: Well, Shiela, you seem to be very upset and anxious about your mother not approving of you. Let me spend a little time explaining to you what causes people to be anxious. Most people believe that they're made anxious by the things that happen to them. You're believing that your anxiety is caused by your mother's disapproval. Actually, we don't think that's true. People usually get upset about things because of what they think about them. For example, 100 people experiencing the same disapproval from your mother wouldn't all feel the same way. Some would feel happy or relieved that their mother didn't care for them and would leave them alone, others would feel terribly upset and suicidal, others would feel kind of indifferent. There could be a whole range of reactions. So that the Activating event, as we call what your mother's doing to you, doesn't cause all these different reactions. It's really what you think—your belief system. Now, different kinds of beliefs cause different kinds of emotions. Illogical or irrational beliefs which exaggerate things cause very disturbed emotions, and rational, logical beliefs cause more appropriate, less disturbed emotions.

Socratic dialogue:

T: OK, Shiela, I understand you feel anxious when your mother picks on you or when you think about your mother picking on you. Now, where do you think that anxiety comes from?

C: Well, from my mother, of course. If she would stop picking on me, then I wouldn't feel anxious!

T: Well, it sure might seem that way, but if your mother picked on me, I wouldn't feel anxious. Now, why wouldn't I feel anxious when you would?

C: Because you don't have to live with her!

T: Well, let's assume I did. I still wouldn't feel anxious. Now, what would be the difference?

C: Well, maybe she just doesn't mean as much to you as she does to me.

T: That could be. The word "meaning" is very important, isn't it? Because it's the *meaning* we put on situations, in this case your mother's behavior, that leads to our emotional feelings. What meaning do you think you're putting on your mother's behavior?

C: (pause) That's a hard question.

T: But you're obviously not saying, "Oh, it's fine that she acts that way. I'm really pleased." Are you?

C: Oh, no!

T: What are you saying?

C: It's not nice at all! It's terrible that she's acting that way!

T: That's right! You're saying it's awful or horrible that she's acting that way. Now we call that "awfulizing" and it's an example of an irrational idea. And irrational ideas are the kind that lead to disquieting, dysfunctional emotions.

Listen to some of your recent therapy tapes with your ear tuned to who was doing most of the talking, you or the client. Are you lecturing too much? Are you talking too little? What is your purpose in doing so?

Now, pick a particular client and determine to use a specific therapeutic style, either Socratic dialogue or lecture, to get across a point. Plan your next session and tape it. Later, review it to see if you met your objectives.

If you speak primarily in declarative sentences (as in lecture format) rather than ask questions (as in Socratic dialogue), you run two major risks. First, you may slip into the role of Expert, who, for example, may be viewed as responsible for holding the patient's marriage together.

Thus, the declarative style may oversell clients so that they unthinkingly accept the therapist's judgment or rely on the therapist to solve their problems. Another disadvantage is that you may set up ideas which clients will perversely deny or debate, even if they are quite correct. Questions are usually the better way to elicit material from clients and to help them learn to help themselves. In order to do Socratic dialogue, it is important to learn how to ask good questions.

FORM OF THE QUESTIONS

The form in which questions are posed is important, and a common error made by new RET therapists is to begin too many questions with the word "why." "Why" questions are difficult to answer; the responses are often redundant, simply reiterating why the patient came to therapy. Examples:

NOT: Why are you anxious?
BUT: What do you think makes you anxious?
OR: Are you aware of the fact that you are in control of your anxiety?

As a handy substitute for the "why," the therapist may always reach for a "how."

Hypothetical questions are also a useful device. For a patient who fears certain life events, the therapist might say, for example: "What would you do if tomorrow morning you woke up and were married (or lost your job, etc.)?" These prospective examinations may aid not only in obtaining cognitive samples but also in directly reducing the patient's avoidance of feared events. Another example, from a depressed patient who suffers from headaches:

T: Suppose you went to a neurologist today and he gave you a new miracle drug which took away your headaches. Tomorrow you'd wake up and have no headaches. How would that change your life? How would you cope?

Such questions may also serve as mini-extinction procedures, resembling low items on a desensitization hierarchy. That is, patients may be avoiding a specific issue or undertaking in their lives, and facing the issue on a verbal level is less fear-provoking than engaging in more direct behaviors.

Try an exercise that Ed Garcia has used with many supervisees: attempt to conduct an *entire* therapy session using only questioning statements and avoiding all declarative sentences. Tape the session and see how close you come to this goal. Note that we are *not* recommending that all therapy be in the form of evocative questions. Too many questions may prove irritating to clients if they believe that you have something to say and are beating around the bush instead of saying it directly. This exercise is merely designed to establish the skill of question asking in your repertoire.

PACING OF QUESTIONS

To stop the client's tangential monologues or to hold back an avalanche of unnecessary information, a useful strategy is to pace questions carefully. Ask the next question as soon as the client answers the last, even if this means interrupting the client's speech. It is difficult to guide the dialogue unless the therapist is willing to be assertive.

See that your client answers your questions. If he or she responds with a non sequitur, this may provide valuable diagnostic information. Why do clients not answer questions? Perhaps (1) they have not paid attention; (2) they may not have understood your question or have misunderstood it; (3) if they have not understood it, they may have been too nonassertive to request clarification; (4) their behavior may be defensive avoidance of a painful topic; (5) they may be unskilled at social conversation; or (6) they may have poor thought habits and routinely think illogically or tangentially.

It is therapeutic to repeat the question; this will teach appropriate skills and help clients to learn to focus their attention or to confront anxiety-provoking situations. To ignore the non sequitur encourages the pathology. If patients repeatedly fail to answer questions, a useful strategy is to stop their tangential thoughts and ask if they remember the question. Then ask how the answer relates to it. This will give you some information about whether the problem is an attentional deficit, an avoidance issue, or a lack of social skills.

Many new therapists are uncomfortable with the advice to stop the patient's digressions and repeat unanswered questions. They often object that it is rude to redirect the client and worry that the client will be offended or even harmed. It might be helpful to remember that it is the *client* who is being rude by ignoring your question. In addition, most clients do not object to redirection, but for those who are offended, the rationale for the procedure can be explained in detail. The important point is that therapy is not a social interaction; with approximately forty-five minutes to work on problems, it is appropriate to stay on target.

Another instance in which rephrasing or repeating your questions is helpful is when you do not understand the client's response (e.g., "I'm not sure I follow you here; could you explain that again?"). In directive therapy, it is important that client and therapist understand one another. If you do not understand the client, your silence may communicate that you do. The client could become annoyed later, when it becomes apparent that you did not understand. You also waste valuable and expensive time by allowing the client to go on when you are unclear about the message. Once again, our experience suggests that most clients are not offended by repetitions of questions for clarification, but instead perceive the therapist more positively for behaving honestly. Both parties benefit from more effective communication.

Maintaining Problem Focus

A prime and often difficult task for the therapist is to keep the patient focused on the problem. Many therapists assume that conversational drifting is a sign of pathological resistance. While this may sometimes be the case, it is more likely that your clients are simply displaying normal social behaviors. To illustrate this point to yourself, monitor some social conversations and note how many different topics are discussed within a twenty-minute period. In therapy, however, conversational drift is inappropriate.

You can increase focusing by not picking up too many ABC's in one session. It is better to take one problem area and focus on it until disputation or some closure has been reached before moving on.

Keeping the client on the topic has benefits in addition to keeping the problem in focus. If the client has a tendency to engage in tangential thinking, the therapist can avoid strengthening this behavior and also may give the client important feedback about this problem of conversational drift. Confront the client genuinely and empathically; for example:

T: Jane, I'm confused. You started out talking about topic X and now you've moved to Y. What's the relationship between them? (Or, which do you want to talk about?)

Being able to contribute to a conversation on one topic and being able to stay with the topic for a period of time is, after all, a prerequisite skill for effective psychotherapy. If this skill is weak or missing, the therapist may have to begin by doing "attention training." This problem is akin to that of working with a hyperkinetic child; nothing will get accomplished until you train the child to attend to a task. The following techniques may prove helpful in this preliminary training:

1. You may listen to tape recordings of therapy sessions with the client in order to sharpen your skills in detecting conversational slippage.
2. Clients may be encouraged to do the same, so that they learn to identify the problem behavior.
3. You can structure the conversation tightly, limiting the discussion to just a few topics.
4. Direct retraining procedures can be used, including rewards for staying on the topic and penalties for digressions. For example, you may say to the client: "My, you've outlined your problem well! That's very good, the way you stayed on the topic; it's helpful to us." On the other hand, you may point out: "You know, you got off the track, and I really don't understand how that follows. Explain it to me again!" As in behavioral training, we recommend putting the emphasis on the positive reinforcers.

Implementing any or all of the above procedures will not be easy, and will require vigilance and strict self-monitoring by the therapist.

Suppose, however, that the patient comes in obviously intending to take over the session with a topic that you believe is a deflection and not as important as another unresolved issue. What shall you do? First, you can give yourself permission to redirect the session by assuming that you know best about therapy. How can you redirect the session? One technique is to remind the client of the goals for the session and to make use of the Premack Principle.* For example:

T: Jim, I'm going to let you talk about your root canal work at the end of the session; we'll save time for that. But first, I have some very important issues which *I* want to discuss about your marriage.

Another approach which at least sets some limits to the client's diversions is the following:

T: Jim, your root canal seems to be important to you. Let's give the first five minutes to discussing your problems with your teeth and then spend the last forty minutes on my topic, the issue of your marriage.

You may also, at this point, ask clients how they feel about the redirection. If they're angry, it may be useful to ask if they experience anger in similar situations—an issue which may indeed be relevant to the main therapeutic problem.

If you sense that the client's new issue is a distraction maneuver, you may confront the client as follows:

T: I get the sense that you're afraid of something.

More directly, you may ask the client how this topic fits in with the avoided one:

T: Jim, what does your root canal have to do with the problems in your marriage?

Ultimately, you may want to share an interpretation of the client's behavior:

*The Premack Principle states that a high-probability behavior can be used to reinforce a low-probability behavior.

T: Jim, it seems like week after week you come in with your agenda
     items which seem to get us off the track of the original problem—
     your marriage! It appears to me you may be trying to avoid that
     problem. What do you think it is you could be frightened of?

If the patient has a persistent tendency to be wordy, flighty, or to
go off the topic in response to the therapist's intervention or question,
strong measures may be needed. You may call for a confrontation by,
for example, forcefully saying, *"Stop a minute!"* to the client. With
difficult patients, the therapist may temporarily have to resort to questions that allow only "yes/no" answers. If you become aware that the
problem focus has already been lost and the conversation has gone far
afield, you may stop and ask yourself two basic questions:

In a few sentences, what is the patient's main problem?
What are the most prominent irrational beliefs?

Another useful tactic to keep patients focused on the task is to keep
asking for specific examples of their main problem.

Redundancy

Therapy, like teaching, often demands a certain amount of redundancy.
It will be important for you to go over rational-emotive concepts with
the patient repeatedly, even though you may feel that you sound like a
broken record. RET philosophy contains subtle points which many patients find slippery to hang onto; rehearsal is therefore very important.
You will want to keep in mind that you are modeling skills for the
patient, such as learning to attend to key phrases and to examine one's
internal dialogue, and these skills require repetition with most clients.
Particularly in the Disputation phase, you may find yourself not wanting to say the same things again and again. It is interesting to contemplate how Dr. Ellis himself has managed to teach the same messages
to so many patients over the many years he has been practicing RET.
Listening to Ellis, one gets a clue; rather dramatic variation in voice

tone and modulation may serve to keep up the excitement and interest of the therapist as well as the patient. In Disputation (as was seen
in Chapters 6 and 7) you can vary the style of phrasing greatly, although you are basically helping to train the client to ask the same
questions (e.g., "Where is the evidence?" "Why is it awful?" "Who
says you must—?").

Language Style

Adjustments in language style will often be made, of course, since
clients vary in their level of sophistication. Take the case of a young
woman, a high school sophomore, who is concerned about getting into a
sorority. She complains of her shyness, explaining that, for example,
she is afraid to go up to the older or stylishly dressed girls and initiate
conversations. It sounds to you as if she has cataloged and ranked people,
and declared herself to fall below some arbitrary and imaginary cutoff
point. Her philosophy seems to be "Some people are better than others," which is expressed in her belief system as "I *should* be as good as
they are! If they don't accept me, it proves that I'm not, and that would
be awful!" With such a client, it might not be profitable to begin by
discussing "irrational beliefs" or "philosophical tenets." You might be
more direct and helpful if you take a more casual approach. The first
query, therefore, might be something like: "What do you think the
others would *do* if you went over to them?"

A question about therapist language often asked by students of RET
is whether it is necessary to use Ellis' jargon (e.g., "should," "must,"
"awful," etc.) Ellis himself, however, has pointed out that clients express their personalized irrational beliefs in their own idiosyncratic language. Adolescents don't often refer to a troublesome person in their
lives as a "shit" or a "bastard" but are more likely to use words such as
"nerd" or "turkey." The meaning is obviously the same. Adults may
also use idiosyncratic language for irrational concepts. Don't wait for
clients to say, "It's awful"; they may have said it many times in their
own words (e.g., "Oh, my God," "That's the pits," "The worst thing
happened," "That sucks," etc.). It is preferable, therefore, to use the

client's language whenever possible. One exception to this rule of thumb: if the client has read books on RET and already employs the jargon, the therapist may continue to follow his or her lead.

Obscenity

Another aspect of style which the therapist will want to be flexible about is the "sprightly use of obscenity" (to use Ellis' phrase). Many RET therapists model closely after Ellis in this regard. We have observed that beginning RET therapists can be discriminated from more advanced students by their liberal usage of four-letter words. In RET terms, it is common to shorthand the patient's self-denigration by referring to his "shithood"; the therapist may ask, for example, how the patient's bad behavior makes him "a shit." Obviously, other terms will do the trick as well, such as "worm," "no-goodnik," and "louse." Here you will want to use your own judgment as to which term will best suit the client.

While Ellis has frequently been criticized for his use of obscenity, he has often commented publicly on the positive reasons for doing so. Ellis hypothesizes that people typically catastrophize in four-letter expletives, even if they rarely use these terms in most conversations. Sometimes even the most subdued and reserved clients find that when they are describing serious life hassles, four-letter words are the most appropriate and evocative descriptors. They often help loosen people up and have a strong emotive—and motivating—quality.

> Reflect on your own subvocal monologue the next time you are late for work and rush from the house, only to discover that you have a flat tire.

A second reason for using obscene language is rapport building. It may sound strange that clients would like a therapist who curses, but remember that most people use obscene language only within their closest circle of peers. It is the more informal language one uses with those with whom one can be relaxed and off guard. Thus, it is a common observation of therapists that once they provide a model for the use of obscenity and thereby give permission for the patient to follow suit, the patient feels more free.

To prove that obscene language can be rapport building, monitor your own use of four-letter words and note in whose presence they are comfortably used.

We do not recommend using obscenity indiscriminately. Its "sprightly use" is best directed at the client's irrational beliefs ("Why the fuck *should* you?") and to characterize the client's self-denigration ("You sound like you think you're really a shit!"). A third use is to underscore significant points ("Isn't the goal of life to get out there and have a fucking ball?"). Realize, however, that obscenity is not directed at the clients themselves *and* that it is not necessary to curse at all, since the same points can be made using other words.

Intonation

A significant aspect of the therapist's verbal behavior to which the RET novice will want to attend is voice *intonation*. A great deal of information about attitudes can be unwittingly communicated in this modality. Particularly, the therapist will want to avoid expressing horror or value judgments. For example, suppose the patient is a young man who is discussing his feelings of guilt about not visiting his parents as often as they would like. The incautious therapist might say: "You only go once a *week*?" or "You don't go frequently *at all*?" Inflections of the therapist's voice may make a great deal of difference in how the patient responds to such questions.

Inflection and intonation can also be used as important discriminative cues in helping clients learn the difference between rational and irrational beliefs. When you listen to one of Ellis' public demonstrations of RET in person or on tape, notice that he uses his voice instrumentally for clarification. Whenever he pronounces one of the words that reflect irrational concepts (e.g., "awful," "terrible," "should," or "need"), he drops his voice several notes, stretches out the word, and increases his volume, producing a dreary, dramatic sound. For example: ". . . and it's AWWWWWFULL that he doesn't like me!" Later, when he changes the "awful" to "unfortunate" or a "need" to a "want," Ellis again pronounces the words, now reflecting rational concepts, in a distinct way. He speaks the key word slowly, enunciates very clearly, and raises the pitch of his voice as well as the volume. Thus, different auditory stimuli are associated with different concepts, making them more salient and, hopefully, more easy to remember. Howard Kassinove of Hofstra University makes a point of encouraging his trainees in RET to model Ellis' vocal style. He points out that variety in style is important in every therapeutic encounter; a significant shift in tone and volume may increase the probability that the client will attend to and learn from the therapist.

Getting the client's attention is crucial when the therapist is about to make an important point. Monitor your typical style. If you are speaking rapidly and loudly and you want to make an important point, dramatically lower your voice and slow down. If your style is typically soft-spoken, on the other hand, you will grab the client's attention by raising your volume and speed. In other words, know yourself and be prepared to shift gears when it is appropriate.

A second strategy is to signal an important concept by the content of your speech and the use of gestures. As in assertiveness training, leaning forward, touching the client on the arm, and making good eye contact are effective nonverbal attention getters. You can also set the stage for a confrontation by verbal "flashers" such as the following:

T: I'm going to do something risky right now and tell you something that most people wouldn't dare to say . . .

OR

T: This is a really important point. Stop and listen carefully to what I'm going to say . . .

If clients habitually interrupt, ask them for five minutes during which they agree not to talk; hold them to this agreement.

Silences

Silence may also be communicative. When you are silent, your behavior may be construed as agreement with the patient. There is a parallel notion in old English law: If your separated spouse continues to sign your name to bills, and this state of affairs goes on for a period of time without your objection, the spouse may win the right to continue to do so since your silence is construed as consent. A similar phenomenon is often true in conversations. For example, if the client loses the problem-centered focus and meanders off into storytelling, your silence may indicate to the client that he or she is making sense, doing constructive work, or even that you are following the story.

Similarly, *inconsistent* silences by the therapist may be unhelpful. Suppose the patient is depressed and frequently makes statements such as: "I'm never going to get better." Inconsistent silence in response to these remarks may provide intermittent reinforcement for this irrational belief, thereby prolonging its existence in the cognitive system. A better plan of action would be to vigorously confront and dispute such remarks or to reflectively paraphrase them rationally (e.g., "It sounds like you're saying that it would be hard for you to change"). The point we wish to stress is that silence is communicative. The problem is that we don't always know *what* we have communicated. Patients may interpret our silence as disapproval, indifference, or agreement. It is wise, therefore, to check on your patient's understanding of your silence and correct misperceptions that you uncover.

Some Final Points

In the above section, we have discussed a variety of stylistic variations in doing RET; it is preferable that the new therapist become comfortable with all of them. Utilize specific variations and change gears when your clinical judgment suggests its effectiveness. The important point is not to behave rigidly—always talking fast, always talking slowly, always using the same intonation, always being funny or glib, always allowing no silent periods. Rigid persistence in one mode of behavior may be less productive for your client and boring for you. Interpersonal style is your tool, and the foolishness of sticking to one modality is analogous to the surgeon who performs a hysterectomy on every patient regardless of the presenting complaint or the physician who prescribes the same medication in every case.

This injunction is consistent with the RET philosophy that there seem to be no absolutes and thus no absolutistic prescriptions in psychotherapy. (Even the belief that there *can* be no absolutes—which is *not* an RET dictum—is dogmatically absolutistic.) Consider some of the following absolutes from other areas of clinical practice:

> There can *never* be secrets in marital therapy.
>
> In family therapy, *all* family members *must* be present at *every* session.
>
> In sexual counseling, a complete sexual history is *always* taken, and sensate focus is useful in *every* case.
>
> Transference *must always* be analyzed.

While certain therapeutic strategies may frequently foster the client's progress, we would echo Ellis' contention (1962) that there appear to be no absolute prerequisites for personality change—even rational thinking.

Rigidity in Other Therapist Behaviors

The practice of psychotherapy usually assumes a forty-five- to fifty-minute hour, but there is nothing sacred about the length of the session. It may be advantageous for you to alter the session length and use a somewhat individualistic approach. Some clients, for example, may require a double session. Perhaps they have many pressing issues to discuss, or they find it very disruptive to their cognitive processes to leave the session before they have actually finished understanding a philosophical disputation. On the other hand, some clients may be unable to sit through a fifty-minute discussion. Therapy may be the first time in their lives that they have undertaken such an endeavor. For such clients, a gradual increase in the length of the session may be desirable before you can get them to converse for a full session. If you do schedule fixed-length sessions, you may wish to spend only part of the time in an intellectual endeavor and the remainder in relaxation training or nontaxing exercise.

Our experience in experimenting with shorter sessions has indicated that the amount of time spent discussing the crucial issues has remained the same, and the amount of time spent avoiding topics or discussing unimportant issues has been reduced. Not only is the client more keenly aware of time limitations and therefore the importance of being succinct and to the point, but so is the therapist. With the shorter session, we have found that we are more directive, more active, more confrontative, and a lot less distracted.

Experiment with sessions of varying lengths to determine what is most beneficial for you and for your clients. Some therapists may well be hyperkinetic children grown up and thus unable to keep their attention span on one topic for more than thirty minutes. Recognizing the limitations of yourself and your client can only benefit both parties.

Similarly, there is no reason to adhere unthinkingly to geographical restrictions in the session. For example, it is not necessary for you to always sit on the same chair or the client to always sit across from you on the sofa. In fact, there appears to be no therapeutic reason why every session must take place in the same office.* Sessions away from the therapist's office may be the most effective at times. For example, in treating clients with social anxiety or agoraphobia, it may be beneficial to go with them into those situations where they actually experience the anxiety and dispute their irrational ideas as they occur. An example of effective therapy involved the treatment of a client with the presenting problem of an elevator phobia. During the first session in our six-story building in Manhattan, the therapist suggested: "Why don't we have

*Check your malpractice coverage on this point, however, particularly if you operate under an institutional policy.

this therapy session standing out in front of the elevator?" As the session progressed in the hallway, the client experienced a gradual reduction in anxiety. Halfway through the session, the therapist had talked the client into the elevator, and they eventually rode up and down while conducting the remainder of the session. This format led to the reduction of the situation-specific phobia in three sessions.

Roles of the RET Therapist

RET practitioners may think of themselves in part as teachers and of RET theory as an educational model. What do you teach? First and foremost, you teach mental health. Second, since the goal of therapy is to enable patients to do an ABCDE analysis themselves, you are a teacher of the logico-empirical method of reasoning. Good teachers not only ask many questions of their students but also question their own performance. Here are some questions you may want to periodically ask yourself:

Is the patient understanding what I have said?

Am I expressing myself clearly?

Am I doing too much of the work?

Does the patient really believe what I (or he) just said?

How can I get the patient to express rational beliefs more strongly?

Am I giving enough homework assignments and are they working?

You may also serve as a behavioral model. Suppose a couple is coming for marriage counseling and the husband expresses a desire to be more emotionally expressive, a goal which his wife wholeheartedly endorses. In addition to suggesting outside models (e.g., encouraging the husband to study the romantic behaviors portrayed in movies), you may role-play appropriate responses (e.g., "If I were in your situation, I might say . . . "). Similarly, in teaching a client the fine art of self-acceptance, you will want to display clear acceptance of clients with their disturbing behaviors. You may thereby model how they can refuse to rate their essence as a person but merely rate their dysfunctional behaviors. Of course, in serving as a model, you had better judge whether you can do what you are asking the client to do. In the case of the inhibited husband, you would be wise to ask yourself honestly if you think you *are* a good model for this particular kind of expression.

Issues of Transference and Countertransference

By transference, we mean that patients react to the therapist as they do to other significant people. It may be very useful to use the transference data and point it out to the patient. The first job is to identify the emotional tone of the interaction and then the belief systems behind the emotion. Once these are specified, you can ask clients whether they relate to others in their lives in the same way as they relate to you. For example: "You know, Bernie, every time we talk about sex, I notice changes in your voice and you become very . . . well, loose with me. I wonder if that's how you relate to other women?" Such a confrontation can provide you with problem areas to pinpoint and question.

Even in a nonsexual context, attitudes toward the therapist may be good indicators of attitudes in other interpersonal encounters. For example, suppose you had given your female patient a homework assignment. She comes back having successfully done it but also exclaiming: "Oh, Doctor, I thought of you and I knew how you'd react if I *didn't* do it!" The patient is really telling you about one of her irrational beliefs: if she failed, you might think she was a shit, and then she *would* be a shit. Thus, you have excellent data to point out that the patient was doing good things but for all the wrong reasons. Essentially the patient is saying that she herself is not worth doing things for, but that you are. Such a patient had better learn that she doesn't have to please the therapist.

Your attitude toward the client—countertransference—is also important, and you may use yourself as a measuring device. Ask yourself: how do you feel when you know the client is coming to see you? Do you look forward to the visit or dread it? For what reasons? What are your feelings about the client during the session? What are his or her major interaction styles? Since the client is probably behaving toward you as to other people, you are in a good position to give direct feedback that others may not be willing to disclose—that is, how his or her behavior influences you. Try, of course, to be as concrete as possible and to pinpoint specific behaviors that can be later monitored (e.g., a whining tone of voice, little or no smiling, poor eye contact, delayed response time).

A shy, inhibited male patient has been discussing his problems in dating when he suddenly looks up at his therapist and asks her: "Would *you* go out with me?" How would an RET therapist handle such a question? Directly! The therapist would either say "No, because—" or "Yes, if I weren't your psychotherapist." In addition, she could discuss with the patient why someone like herself might or might not date him. Subsequently, the therapist will also raise the issue of what the question meant and if it were asked with some serious intent.

It is certainly permissible for you to indicate your feelings. In response to a serious question about dating such as the one above, you might say, for example: "Yes, if I had met you in other circumstances or before we started therapy, I probably would have wanted to date you. That would have been nice, but the reality is that we are involved in a therapeutic relationship and I *will not* have personal relations with any of my clients. Those are the facts, and we'd better accept them."

Achieving this agreement may help the patients to freely and fully self-disclose. If the issue is left unresolved, they may withhold information in order to put their best foot forward and keep alive the possibility of a personal relationship with you. In addition, by reaching closure in this way, you are also modeling a discrimination between thoughts and actions—for example, "I may have a nice sexual fantasy, but I *choose* not to act on it." This may be a very educational message about how to deal with desires; just because they exist does not mean you *have to* act on them.

Suppose the patient asks the therapist if she is attracted to him, and the therapist is not; what might she say in this case? Quite simply and gently, she may say: "No, I'm not." If the patient reacts to this information by becoming more depressed, the therapist has a perfect inroad to a major irrational belief, for surely she will not be the only female ever to reject him. His reaction may allow her to challenge him with statements such as: "Are you believing that because *I* don't find you attractive, no one else will?"

Perhaps the reader is surprised that we recommend that the

therapist respond immediately to such questions with a yes or no. One rationale is that with such a reply, the therapist is modeling good communication in an open, spontaneous relationship. This position, of course, is quite different from that taken in more psychodynamic therapies. Yet to first inquire, as an analyst might, "Why do you want to know if I'm attracted to you?" may seem like a phony dodge to the patient. The question may be a good one, but it would be better to ask it at a later time. A good, trusting relationship is not developed by being "clinical," such as by asking, "Why is that important? Why do you want to know?" Thus, the therapeutic relationship had better be built on sincerity. It is usually preferable, therefore, to answer client questions directly and honestly, and then deal with the individual's subsequent thoughts and feelings.

Let's put such interchanges into somewhat different environments and examine them:

Suppose you are sitting with a good friend over a cup of coffee and your friend asks, "Do you find me attractive?" A "clinical" answer that dodges the issue would probably make the other person think: "Hey, she's not really my friend. She won't even answer my question!"

Suppose that you, as a therapist, go to your supervisor and ask: "How am I doing?" If your supervisor says: "Why do you want to know?" what might you suspect? Wouldn't it cross your mind that the answer is not positive?

Patients may also ask many personal questions of the therapist. Are there any limits to the therapist's self-disclosure? Probably not; the RET therapist knows that there is nothing inherently shameful in this world, so what could the patient ask that would be nontherapeutic? On the other hand, a barrage of such questions may be distracting. After answering them directly, you might ask patients how they feel about this new information, how they feel about you, and what were their reasons for asking. For example, perhaps the patient looks on you as a mystical deity and then rejects you after learning that you are a mere mortal. This pattern may very well reflect what the patient does in everyday relationships, and you would do well to dispute the irrational beliefs associated with this problem.

Patients may have an authoritarian dependency such that they cannot take orders except from Perfect People; this style often leads to a kind of self-downing philosophy. It might be profitable to ask such clients if they think they are as good a person as you are. If the patients respond, "Oh no, why you're a doctor and I'm just a lowly slob," you can guess that they are doing the same thing with other people in their lives, such as their boss, the president of the company, or the provost of the university. It will be important to demystify the rest of their gods in addition to yourself.

If patients do not bring up transference issues, you may choose to do so. For example: each time you give a male client a homework assignment, he appears to sulk and accepts the assignment with resignation in his voice. At this point, you might inquire: "You know, John, each time I give you a homework assignment, I hear some resentment in your voice. How are you feeling toward me right now?" Once these feelings have been acknowledged, you may proceed to identify the irrational beliefs which cause his feelings and inquire whether he has similar beliefs and feelings about other people. It will also be important to identify the beliefs that led to the inhibition of direct expression of these feelings. Thus, exploring the transference issue is not done for any curative reasons but to help the therapist recognize relevant A's, C's, and, most important, B's.

Concluding Therapy Sessions

Two helpful hints to keep in mind as the therapy session is coming to an end are the following:

1. Try to end each session, group or individual, by giving the clients a homework assignment or having them design one themselves. Assignments may be in the form of thinking, reading, writing, or trying new activities (see Chapter 11). In any

case, their purpose is to strengthen or extend the skills learned in the session and to bridge the long gap between sessions.

2. As feedback, you may ask: "Was there anything I did or said in the session which bothered you in any way?" Also, "Was there anything I did or said today which seemed particularly useful to you?" And most important, "What did you learn from today's session?" Questions such as these may (a) enable you to adapt your style to your patient, (b) provide information to be taken up in the next session, (c) give an opportunity for a brief rehearsal by the patient, and (d) help identify other B's which can be taken up later.

Summary: Common Errors to Avoid

1. *Failure to listen.* Among other problems, you may misdiagnose if you fail to listen critically. Patients may say they are "angry," for example; you may inquire carefully what they mean by this term because they may be mislabeling their state and therapy may take off in the wrong direction. Similarly, you can be carefully attuned to key words, such as clients' idiosyncratic phrases, which indicate their irrational beliefs.

2. *Failure to develop goals.* It will be important to ask, rather than assume, what the client's goals are. You will also want to determine the client's expectancies of therapy. It is important to know these concepts so that you can clarify or correct them, or if agreement cannot be reached, the patient can be referred elsewhere.

3. *Errors in information gathering.* New therapists may err in either direction, either spending too many sessions gathering data before planning an intervention or failing to get sufficient information and jumping too quickly into disputation. In either case, they run a risk of alienating or losing the client or at least of doing inefficient therapy.

4. *Errors in assertiveness.* Again, errors may be made in either direction, either allowing clients to ramble or cutting them off too abruptly. What is happening when you are not sufficiently directive and allow the client too often to lead? Perhaps you have forgotten your game plan and are caught up in the patient's stories. Perhaps you are afraid of offending clients if you interrupt and do not want to appear rude. Asser-

tive clients will often let you know your error, either by criticizing or asking what you thought at the next session or by complaining that you interrupted too often. You might keep in mind, however, that each therapy session is not a win-or-lose game; there's always a next time.

5. *Errors in questioning.* You will want to avoid the following mistakes: (a) asking irrelevant or overgeneralized questions (e.g., "How've you been?") instead of asking directly relevant questions; (b) overusing rhetorical questions (e.g., "Where does your getting upset get you?"); (c) using too many "why" questions, which generally lead only to "because" excuses. It would be better to use "how," "where," or "what's the evidence" questions or to ask, "What are you telling yourself?" or "When you do this, what are you thinking?"; (d) overusing "yes/no" questions; queries that require fuller participation or richer answers are better; (e) asking multiple questions, such as bombarding clients with three or more questions without allowing them to answer any one of them; (f) answering the questions for the clients instead of letting them grapple with questions on their own or helping them by breaking questions down into simpler components; (g) failing to note whether the client has, in fact, answered your question or simply zig-zagged off into a story. If the question was unanswered, bring the client back to task.

6. *Errors in lecture style.* Avoid lengthy lectures, particularly when you fail to check and see if the client is following you. Educators tell us that the best way to learn something is to teach it; the best way for the patient to acquire RET principles, therefore, is not to listen to a long didactic lecture.

7. *Failure to check understanding.* It is important to get frequent feedback from clients to assure that they are understanding you. Listen to tapes of what you think are your good sessions; make sure that clients weren't "Um-hmmm-ing" you into thinking that they understood. It is useful periodically to ask clients to restate what you have just said or to ask: "What's your understanding of what I've just said?" or "What is your feeling about what we've been discussing?"

8. *Errors in being too wise.* You can avoid trying to be the Wise Person. It might be preferable to ask patients to try to convince you, for example, why they are a worm. You may have a wise thing to say, but be wiser not to say it. It is generally preferable to lead the client, by Socratic questions, to the same insight.

9. *Attitudinal errors.* You will want to avoid the following: (a) blaming and condemning remarks (e.g., "You know how to challenge those ideas"); (b) scare tactics (e.g., "You have a BIG problem; it's going to take a long time to work this out"); (c) being unrealistic and offering false hopes (e.g., "Oh, we can fix you up in no time"); (d) judgmental remarks (e.g., "Why do you need the approval of a *creep* like him?"); (e) overgeneralization (e.g., "You *are* smart"); and (f) argumentative power struggles in which you try to force the client to accept your views (e.g., "I'm the therapist here; I'll tell you what's wrong with you").

10. *Errors in the use of humor* Use humor frequently, but don't direct it at your client. Try not to be too giggly. See that your humor is therapeutic and not used for entertainment purposes.

The reader is encouraged to listen to a recent therapy tape and check performance on each of the categories above. You won't be able to listen for all of these errors at one time; monitor each error separately.

10 Comprehensive Rational-emotive Therapy

The early writings of Ellis focused almost exclusively on the *elegant solution* and the logical, persuasive model of therapy. In fact, it is this focus on philosophical content which distinguishes RET from other cognitive and cognitive-behavioral systems of therapy. The reader will recall, from our discussion on page 40, that the elegant solution entails the assumption that the Activating event is true and will remain so ("assuming the worst") and encourages clients to change their evaluation of the given reality. In Ellis' more recent writing (1973, 1977f, 1979b), he has expanded his theory to include both elegant and inelegant solutions, recognizing that clinical realities may dictate both to maximize therapeutic effectiveness. *Inelegant solutions* are attempts to help clients change their misperceptions of the A and, if feasible, to change the A.

Up to this point, you have been guided through the process of an elegant disputation, and you are probably aware of more therapeutic help required by your client. Therefore, we now turn our attention to other therapeutic modalities used by the rational therapist.

After reviewing the psychotherapy literature, we have discovered that cognitive-learning therapies appear to fall into four categories:

1. Elegant RET, with its emphasis on the philosophical solution.
2. Self-instructional training programs which attempt to guide clients' behavior directly by teaching rational self-statements and establishing a mediational influence between internal self-talk and behavior.

3. Analyses of clients' perceptions of reality, with efforts to help them develop more realistic schemas for their world.
4. Problem-solving approaches which help clients develop more efficient skills and guide them through the problem-solving process so that they may more efficiently deal with their world.

Rational-emotive therapists try to utilize all four modalities of cognitive-learning therapy. Thus, we will include a brief description of work in each of the three areas not covered so far. This presentation is not meant to be all-inclusive of other cognitive-learning therapies but to provide what, in our estimation, are representative examples.

Self-Instructional Training

Some clients may not understand or profit from the disputation phase of therapy. Among the reasons for the difficulty are: the client is too young, is intellectually limited, is overwhelmed by anxiety and unable to think clearly, or is confused by an overlay of psychotic thought disorder. In other words, RET therapists do fail in communicating the elegant solution to some patients, and the reasons for the failure may not be obvious; contraindications are often unknown. When little or no progress has occurred or is clearly predicted, the RET therapist may turn to *self-instructional training* as an alternate solution.

Self-instructional training is a procedure developed by Donald Meichenbaum (1977) in his work with test-taking and public-speaking anxiety. Other examples of self-instructional training include Novaco's (1975) work on anger control, Camp's (1975) work with hyperaggressive children, and Maultsby's (1975) work in rational behavior training. Essentially, clients are asked to imagine troublesome situations, to experience their emotional impact, and to recite coping self-statements. In Meichenbaum's therapist manual (1973), three types of coping self-statements are outlined:

1. *Confronting and handling the stressor.* These self-statements help the client focus on the task rather than on the anxiety. The principle is that task-relevant cognitions will be incompatible with anxiety-producing cognitions. For example:

What is it I have to do? Just think rationally.

Don't worry; worry won't help anything.

I'm not sure how to begin. Well, I'll just get started and maybe it'll become clearer as I go along.

2. *Coping with the feeling of being overwhelmed.* These self-statements are designed to help the patient cope with anxiety and reinterpret it. The message is that anxiety itself is not awful. For example:

Don't try to eliminate the anxiety totally; just keep it manageable.

This is the anxiety I thought I'd feel. It's a reminder for me to cope.

Slow down a little. Don't rush and get all in a panic.

I'll label my anxiety from 0 to 10 and watch it change. There, now I'm in better control.

3. *Reinforcing self-statements.* These coping sentences are an important component since the processes the patient is using are internal and others may not be able to reward the patient for small increments of control. Examples:

It's working. I can control how I feel.

I did it!

I am in control. I made more out of my fear than it was worth.

It's getting better each time I try these procedures.

The procedure for doing one form of self-instructional training is as follows. First, the client learns relaxation techniques. While this skill is being developed, client and therapist construct a hierarchy of anxiety-provoking situations from least to most threatening. For example, for a test-anxious student, the lowest item on the hierarchy may be "sitting in class when the instructor announces that a test will be given in two weeks." The highest item on the hierarchy might be "taking the exam and seeing other students finishing and leaving the room." Hierarchies typically consist of at least ten items, arranged on spatial, temporal, or thematic dimensions. While the patient is relaxed, each hierarchy item in turn is presented imaginally, and the patient practices reciting aloud, and later covertly, self-statements from each of the above three categories.

The technique of coping self-statements does not provide the patient with a philosophic understanding, and therefore behavior change may be unlikely to generalize across problems. The patient has instead acquired specific covert responses which are cued by specific environmental stressors. It may be obvious that these techniques are derived from a behavioral model. Meichenbaum's procedures place less emphasis on thinking and logical analysis than does RET, and they treat covert stimuli, responses, and reinforcers in the same manner as external stimuli, motoric responses, and externally applied reinforcers.

Case example: Helen was an obese twenty-year-old woman who avoided all contact with men. She had had a traumatic upbringing with an alcoholic father and had been raped by a stranger at the age of fourteen. Initial attempts at RET helped her to feel less depressed and guilty about the rape experience, but her fear in the presence of men continued unabated. A fear hierarchy was constructed. The first item was walking alone on a beach and seeing a man about 200 yards away; across items, the man was imagined to come closer and closer. The highest item was sitting in a school cafeteria, talking to a man. After relaxation training, each item was imagined and paired with the following self-instructional statements: "This man is unlikely to hurt me. There I go again, overgeneralizing. All men aren't the same. Relax; enjoy the walk (or lunch). What could I say to introduce myself? I'm doing fine. Isn't it great that I'm in control." After five sessions, the

---

The reader might try to suggest some coping statements, utilizing each of Meichenbaum's three categories, for clients with each of the following types of problems:

Dealing with an argumentative spouse.

A child afraid of sleeping alone in the dark.

A man afraid he won't be able to satisfy his sex partner.

A client who is afraid to disagree with her supervisor.

A client you are presently treating.

See Answer Key, p. 286.

client was able to have lunch with men in the school cafeteria with minimal anxiety.

A less elaborate version of Meichenbaum's procedures used by RET therapists is known as the Rational Barb (Kimmel, 1976); here the therapist deliberately tries to re-create specific Activating events. To illustrate this technique, consider the case of a child who becomes upset when her peers call her names. The therapist might ask the child to do some name calling to him; the therapist can then model both coping self-statements and the absence of emotional overreactivity. The therapist may then tell the child that he will call her a name (give her a Barb) so that she can practice the same responses (e.g., "Well, you might think I'm a four-eyes, but that doesn't make me a bad person").

Dealing with the A

If clients have understood and profited from a disputation, yet perceive that their world contains many unpleasant Activating events (which may be a reality), the work of therapy is not completed. They may feel sad (rather than depressed), annoyed (rather than angry), and apprehensive (rather than anxious), and may feel this way a substantial proportion of the time. In such cases, even though clients think rationally and feel an appropriate level of emotion, certain aspects of their lives are still unpleasant and worthy of psychological intervention. Two major procedures to which the rational therapist may turn are (1) helping them to examine the accuracy of their perception of the A, and (2) helping them to develop strategies to change those A's that can be changed.

PERCEPTION OF THE A

In drawing the distinction between elegant and inelegant solutions (see Chapter 3), we used the example of a male client who believed that everyone in his office hated him. Using the elegant solution, we assumed that his perception of the A was correct and attempted to de-awfulize his evaluation of this situation. Even if the disputation were successful, however, the client would be left with unpleasant emotional effects and would undoubtedly be uncomfortable when he went to work every day. This level of affect would be needless if the client were misperceiving the situation; other procedures would be warranted to correct the misperception. The additional task of RET, therefore, is to encourage the client to be more scientific in his examination of data and his conclusions from them.

Psychologists such as Kelly (1955) and Wegner and Vallacher (1977) believe that we human beings function as scientists in our approach to the world around us, although we may be unaware of performing this role. Scientists are interested in the classification, prediction, and control of events in the physical or social environment. All persons are interested in the same phenomena but may not know how to function as good scientists. Without careful monitoring, we can easily slip into habits of poor observation, inaccurate classification, incorrect predictions, and inept attempts at control. These errors can produce the very problems which bring patients to the psychotherapist's office, and one way to conceptualize psychotherapy is to view the therapist's role as a teacher of scientific methodology.

One of the first axioms in the philosophy of science is that there are no immutable facts; all facts are viewed as hypotheses. In the logic of science, a hypothesis can never be confirmed; data which fail to disconfirm the theory provide support for it but never proof of it. The scientist recognizes that even repeatedly observed events exist in a world of change; thus, even scientific "laws" are regarded as temporary and subject to revision. Scientists, therefore, can be seen as individuals who are prepared to *change their minds* as they adapt their beliefs and their behavior to accommodate changes in reality (Johnson, 1946). Now, let's see how these principles apply to therapy.

One of the first principles to teach the client is the distinction between facts and hypotheses. In working with our hypothetical male client discussed above, we would first attack his notion that it is a fact that no one likes him; this "fact" is merely a hypothesis. If our client is willing to accept this view, his job is to determine the validity of the hypothesis by gathering data and drawing appropriate conclusions from them. These steps are precisely the ones used by therapists such as Raimey (1975), Maultsby (1975), and Beck (1976) in their cognitive therapy. In this work, therapist and client search for two major kinds of cognitive errors: errors in gathering data and errors in drawing conclusions.

A good scientist gathers data impartially, attempting to observe and report his or her observations objectively and accurately. The scientist's precise use of language, therefore, is of the utmost importance. In therapy, the patient in our example would be asked for data to support his hypothesis that no one likes him, and the therapist would listen carefully to these reports. How does he know that no one likes him? Clients typically respond to this question with a list of persons who they believe dislike them. This evidence, however, is hardly objective, and there is a hidden conclusion in each datum—that the individual does not like the client. The same question deserves to be repeated, therefore: how do you know that she or he doesn't like you? In other words, the therapist is attempting to get the client to report the data objectively before he evaluates them.

Beck (1976, Beck et al., 1978) has indicated two primary ways that patients distort data: *selective abstraction* and *magnification/ minimization*. Selective abstraction "consists of focusing on a detail taken out of context, ignoring other more salient features of the situation and conceptualizing the whole experience on the basis of this element" Beck et al., 1978, p. 7). Magnification/minimization "is reflected in errors in evaluation that are so gross as to constitute a distortion" (p. 8). In both types of cognitive errors, patients are ignoring certain features of the world around them, so that they are gathering biased data. In selective abstraction, clients focus on one category of data and ignore others; in magnification/minimization, clients ignore information within a category.

For example, our hypothetical client may selectively attend to only certain features of his co-workers' behavior; perhaps he ignores their greetings, their nonverbal cues of approval when business is being discussed, or the times they seek his professional advice. He may inaccurately discount these data as being irrelevant to his hypothesis. In addition, the client may minimize when he states that he is never asked out to lunch; in fact, he may have been approached one or two times over the past six months. Statements such as "They always avoid me" indicate maximization.

If your job as a therapist is to teach the client to gather more accurate data, what techniques will you want to use? For one thing, you and the client had better agree on which data are relevant to the hypothesis, thus avoiding selective abstraction (e.g., eye contact, greetings, minutes spent in conversation, relaxed intonation in speech). Second, frequency counts in logbooks will help the client keep accurate records and avoid the problem of magnification/minimization.

If the client returns to therapy with more accurate accountings, he may be able to report that, in fact, four co-workers made good eye contact with him while two did not; verbal interchanges were very brief with three of the first group and longer with the remaining three; and he was invited to lunch once in the past week by one co-worker. With such specific data, the client may already have abandoned his hypothesis that *no one* likes him, but if he still believes it, he is making logical errors in drawing conclusions from his data.

If the frequency of social interactions is, in fact, low, many hypotheses could be entertained as explanations. For instance, the client may behave unsociably in the office and his co-workers may believe that *he* does not like *them*. Another possibility is that the client's role in the office may preclude social invitations from others—because of status differences, for example. Other hypotheses that come to mind include an office norm of minimal social interchange set by the pressures of the work itself or by administrative fiat. The behaviors of the co-workers may have more to do with the intrapsychic problems of the individuals than with interpersonal dislike for the client. In other words, the therapist can help the client generate numerous alternative hypotheses to account for the objective data, and the *habit* of hypothesis generation will be a particularly important skill for the client to develop.

Beck has outlined three logical errors commonly made in drawing conclusions from data, all of which are errors in inductive logic. Induction is a tricky process because to make an accurate judgment, it is necessary to examine every instance of a particular phenomenon from which you are attempting to draw a conclusion. For example, if your hypothesis is that all little red hens have high IQ's, it is logically necessary to examine the IQ of each and every little red hen. Since such a task is formidable at best, conclusions drawn inductively are usually based on a sampling procedure, subjected to inferential statistics, accepted within probability limits, and therefore always tentative. Clients, however, rarely follow these canons of science.

The errors of conclusion drawing to which Beck refers are:

1. *Arbitrary inference:* the process of drawing a conclusion in the absence of supporting evidence or in the face of contrary evidence.

2. *Overgeneralization:* the pattern of drawing a general conclusion on the basis of a single incident.
3. *Personalization:* a tendency to relate external events to oneself when there is no basis for making such a connection.

The reader can easily see that our hypothetical client above was making these kinds of logical errors about the behavior of his co-workers.

One way to teach the client to view his cognitions as hypotheses to be tested is for the therapist to model this very behavior. Beck et al. (1978) suggest that therapists offer their own interpretations of the client's behavior as hypotheses to be tested. For example, with our client above, the therapist has hypothesized that the client draws a conclusion ("no one likes me") when certain social interchanges at work fail to take place. This theory can then be tested by having the client record how often he draws this conclusion in the actual situation. Thus, the therapist's conclusion is subject to a test; in like manner, the client's cognitions are objectively validated. The point of these procedures is to train the client to objectively test his perception of the A in a much more rigorous fashion than he is likely to have done.

In summary, two major procedures have been outlined: (1) training the patient to objectively collect and accurately label data outside the therapy session, and (2) training the patient to question his or her automatic conclusions from these data. The first procedure evaluates whether the A as reported is true or if the patient has cognitively distorted the A. Consider the following examples of cases of self-downing:

> The client, Georgina, reports that she acted very selfishly. It would be wise, first of all, to examine what the client actually did. A useful discussion might involve asking the client to define *selfishness* and to discriminate it from *self-interest*. It might be pointed out to her that selfishness implies total disregard for other human beings, while self-interest implies simply choosing to put oneself first, even if others are temporarily inconvenienced. Discriminations such as these encourage clients to carefully examine their perception of the A (in this case, their own behavior) and to determine whether or not they have correctly labeled it.

> The client, Bill, who works in the art department of a large New York advertising agency, claims, "I'm no good at snappy conversation!" Is this statement correct? If so, his deficit may be a result of

inborn or acquired tendencies, or possibly, since he views the deficit as awful and is anxious, he may be editing out verbal repartee. More likely, however, is the possibility that the client is misperceiving. He may be better than average but does not notice it because he is comparing himself against a talented reference group—New York ad men, who make their living at this very skill.

The patient, Ron, reports that someone criticized him and he accepted the other's evaluation as fact. There are two parts to this challenge: (1) determining if the other's comments were indeed critical, and (2) determining if they made sense as statements of fact. In the first instance, for example, the patient might say that someone insulted him; questions the therapist may use as challenges include: "What actually happened?" "How was that an insult?" In the second instance, the therapist might consider use of an analogy such as the following:

"Suppose a little child came in at 4 P.M. and began whining for cookies, but his mother told him 'No.' The child threw himself on the floor and began screaming, 'You're a bad mother . . . you're mean . . . you're stupid!' That's an Activating event. Do you think Mom will react badly to it? Probably not, because she knows differently. In fact, isn't she acting like a good mother by restricting sweets to protect the child's teeth, and especially just before dinner so he won't spoil his appetite? Now, let's see if what Mr. X said to *you* made sense."

The second procedure, questioning the patient's conclusions drawn from the data, is best done by Socratic dialogue. As early as 1946, in Wendell Johnson's work on semantic therapy, it was pointed out that two important questions for the therapist are: (1) what do you mean? and (2) how do you know? The reader can find these questions embedded in the following sample transcript, in which the client is a young woman obsessed by jealous feelings for her husband:

T: Just because he meets her for lunch, does that mean they're having an affair?
C: We-e-l-l, no.
T: There's no way you can hang onto a lover and not have him enjoy members of the opposite sex in any way—can you?
C: I can expect him not to have sexual relations!
T: OK, but if you're going to suspect that every time he talks to a

person, what's going to happen to you? You'll constantly be on
guard, won't you?

C: Yes, I guess so.

T: And it *is* possible that an affair might happen. What does one
sexual encounter mean?

C: That he doesn't care for me anymore.

T: Does it really mean that? If I say "blue means green," does that
make it true?

C: But if he has an affair, that means I'm not enough for him.

T: No, that's your perception of that, and you think that's what it
means. Because you believe it, that doesn't make it true. You're
assuming that a person (1) can only love one person at a time, and
(2) can only have sex with people they love, and (3) will not love people
if they're having sexual relations with someone else. All these
assumptions are in your thinking.

C: It could mean he didn't think enough of me to abide by my wishes
and not have outside sex.

T: Right. It could also mean that he thought he could get away with it!

C: I want him to be only mine.

T: I would like that too with my mate. Maybe that's not possible. It
doesn't mean we can't enjoy them at all.

C: But if he does that, I'm going to be very upset.

T: I think it's appropriate for you to be disappointed, but do you have
to be really upset?

C: I don't want him to do it!

T: You didn't answer my question.

C: I don't have to be very upset, but so far I've been doing that.

T: What do you think would happen if you weren't so upset?

C: Maybe he wouldn't be so careful—maybe he wouldn't do what I
want him to.

T: How does that happen?

C: He won't take any chances—he knows I'll get really upset.

T: You know that?

C: He takes me seriously because he knows I'll get really upset.

T: You're repeating your position, but you still haven't told me how
you know that. Have you tried out both?

C: No, but I just don't want him to.

T: From what you've told me, it sounds like you're upset most of the
time now, and your upset seems to result from some of these
unwarranted assumptions that you seem to make. Let's go back and
talk about some of these assumptions again in detail.

Most RET therapists seem to engage in procedures such as those outlined above, perhaps not realizing that they are working very similarly to Beck, Johnson, and others. We hope that this description will make clear to them what they are doing, as well as inform the new therapist how to go about clarifying perceptions of the A more efficiently. We might point out that the process of correcting misperceptions of the A is also used in challenging irrational ideas at B—namely, posing the question to the client in many different forms: "Where is the evidence that what you believe is really true?"

CHANGING THE A

Once you have helped the client examine the accuracy of his or her perception of the A, it will be clear that A's are rarely black-and-white issues. Absolutistic hypotheses (always, never, everyone, nobody, etc.) are rarely confirmed. Thus, our client may discover that while some people in his office like him, the percentage may still be lower than he desires, and a psychological intervention may be appropriate. Helping the client change those A's that can be changed is a legitimate and important endeavor for the rational therapist. This cue has been taken from Ellis, who, in his therapy groups, spends a significant proportion of time helping clients develop social and survival skills. Changes in the A are of two basic types: (1) attempts to change the environment in which the patient operates and (2) attempts to change personal aspects of the client.

Changing the world.   Clients are frequently beset by real-life adversities which can be changed. There may be severe financial problems, legal problems, in-law problems, medical problems, educational problems, career problems, and marital or family problems. In dealing with such issues, the RET therapist can serve two basic roles: giving information where appropriate and, more importantly, teaching problem-solving skills.

Perhaps one of the first skills clients may profit from is discrimination training—that is, deciding when they have reached the limits of their expertise and had better consult an *outside expert*. Seeking advice may be difficult for some clients; they may not even know that there are resources to which they can turn. We recommend that all therapists develop a list of specialists (medical, legal, financial, etc.) as resources for handy reference.

The second skill clients may profit from is maintaining a *problem-oriented set*. By this phrase we mean three important cognitive realizations:

1. Clients are not helpless; they can do something about the situation. As we stated earlier, rational living does not entail passive acceptance of unfortunate or unpleasant events and certainly does not mean endorsement of them. If direct change of an unpleasant environment is not possible, one can at least selectively encounter that situation. For example, although clients cannot remove the pollution from the air in Manhattan, they can choose not to live there. Similarly, they may never change obnoxious behaviors in their mothers-in-law, but they can at least limit their contact with them.

2. Clients had better realize that in many instances only limited change is likely within a limited period of time. Holding unrealistic expectations and awfulizing when they are not reached can be detrimental to one's mental health.

3. Clients had better understand that there are no perfect solutions, merely better or worse alternatives.

Many of the difficult A's which patients present are *conflicts*, either approach, avoidance, or a mixture of these elements. Conflict resolution training utilizes many elements of rational-emotive therapy. Part of the difficulty clients have in resolving conflicts or reaching decisions involves failure to take risks, beliefs in the necessity for certainty, a belief in foretelling the future, and awfulizing about making the wrong decision. These concerns are dealt with by disputations of the irrational beliefs. Once clients have learned that there is no such thing as a perfect solution, no guarantee of a given outcome, and no shame in choosing the wrong road, they may still lack the ability to draw up what Ellis has called a *hedonic calculus*.

A hedonic calculus is a fancy way of saying that sensible decision making entails listing all the elements that enter into the decision, their relative value to the patient, and the relative probability of various long- and short-term consequences; tallying up the pro's and con's; and then being brave enough to act upon these data. Each of these steps may entail elaborate discussion between the client and therapist, the client and outside experts, and the client and others involved in the decision.

For instance, suppose the client is a divorcee with two children who is considering marrying a new partner who lives in another city several hundred miles away. In addition, the prospective spouse is a workaholic with a medical disability. The contemplated marriage might involve changing the residence, leaving a stable job, and disrupting the children's schooling. These negative factors are balanced by her affection for the man, their shared professional interests, sexual compatibility, and his excellent rapport with her children. In drawing up her hedonic calculus, she discussed with her therapist the relative probabilities of various outcomes, such as the effects of remarriage on the children, the probable level of commitment by her partner, her need for guaranteed longevity in the relationship, and so forth. With her physician she discussed the import of the medical disability; with her children she discussed their reaction to the contemplated union; and with others in her profession, she investigated the probability of finding remunerative employment in the new location. Once the data were amassed, she and the therapist worked on the hedonic calculus until it was clear that greater happiness could be achieved by taking the risks of entering into the new relationship.

A major change strategy which clients can be taught in order to make their world a little brighter is the use of principles of *contingency management*. Many interpersonal difficulties can be helped by the judicious use of contingency management to shape new behaviors and extinguish or punish undesired behaviors. Parents may find lessons in behavior modification helpful in reducing conflicts with their children, and children can profit from the same principles in attempting to change interaction patterns with their parents, teachers, and siblings. In other words, learning to establish reinforcement systems may be useful for clients of any age in virtually any interpersonal situation. If the reader does not understand these basic behavioral systems, helpful references will be found in the Appendix.

Here is an illustration of the use of RET which includes behavior modification (as RET usually does, since it is almost invariably cognitive, emotive, *and* behavioral). In this case, the client was a young mother of three children recently separated from her husband. Among her emotional complaints were depression, guilt about the dissolution of the marriage and its possible negative effects on the children, and increasing anger at the children as they began to misbehave more and more frequently. As she and the therapist began to explore and sample her child-rearing skills, it became apparent that although she was a warm and caring parent, she had begun to refrain from punishing or containing the children's unwanted behaviors. The motivation for this change in her behavior appeared to be avoidance of guilt, and the guilt, in turn, resulted from some irrational cognitions she held. For example, she implicitly believed that she had to provide twice as much love for her children since her husband was no longer living at home. Her definition of love apparently meant that she must not disapprove of her children's behavior and certainly must not yell at or punish them. As might be expected, the children got more and more out of hand until, at the point of exasperation, the mother lost her temper and then immediately chastised *herself* for being a cruel witch. The client was therefore "doing herself in" by an unfortunate choice of an interpersonal and intrapersonal system; she was punishing herself instead of appropriately disciplining the children.

Cognitively, the RET therapist helped her to explore her definitions of concepts such as "love," "punishment," and "mothering"; it soon became clear to her that good mothering included not only demonstrations of affection but appropriate use of punishment. It was in her children's ultimate best interest to be temporarily discomforted by parental control if an important behavioral lesson were to be learned. After all, it would be important to immediately scold or penalize a young child for crossing a street without looking for oncoming traffic. Similarly, the learning of social behaviors may occasionally require a firm hand. It is an act of a loving parent to take the responsibility and the risk of confronting a child's misbehavior, giving direct feedback, and implementing a contingency to change it. Once the client had thus given herself permission to manage her children, she and the children, with the help of the therapist, worked out a constructive set of mutual responsibilities with appropriate reward and penalty arrangements to deal with the specific problems. The children's allowance, instead of being handed out as a dole, was made contingent upon desired behaviors. A potent penalty turned out to be loss of TV privileges for a specified number of hours. Even after her cognitive challenges, however, this mother remained a "softie" and became uncomfortable with the prolonged penalties she had assigned. Accordingly, an amendment to the system was added whereby the children could work off some of their penalty time by a constructive behavior, such as extra helping around the house or doing something nice for someone else.

To summarize, attempts to change the A which involve changing the client's environment may be accomplished in two major ways: (1) by teaching the client problem-solving skills, such as gathering information, weighing consequences, and choosing a course of action; (2) by sharing information with the client, such as the use of operant technology to attempt to change the behavior of others in the environment. Another major aspect of changing the A entails making changes in the clients' behaviors so that, hopefully, their world will react differently to them. We turn now to this second strategy.

Changing the client.   If your clients are performing poorly in some life endeavor and are denigrating themselves for their poor results, the first order of business in therapy, as we have said, is to work on the self-downing. If the work of therapy were to stop there, however, the clients might very well accept themselves but remain what Goldfried and Davison (1976) labeled a "relaxed incompetent." The question the therapist will want to ask is: "Is my client investing significant effort and does he or she have sufficient skills to change a poor performance?" We turn now to some common skill deficits that may hinder the client from achieving desired goals.

A primary area of concern is often a deficit in *social problem-solving skills*. While a number of researchers and therapists have worked in this area (e.g., Allen et al., 1976; Mahoney, 1977; D'Zurilla and Goldfried, 1971), we will focus primarily on the work of Spivack, Platt, and Shure (1976) of the Hahnemann Medical School. These researchers indicate that there is no correlation between the ability to solve interpersonal problems and the ability to solve practical problems (such as the one presented in the previous section) or problems involving inanimate objects. Thus, one may be a brilliant research physicist and yet be unable to solve the problem of getting along with one's secretary. Social problem solving is not correlated with IQ but has been shown to correlate with other measures of psychopathology and poor social adjustment. Nevertheless, deficits in social problem-solving skills may be present even when there is no strong emotional component. Clients may not be upset about their behavior, but they may continue to behave in a manner which is self-defeating and which society may define as inappropriate.

Spivack describes an encounter with a youngster which inspired him to investigate the role of social problem-solving skills in behavioral disorders. While Spivack was employed as a psychologist in a residential treatment facility, one of his patients went AWOL and walked to the nearby town late one night. Spivack was subsequently summoned to help find the child; after a search by the police, the boy was discovered walking down the railroad tracks at 11 P.M. toward the center of town. The following day, Spivack discussed with the child his reasons for the trip. As a good analytic psychologist, he had many hypotheses to explain the child's aberrant behavior. Possibly the boy was behaving masochistically and desired to be punished for his behavior, or was acting out his anger toward his caretakers. As the therapist proceeded to gather information in support of these notions, he asked the child many questions about his behavior. The boy reported that he was going to town to buy an item that he had seen in one of the stores. The therapist asked, didn't he realize that the store would be closed at that hour of the night? The child responded that he hadn't thought of it. Didn't he realize that he was breaking a rule? The boy responded that he hadn't thought of it. Didn't he realize the consequences of his actions—that the staff would be angry with him and that his privileges would be curtailed? The boy responded that he just hadn't thought of it. Didn't he realize that there were other ways to get the desired item? The boy responded again that he just hadn't thought of it. At this point, Spivack reported having a dramatic insight. Possibly his own hypotheses concerning the child's behavior were wrong and the child's were correct. Could it be that instead of some intricate masochistic motivation the child *simply didn't think?* This simpler hypothesis ultimately led Spivack and his co-workers to conduct a large research project investigating cognitive factors in problem-seeing and problem-solving skills.

The results of these studies have suggested a number of hierarchically developed cognitive skills which, when absent, lead to psychopathology. The preliminary step, of course, is the ability to recognize that a social problem exists, that there are two or more people in conflict. This step entails the ability to interpret others' feelings from their verbal and nonverbal cues. A number of other prerequisite skills are important, the next being the ability to stop and think (e.g., "OK, here is the problem, now how am I going to attack it?"). Another skill is the ability to discriminate facts from opinions. A fact is an observable or verifiable phenomenon or act which can be agreed upon by at least a majority of those who observe it. Finally, a related skill is the ability to recognize that others will have different opinions than oneself about the same facts.

Once recognized and acknowledged, the first necessary skill for *dealing* with the problem is labeled *alternative-solution thinking*. This skill involves the ability to *generate* (not merely recognize) a number of possible solutions to a social problem. The more alternatives the client can devise, the more likely he or she is to function adaptively. Consider the example of a child who sees another child playing with a toy that he or she wants; this is a social problem. Spivack's research showed that a socially well-adjusted child could generate many alternative courses of action to deal with the situation; for example, he or she could (1) ask the child for the toy, (2) trade for the toy, (3) hit the child and grab the toy, (4) ask to play with it when the child is finished, (5) play with something else, and so forth. The disturbed child is more likely to simply grab at the toy and not consider other alternatives. The suggestion is that the disturbed child has not learned the cognitive skill of generating alternatives. Don't be misled into thinking that once you have cleared up a client's irrational beliefs, you can assume that more appropriate behaviors will follow. Spivack's notion questions this assumption and points out that alternative thinking is a skill which the client may need to acquire and practice. The skill is akin to what has been called "brainstorming." The therapist encourages the client to suggest as many behavioral alternatives as possible, without censoring or evaluating them. Crazy ideas, silly ideas, impractical ideas, and imperfect ideas are all encouraged before the therapist leads the client to the next step in the hierarchy.

The second step in developing problem-solving skills is labeled *consequential thinking*. This term refers to the ability to predict the consequences of one's behavior, particularly its effects on other people. Will the other person respond positively or negatively? How is the other likely to feel? Will he or she become angered by the behavior? Is the behavior likely to elicit compliance? Is the behavior likely to get you what you want? Consequential thinking thus involves making predictive inferences about the relationship between social behaviors and social consequences. The therapist's knowledge of behavioral principles may also provide useful data to help the client make these predictions. For example, consider the case of a mother who is trying to decide how to react to her son's persistent habit of whining. Among the behavioral alternatives she generated was the idea of simply ignoring the child when he whined, thus using the concept of extinction. What might be the consequences of her action? The literature on operant extinction clearly suggests that the *immediate* effect of this procedure might well be an initial increase in the very behavior the mother dislikes. An additional problem to be guarded against is the possibility that the mother might not be entirely consistent in her plan, and might intermittently attend to the child when he whined. It could be pointed out to the mother that intermittent reinforcement significantly increases a behavior's resistance to extinction, thus prolonging the problem. Thus, in consequential thinking, the patient is essentially evaluating the pro's and con's of each of the alternatives previously generated.

Once the client has evaluated the various alternatives and selected one(s) that appear to have the best probability of success, the next step entails doing *means-ends thinking*. Cognitively, the client analyzes the sequence of events that will happen, identifying the step-by-step process required to achieve the goal. The mother in the example above would cognitively rehearse exactly how she will implement her extinction plan and how she will respond if her child escalates his whining. For example, how would she cope with the whining if she is in a public place with the child?

Finally the client learns the skill of *verifying* the solution. The plan is implemented and its effects are evaluated. How did it work? What went wrong? Can it be fixed? If the results are negative and the plan appears to be ineffective, the client is led back again to step one, alternative-solution thinking, to generate new approaches to the social problem.

A theory of psychopathology that focuses only on cognitive elements which inhibit or interfere with appropriate functioning assumes that more appropriate responses are available to the individual. If the client thought rationally and were freed from inhibiting processes, he would, theoretically, be able to behave competently. The work of

Spivack and his colleagues points out, however, that personal problem-solving skills may be necessary to add appropriate, adaptive behaviors to the client's repertoire. This model suggests that dysfunctional behavior can be caused by the *absence* of appropriate cognitions as well as by the presence of dysfunctional ones.

Many of the elements of the Spivack et al. training program in social problem-solving skills overlap with rational-emotive theory. For example, differentiating facts from opinions, stopping to think before acting, and specifying problems are routinely taught by rational therapists. It is unfortunate that the RET literature has neglected to report the social skills training that RET therapists have done with clients for years. In particular, Ellis has conducted a workshop called "Creative Contacts for Singles," one of the most popular ones given at the Institute for Rational-Emotive Therapy. In this workshop, he first helps people identify and challenge their inhibiting thoughts and then teaches them and allows them to practice social skills in contacting members of the opposite sex. Since the literature on RET has been imprecise in specifying the steps entailed in social problem solving, the work of Spivack, Platt, and Shure provides a significant complement to it.

When RET therapists teach problem-solving skills, however, they go one step further and also teach the client *how to cope with failure*. On many occasions clients will find that they have only a choice of very imperfect alternative solutions, that each solution has a probability of producing undesirable consequences, or that the problem is simply unsolvable. Cold reality sometimes thwarts the best problem solvers. When this is the case, the elegant solution (e.g., anti-awfulizing and anti-catastrophizing) is an indispensable tool.

ASSERTIVENESS TRAINING

One generalized behavioral skill that may be important in the client's adaptation to the environment is that of assertiveness, or the *appropriate expression* of feelings and desires. Deficits in this skill may result from (1) lack of verbal and/or nonverbal repertoires, (2) cognitive factors which impede the expression of these behaviors, or (3) both. In addition, the therapist had better recall that deficits in assertiveness may be situation-specific. Thus, clients may be quite assertive with their employees at work yet meek as a mouse at home. The assertive female professional may fall prey to unselective sexual encounters because she "cannot say no." The client may be quite adept at expressing negative feelings but tongue-tied when it would be appropriate to express tender, gentle, or loving messages. Changing this aspect of clients' behavior, therefore, may help them to change their A's as long as two anti-absolutistic notions are kept in mind:

1. Behaving assertively is no guarantee that one will get what one wants, although it may increase the probability of a favorable outcome.
2. If one knows how to behave assertively, that does not mean that one must behave this way all the time. In some instances, discretion may be the better part of assertion. In other words, the skill of consequential thinking will be relevant.

The first step in teaching the client to behave more assertively is to outline the differences between assertive, nonassertive, and aggressive behavior. *Assertive behavior* is characterized as a statement of a preference or a request for change from another person, which is communicated directly yet not hostilely or defensively. *Nonassertive behavior* is characterized by indirect communication, overinhibition, anxiety, and perhaps not attempting to get what one wants at all. *Aggressive behavior* typically reflects demands rather than preferences, is usually righteous or hostile, and often has the intent of punishing the other.

A second task in assertiveness training may be to correct the client's self-statements: irrational notions which lead to unassertive, hostile, or aggressive responses, or ideas with which the client punishes himself for inept assertive responses, for assertions which don't prove immediately successful, or for failures to respond at all.

Clients may then find it useful to perceive their right to be assertive, a step which may be an eye-opener for some clients. What are their rights as persons? What are their rights in specific social roles—as spouse or as parent? Such questions often provide a provocative homework assignment. The following suggestions may help the client get started: "I have the right to have feelings and express them, including complaints and criticisms. I have the right to set my own priorities. I have the right to say no without feeling guilty."

The next step in assertiveness training may entail assessing the client's strengths and weaknesses in assertive communication and developing training procedures to bridge the gaps in his or her skills. The following list, adapted from one prepared by Janet Wolfe, may act as a checklist for both therapist and patient in determining skills and skill deficits in verbal and nonverbal behaviors.

Guidelines for Behaving Assertively

1. When expressing refusal, express a decisive "no"; explain why you are refusing, but don't be unduly apologetic. When applicable, offer the other person an alternative course of action.
2. Give as prompt and brief a reply as you can, without interruption.
3. Request an explanation when asked to do something unreasonable.
4. Look directly at the person you're talking to. Check your other body language for things that might convey indirectness or lack of self-assurance (e.g., hand over mouth, shuffling feet). Watch your vocal tone and inflection, making sure that you speak neither too loudly nor too softly.
5. When expressing annoyance or criticism, remember: Comment on the *behavior*; avoid a personal attack.
6. When commenting on another's behavior, try to use "I statements." Example: Instead of saying, "You rat—you made me so mad!" try, "When you keep canceling out on social arrangements at the last minute, it's extremely inconvenient and I feel really annoyed." Where possible, offer a suggestion for an alternative behavior ("I think we'd better sit down and try to figure out how we can make plans together and cut down on this kind of inconveniencing").
7. Keep a log of your assertion-related responses. Review them and talk them over with a friend. Watch good models. Remember: you don't unlearn bad habits or learn new skills overnight.
8. Reward yourself in some way each time you've pushed yourself to make an assertive response—whether or not you get the desired results from the other person.
9. Don't berate yourself when you behave nonassertively or aggressively; merely try to figure out where you went astray and how to improve your handling of the situation next time.

Obviously, lists such as this are intended merely to refresh your memory; they will not be sufficient guidance if the area of assertiveness training is new to you. A more extensive bibliography is provided for the newcomer to assertiveness training in the Appendix. Remember, assertiveness training is one technique that the RET therapist can use in helping the client to try to change the A.

GIVING PRACTICAL ADVICE TO HELP CHANGE THE A

Suppose you, as a therapist, think that the client could make some physical changes to improve his or her chances of reaching goals. Would you feel comfortable giving your client honest feedback or initiating such discussions?

> How would you feel about confronting and openly discussing any of the following topics with a client?
> Homeliness
> Overweight
> Physical deformities
> Brain damage
> Psychosis
>
> Do you give yourself the freedom to tell your clients that some aspect of their behavior or appearance is socially unacceptable or goal-defeating? Be alert to whether or not you are avoiding such topics because they are uncomfortable for you. Are you afraid of your client's reactions? If so, is your hesitancy based on rational reasoning or an irrational need for your client's approval or an irrational belief that your client would be "damaged" by such feedback?

For example, suppose your client is an older woman who is looking for a mate, yet has allowed herself to become a bit dumpy and dresses in a dowdy fashion. Wouldn't you be irresponsible if you withheld practical advice that may be relevant? How could you tactfully suggest changes that might enhance her chances of reaching her goal? You might say something like the following: "You know, Mary, it's been my experience that women like you have a better chance of getting into a relationship if they lose some weight, get a new hairstyle, and learn what they can about putting their best foot forward. Does that sound like anything that would appeal to you?" or "Is that something you'd be interested in?" In other words, without being critical, you can make suggestions in the third person, not directly to the client. The suggestion implies, "You can do what you wish, but this might be helpful," and allows the *client* to make the decision to change.

If the client accepts the suggestion, be sure to reinforce any positive changes that you observe from week to week. For example, "Mary, what an attractive dress you're wearing" or "I like the way you've done your hair; it's very flattering." The changes made may also begin pleasing the client herself.

In other cases, useful feedback may be more direct. More seriously disturbed clients may be grossly unaware of the effects of their appearance or behavior on others, and your confrontation may preferably be more forceful and more persistent. Remember, few people, if any, in the patient's life will be brave enough to provide such feedback; your timidity in the guise of "unconditional acceptance" will be counterproductive.

In a recent example, the client was a young anorexic woman whose emaciated appearance immediately struck the therapist. The presenting problem given by the patient was her lack of friends, about which she was puzzled and depressed. Now, a hallmark of anorexia is a distorted body image; the slimmer such patients get, the more beautiful they appear in their own eyes, even when their physical state has deteriorated so much that hospitalization is required. The therapist in the present case confronted the client with his own reaction to her appearance: a sense of discomfort of the sort he might feel in visiting someone wasting away from a terminal disease—hardly the sort of reaction a young woman in search of friends would desire. At first the patient vehemently denied that her appearance played any role in her social difficulties, but with repeated and vigorous challenge by her therapist, she finally recalled a recent interaction with a co-worker. The other woman had timorously inquired whether the patient was suffering from leukemia. In the ensuing weeks, with persistent confrontations by the therapist, the patient began clearly to realize the impact of her appearance on others, and although she preferred her cachectic state, she became determined to make some changes in her diet and choice of clothing.

The psychotic patient may similarly be unaware of the social discomfort of others in responding to peculiarities of speech, movement, or appearance. In fact, some psychologists refer to psychotic behavior as "disturbing" rather than "disturbed." Obviously, such behaviors will be socially detrimental to the patient in many areas of life. Here you may serve three important roles. First, the therapy session, as it progresses, may serve as a training ground for social interaction, with the therapist giving immediate feedback to undesirable behaviors. The dyad may work out a signaling system; for example, you may snap your fingers every time the patient mumbles, goes off the topic, or inappropriately breaks eye contact. Second, you can train the patient to become a more careful observer of the reactions of others. Reports of these verbal and nonverbal reactions to inappropriate behaviors can then be discussed in therapy. Finally, you can train the patient to use some self-statements which may function to reduce the discomfort of others as well as self-instruct the patient. Meichenbaum (1977) reported successfully using phrases such as "I'm not making myself understood. It's not clear; let me try again."

In summary, in addition to the elegant disputations and philosophical restructuring used by the RET therapist, many other skills and techniques may be helpful. Among these, we have considered the use of coping statements (or self-instructional training), improving the client's distorted perceptions of the A, and helping the client to change those A's that can be changed. In the latter category we discussed techniques for helping clients change their world (e.g., problem solving and contingency management) and techniques for helping clients interact more favorably with their world (e.g., social problem solving, assertiveness training, and providing direct feedback). In discussing these varied techniques drawn from the work of psychologists such as Beck and Meichenbaum, we realize that we have not been able to do them justice, but we do want the reader to understand how the RET therapist incorporates their work. We suggest that readers familiarize themselves with these other techniques, and consequently have provided lists of recommended readings on many of the above topics in the Appendix.

11 Homework Assignments

Rationale

Rational-emotive therapy is a cognitive-learning system. A major tenet in RET, therefore, is the principle that unless clients put their philosophical restructuring to the test of practice, the effects will not be meaningful or durable. If clients say that it "wouldn't really be awful to be turned down for a date" yet continue to avoid calling prospective dating partners, the therapist would first check whether the correct IB has been disputed. If it has, the therapist would doubt the conviction of the client's new beliefs. Thus, RET is not merely a "talk therapy"; rather, it stresses that meaningful cognitive change is unlikely unless the client behaves differently. In fact, following a cognitive-dissonance model, behaving differently will often lead to thinking and feeling differently. One of the principal means of helping the client to behave differently is through the use of homework assignments, thus giving the client a means of generalizing the work of therapy beyond the confines of the therapist's office. Homework assignments are a routine element of RET.

The specific goals of the homework assignment may be (1) to change a dysfunctional behavior or establish an adaptive behavior; (2) to reduce irrational cognitions and replace them with more helpful ones; or (3) to determine how well the client has understood the basic principles of rational-emotive therapy. Accordingly, homework assignments may be drawn from any of the following categories:

Reading assignments
Listening assignments
Writing assignments
Imagining assignments
Thinking assignments
Relaxation and other distraction assignments
Action assignments

As we suggested above, major emphasis is placed on the last category. If that is so, you may ask, why do RET therapists use the other types? Different assignments may accomplish different goals, but even when various assignments are aimed at the same goal, the therapist may use various types of homework. RET is, in part, based on an educational model, and good educators know that the use of multiple modalities and multiple learning trials will maximize learning. After all, how much can the client learn in one forty-five-minute session per week? In college courses, students are given lectures, field or laboratory exercises, and reading assignments; the RET therapist will want to do the same. The question the therapist will be asking himself or herself in each meeting with the client is, "What can my client *do* this week to put into practice what we have discussed during this session?"

Before we move on to discuss specific homework suggestions, let us point out that useful homework assignments share four important characteristics:

1. *Consistency*. The assignment is consistent with the work done in the session and is not irrelevant or arbitrarily assigned. Try to devise an assignment that leads naturally from the main theme of the session.
2. *Specificity*. The assignment has been given in sufficient detail and with clear instructions. For example, if the client is asked to generate possible solutions to a dilemma, do *not* vaguely say, "Think of as many as you can." It would be preferable to say, "Think of at least five possible solutions." In this way, the client has specific instructions and may be more likely to stretch his or her creative faculties.
3. *Systematic follow-through*. Try to be systematic about giving a homework assignment each week *and* check on the last assign-

ment at the next meeting. Also, do not assume that completion of one homework assignment in a problem area will do the job. It may be wise to systematically repeat the assignment (or variations of it) for a number of weeks.

4. *Large steps.* Rational-emotive homework assignments tend to follow a flooding model rather than one of gradual shaping. The RET therapist is likely to encourage the client to take large steps rather than small ones—for example, to "ask four women out on a date this week" rather than "try to speak to one woman this week." The rationale for this maneuver is that it is usually more efficient in producing change. Feedback from the client's weekly homework assignments will help the therapist to set the size of the next step.

When helping the client to design homework assignments, it is best not to do so in an off-the-cuff or apologetic manner. Explain the assignment carefully, including the rationale for selecting it; understanding will help increase your client's compliance. It is also helpful to ask the client, "Do you think you can do that?" If the answer is "No," you have more work to do. Perhaps you can help the client rehearse the assignment in imagery (with the client narrating the scene aloud) or by role playing. Perhaps the client will agree to do *part* of the assignment or can suggest a variation of it that is acceptable. Once agreed upon, a useful question to ask is, "How will you remember to do that?" One technique to help the client remember the assignment is for the therapist to write it out in the manner of a medical prescription. Some therapists have pads of paper printed with the inscription "Behavioral Prescription from the Desk of John Jones, Ph.D." for this purpose. Formalizing the assignment procedure in this way not only aids the patient's memory but also underscores the credibility and importance of the homework.

Examples of Homework

READING ASSIGNMENTS

Patients may strengthen their comprehension of the basic principles of RET and its application to specific problem areas by reading assignments.

At the Institute for Rational-Emotive Therapy, for example, new clients are given a free packet of materials to read at the end of their first therapy session. Additionally, clients are encouraged to purchase a copy of *The New Guide to Rational Living* by Ellis and Harper (1975). Thus, before their second therapy session, it is hoped that they will have had some opportunity to become familiar with the ABC model of emotion.

Many suggested books and articles that clients may find helpful at various points in therapy are given in the Appendix. However, it may be difficult or time-consuming for your client to locate some of these materials. Purchase a few copies of the books that you are most likely to recommend. These can then be given, sold (at your cost), or loaned to the client.

LISTENING ASSIGNMENTS

The reader will recall our earlier suggestion to tape-record therapy sessions after getting the client's permission. Clients are also encouraged to bring in their own recorders and simultaneously tape the session. In either case, it is useful to encourage clients to listen to their therapy tape between sessions. Multiple trials of the same lesson are beneficial to learning.

Listening to prerecorded tapes can also be used as a homework assignment, either to supplement reading work or to replace it for clients with reading or vision disabilities. Tapes of RET lectures (and even rational songs sung by Dr. Ellis himself) are available from the Institute for Rational-Emotive Therapy. An annotated listing of some of these tapes is given in the Appendix.

Listening to tapes is particularly valuable when the therapist is teaching the client relaxation techniques. A prerecorded tape, such as the one by Arnold Lazarus (see p. 283) may be recommended, or the therapist may record his or her own relaxation instructions or, most simply, record a session of relaxation with the client. The last procedure may increase the effectiveness of the training for some clients, since the therapist's voice is associated with the procedure and may thereby aid in generalization from the therapist's office to the patient's home. The patient may then be instructed to play the relaxation tape each night, perhaps just before bedtime. At the next therapy session, the patient can bring in the tape and demonstrate its use to the therapist. In this way, the therapist can periodically stop the tape and check out the client's degree of relaxation. Teaching relaxation techniques can become a tedious chore for the therapist and can use up much valuable session time; both of these problems can be minimized by having the patient do much of the work as a homework assignment.

WRITING ASSIGNMENTS

Writing assignments are very often used by RET therapists and generally take one of three forms: self-help homework sheets, written essays, and log books.

Self-help homework can be done on a sheet of notebook paper which the client can label "ABCDE" or "What happened—what I felt—what I was thinking—what was wrong with those thoughts—what thoughts would be more accurate and helpful." In either case, the self-help homework exercise allows the therapist to determine if the client really understands the ABC's of RET. Clients may, for example, have trouble identifying the relevant rational and irrational beliefs. They may write "I feel" when they really mean "I believe." Linguistic confusions and misunderstandings of the theory become clear in such an assignment and offer the therapist a chance to do much invaluable teaching when the assignment is reviewed during the next therapy session.

A client has filled out a homework form and given it to you, the counselor. A portion of the form is reproduced below. What would your response be? What corrections, if any, would you make?

Activating event = I went for a job interview.

Rational belief = I was turned down.

Irrational belief = It is horrible that I didn't get the job.

Emotional consequence = I felt depressed.

Disputing = I didn't care that I didn't get the job.

Answers are given on page 287.

A related assignment is the use of *written essays,* which can also take a number of forms. For example, clients may be asked to write out a debate to one or more of their irrational ideas. They can be told to pretend that they are on a debating team and their job is to argue the opposite side, *whether they believe it or not.* The therapist is thus employing principles of cognitive dissonance with clients who claim that they could write the debate but wouldn't believe it. Attitude-change research suggests, and clinical experience verifies, that performing such a debate often convinces debators of their own arguments. Thus, at the end of a therapy session, the therapist can write out the statement to be challenged at the top of a sheet of blank paper (using a separate sheet for each debate); the client fills in the debate below. In this way, disputations that are unfinished in the session can be continued at home, or the work of a completed disputation can be consolidated. Here is a sample of an actual debate written by a female client:

Statement: If my children make mistakes in their lives, it proves that I am a bad mother.

Challenge:

1. Everyone makes mistakes, whether they had good or bad parents. It is a human characteristic.
2. My children need to learn by trial and error. Mistakes that *I* have experienced had a positive growth aspect. I learned to try not to repeat the mistake. Pain helps develop aversion to the pain. Also, having experienced mistakes has made me able to be more compassionate and insightful with others. I feel more sharing with people and enjoy more maturity. The same may be so for my children.
3. I am not the only influence on my kids. They have had input from many formative sources besides me. The difference between my two children shows that I couldn't have fully created their personalities or they'd have to be more alike. They continue to have even greater input from other people and experiences, and from themselves. As they meet each new life situation, they respond and make subtle adjustments called for by the moment. So I am not totally responsible for their problems. My *kids* have even indicated to me that I'm not a bad mother because they make mistakes—"that's silly!"

4. I might as well take some credit for their good qualities too, if I were to insist on responsibility for their negative qualities. I know I've done much good for my kids.
5. If I concentrated on my finished mistakes as a mother, I would trap/freeze myself in the past. I would deny recognition of time elapsed, growth and change taken place. That would be living the life of another (albeit someone I knew most intimately). And continued guilt amounts to self-pity. That's bor-ring!

In a related form of essay, the client can be asked to reverse a "should" and defend it. For example, if a male client has been complaining that his mother shouldn't act irascibly or nag at him, the therapist may prescribe an essay in which the client describes why his mother should be exactly the way she is. He might explore what he knows of her upbringing and the history of his interactions with her, and he will undoubtedly find that her behavior is quite understandable. Such an exercise may be an important empathy-building experience to illustrate to the client that the behavior of others is not mysterious or arranged for his personal inconvenience but is a logical outgrowth of preceding events and of people's ways of reacting to these events.

Written homework assignments are often useful when the therapist is teaching problem-solving skills. The client can be given the assignment of generating five alternative solutions to a problem. For example, an agoraphobic client who refused to drive her car for fear that it might break down while she was away from home alone generated these solutions:

1. I could walk to the nearest phone booth and call a family member.
2. I could walk to a nearby house and ask to use the phone.
3. I could walk to where I was going.
4. I could flag down a passing motorist and ask for help.
5. I could walk to the nearest garage and get them to fix the car.

Similarly, the mother of a young sleepyhead who wouldn't get out of bed in the morning generated these alternatives:

1. I could drag him out of bed (that's what I do).
2. I could reason with him.

3. I could ignore him and let him take the consequences of being late.
4. I could do what he wants (wake him again in twenty minutes and meanwhile fix his lunch for him).
5. I could pour cold water on him if he doesn't get up.
6. I could promise him a treat if he's up within three minutes.
7. I could buy him an alarm clock and make him responsible for his own wake-up.

Homework assignments can also be given for the next stage of problem solving, consequential thinking. Clients can be asked to write out their prediction of the consequences to the alternative solutions generated and then seek out cross-validation by discussion with other people.

The third form of written assignment used by RET therapists is the *log book*. Clients can be asked to keep track of specific events and evaluate whether or not their predictions of events were accurate. The client may complain, "Every time I call up a woman to ask for a date I get turned down!" What are the data? How many women did he actually call, who were they, and how many refusals did he get? Similarly, the depressed patient who claims to be depressed "all the time" may discover useful information by keeping track of happy moments or times in the day when the despairing mood lifts (cf. Beck et al., 1978). The obese client can keep a log of foods eaten, the amount, kind, time and place of eating, and so forth. Accurate data records may serve many functions: (1) to correct the client's distorted perception of the A; (2) to correct the client's schemata for doing consequential thinking more accurately; and (3) to identify the antecedents and consequences of a troublesome behavior.

IMAGINING ASSIGNMENTS

Homework assignments of imagery or fantasy are employed by RET therapists as a form of imaginal disputation or imaginal desensitization. After the therapist has led the client through rational-emotive imagery (see page 102), an assignment can be given to practice this skill for ten minutes every day. The client thus imaginally produces the troublesome emotion, changes it, and rehearses the cognitions which effect the change.

Clients can also be asked to do cognitive rehearsal of new behaviors before attempting them, to repeatedly confront their worst fears in imagination for desensitization, or to use the techniques of covert conditioning. In covert conditioning, the stimuli, responses, reinforcers, or punishers may be imaginal. Here are some examples. The therapist is hoping to help change the valence of a stimulus for a client; perhaps the client is a woman with vaginismus who fears the insertion of any object into her vagina, yet who is orgasmic with manual stimulation. The client can be instructed to imagine that her partner is inserting his finger (and later, his penis) into her vagina, and to do so just at the point of her orgasm. By pairing the aversive image with the positive experience of orgasm, the concept of penetration may lose some of its sting. Similarly, if the man has a fear of penetrating the vagina, he can imaginally rehearse this act just at the point of his manually induced orgasm, thus changing the valence of a response. Conversely, clients can also be instructed to pair stimuli with aversive images, as in the technique of covert sensitization (Cautela and Baron, 1977). The alcoholic can imagine himself drinking a mug of beer and discovering dog feces in the bottom of the glass. More detailed instruction on the implementation of covert conditioning can be found in some of the behavior therapy reference sources listed in the Appendix.

THINKING ASSIGNMENTS

Clients can be asked to keep records of the irrational or disturbing thoughts they have between sessions. This record can then become the starting point for the next therapy visit. Alternatively, clients can write down what they have found to be helpful thoughts, either self-generated or recalled from discussions with the therapist or others. The therapist may even prescribe a list of helpful ideas for rehearsal.

Thinking assignments are often easy for clients to forget since the response is covert. What is the best way to remember something? Write it down. As an aid to memory, therefore, encourage clients to make a checklist of "Things to Remember to Think." After all, pilots use a checklist of things to do before takeoff; why not a list of things to think?

RELAXATION ASSIGNMENTS

As mentioned above, under "Listening Assignments," relaxation is often taught by having patients listen to a prepared tape of instructions. Soon, however, the patients can do the exercises without the external cueing. In fact, as their skill at relaxation increases, they may find that they can best work at it at their own pace. They may not need to work at isolated muscle groups (e.g., the right hand) but can combine them into larger units (e.g., both arms).

An important part of giving a relaxation homework assignment is assuring that clients have structured their time to allow for the exercises and have structured their environment to maximize the probability of doing them successfully. Ideally, they will want to find a quiet room, away from distractions, in which they can recline. Family members can cooperate by not disturbing clients and by taking phone messages while they do their homework.

ACTION ASSIGNMENTS

Two of the most widely used action assignments in RET are risk-taking and shame-attacking exercises. Although these are often interchangeable, one can discriminate between them on the basis of the client's underlying fear. The *risk-taking assignment* challenges patients' temerity, encouraging them to reevaluate their *definition* of certain behaviors as terribly dangerous (when in fact they are not). Such assignments often encourage clients to be more assertive and to push themselves to take risks, particularly social risks, that they may have been avoiding. A unique aspect of risk-taking assignments is that many times the exercise is designed *to have the patient experience failure*, especially in cases of perfectionism or fear of failure. The reader will recall that in a learning paradigm, people learn to reevaluate by experience. If they never have the experience of failure, they will be unlikely to change their conceptualization of it and their avoidance of it. Thus, it is difficult to work on the fear of a negative event unless the client experiences it.

Consider the case of a young man with dating anxiety who, after some social-skills training, is instructed to make three social contacts in the next week. If he is successful, that will be nice, but he may have missed an important lesson, since the probability is that he will not *always* be successful. He will not have been immunized against the stress of failure and may continue to be vulnerable to it. The RET therapist may instead suggest that the client go out and collect three *rejections* in the next week. Such a suggestion may bring a twinkle to the client's eye and, by itself, produce a change in attitude. Notice that such an assignment sets up a positive Catch-22, since the client will succeed even as he fails. If his social overtures are accepted, he has made progress toward his goal, and if they are rejected, he has succeeded in doing his homework and can bring in these incidents for analysis in therapy. Thus, the RET therapist may prescribe failure experiences for two major reasons: (1) they are instructive, and (2) they allow for desensitization, since if the client is afraid to fail, he will probably not try in the first place.

Risk-taking assignments used by the RET therapist often have a paradoxical nature, encouraging clients to do what they view as a bad behavior *and* simultaneously to work at not catastrophizing or putting themselves down. The insomniac may be instructed to try to stay awake all night, the obsessive to obsess 100 times per day, the impotent male to not get an erection (Fay, 1978). Being given the assignment to do the very thing which troubles them often removes the "horror" of the behavior, and clients commonly report, with surprise, that they found it hard to do the assignment.

Consider the case of a certified public accountant who had a dread of making errors, a serious case of perfectionism. His assignment was to deliberately make mistakes and to practice accepting himself nonetheless. Although the client insisted that he made mistakes routinely and did not have to try, when he came back the following week he reported that in fact he had made *no* mistakes. As the therapist had predicted, he was extremely fearful of what was in reality a low-probability event. In the ensuing weeks the assignment was continued, and the client forced himself to make an occasional error. He reported experiencing a revelation: that an error was not a catastrophe and he was not a failure for making one.

Shame is a form of self-downing, and the *shame-attacking exercise* (Ellis, 1973, 1977b) is designed to teach clients that if they actually perform a silly or foolish act, even in public, their world will not come to an end and they needn't denigrate themselves. The central tenet is to teach clients to discriminate between their behavior and their worth as a human being. They are not at stake in anything they do. Clients can thereby apply the principle of learning to rate their behaviors, not themselves.

The shame-attacking assignment is also designed to challenge the dire need for conventionality. We often exchange conformity for approval, which is a strong social control device but which can also be unnecessarily stifling as we punish ourselves with anxiety and shame. What might happen if we challenge conformity? People might think poorly of us; people might frown. But people's thoughts and facial expressions cannot hurt us; often, however, we *believe* they can. The shame-attacking exercise can help the patient to challenge this belief. Additionally, these exercises are fun and can help the client to take social disapproval less seriously.

Here are some examples of shame-attacking exercises often used by the RET therapist:

1. Go up to a stranger and greet him or her warmly. Ask about his or her health. Be effusive.
2. Stand on a busy street corner. Stretch out your arms and say, five times, "Your messiah has come. Follow me."
3. In a restaurant, go up to an attractive person's table and inquire if the meal is satisfactory and if you can bring him or her anything.
4. Go to a nearby shopping center and try to sell someone a copy of yesterday's newspaper.
5. Go to a store and announce to the salesclerk that you are a transvestite or fetishist. Buy something typical of the opposite sex (e.g., high-heeled shoes or sexy men's briefs).
6. Go into a large department store and announce the time, five times, by saying, "Ladies and gentlemen, the time is now 1:15 . . . 1:16 . . . 1:17 . . . etc."
7. Tie a long red ribbon around a banana and "walk it" down a busy street.
8. Ride a crowded elevator standing backward (facing the rear).
9. Yell out five successive stops in the subway or on the bus.
10. Go to the local library and, in a strong voice, ask the librarian to see two books: *The Illustrated Version of the Marquis de Sade* and *Sex and Perversion in Contemporary America*.
11. Find a restaurant that offers "two eggs any style." Ask your waiter for one fried and one scrambled.

If clients are being seen in a group, shame-attacking assignments can be given to all group members and often can be done in the group setting. For example, clients can be asked to sing a song, do a dance, or perform a "spotlight" act.

Clients can adopt one of these stock assignments or, preferably with the help of the therapist, design one that is more personally relevant. For example, one client claimed that she could not be assertive with her mother for fear of harming her mother's health, which in turn would lead others to conclude that she was a bad daughter. Her homework assignment was to tell her friends that "dear old mother had a nervous breakdown because of my bad behavior"; she was to watch their reactions and practice accepting herself nonetheless.

An important warning about shame-attacking exercises: be certain that the client is not planning to do an exercise that will result in loss of a job, expulsion from school, or arrest. If the real and likely consequences of his or her behavior are disadvantageous, the assignment will be harmful, not helpful. It would not be wise to do a shame-attacking exercise, such as wearing a pillow on your head, in front of the boss who is likely to rule on your promotion. There would be fewer practical negative consequences if the pillow were worn while walking on a downtown street.

Thus, the shame-attacking assignment is designed to accomplish two things, the first of which is to help clients behaviorally dispute their sense of shame. The goal is to do the exercise as prescribed. Thus, cognitive rehearsal and a cognitive ABCD analysis may prepare the client to achieve this end.

The second goal of the exercise is to help clients evaluate the accuracy of their predictions of how the world will react to them. Most of us overestimate the extent to which others care about or even notice our behavior. For example, Ellis tells of one of his clients who, for weeks, tried to find the courage to call out the stops in a New York subway. Finally he succeeded in calling out one stop and saw that nothing disastrous happened. The next week he gave himself the assignment of yelling out each of the seven stops between his home and his work. What happened? No one on the subway said anything to him—except some teenagers who came over and inquired, "What's the next stop, Mister?"

Other kinds of action assignments are also used by the RET therapist. The married couple caught in a spiral of "getting-even" behaviors may be instructed to do three "caring" acts for the spouse in the

To get the reluctant client to do a shame-attacking assignment, the therapist may want to set an example. The therapist may go out on the street with the client and model unusual behaviors to show the client that people are more tolerant of our behavior than we think. Could you do this?

We suggest that new RET therapists follow the training example at the Institute for Rational-Emotive Therapy and set themselves the task of doing a series of shame-attacking or risk-taking assignments. Pick from the list above or design your own project, and *do an exercise this week yourself.* In fact, it is a good idea to schedule a shame-attacking exercise for yourself at periodic intervals to keep up your skills.

next week. The reluctant job seeker may be asked to write up a résumé. The woman experiencing guilt about being "selfish" may be told to do something nice for herself before the next session. The sexually troubled couple may be given sensate focus assignments. The client with a self-image of ugliness may be instructed to practice looking in the mirror for ten minutes a day and practicing self-acceptance while acknowledging certain physical defects. The list of such assignments is long and varied, but in all of them the therapist encourages the client to behave differently in order to think and feel differently.

Trouble-Shooting Homework Problems

When clients return to therapy each week, be sure to check up on their homework assignments first. Unless the client brings up a new issue which is clearly of greater importance or is in obvious emotional distress, follow-through on old assignments provides the therapist with a systematic way to integrate therapy visits.

Patients may expect their homework assignments to change each week, as they do in a classroom situation or in a physician's office when medication or dosage level is adjusted. In fact, however, the client may work at a behavioral assignment for a number of weeks before cognitive or emotional change occurs. Be sensitive to your client's expectations; if uncorrected, they may lead to depressive cognitions (e.g., "Oh Lord, I'm not making progress") which may increase the client's distress.

What do you do if clients have failed to do their homework assignments? You investigate; such failures often provide valuable diagnostic information about their belief systems. The uncompleted assignment may be treated as a new Activating event which may have resulted in additional emotional stress to the patient. Thus, a useful series of questions the therapist may ask include the following:

T: How do you feel about not doing the assignment?
C: Terrible.
T: Terrible? In what way?
C: I feel guilty. I should've done my homework.
T: You believe you should have done it? Well, why *should* you?
C: Because I feel so terrible about not doing it.
T: Do you think you'd feel differently if you didn't say *should've*? Try it now—it would have been nice if I did it, but I didn't. Too bad. I'll try it again next week.
C: I didn't do it. Too bad. I'll try it again next week.
T: Do you think you'd feel better if you just stuck to that belief?
C: Yes; it would be better if I thought about it that way.
T: Well, can you remind yourself to think that way?
C: How?
T: What would you do if you wanted to be sure to remember to buy milk at the store?
C: I'd write it down! I'm going to do that now. Now, what was it we just said . . . ?

Depressive cognitions may follow failure to do a homework assignment, as in the example above, or may be the *cause* of the failure. Thus, the patient may have been stopped by the cognition: "It's hopeless—why try?" Typically, the patient will not have answered this question, and the therapist may help the patient to challenge the notion of helplessness and to review the reasons why it would be beneficial to try.

Do not be afraid to confront your client and ask why the assignment was not completed. Why was it so difficult to accomplish? One hypothesis to investigate is that the client has defined the required step as *too large*. As we stated earlier, RET therapists tend to follow a flood-

How do *you* feel when your patient fails to do a homework assignment? Do you find yourself getting angry? If so, it would be wise to examine your own "shoulds" and dispute them. Or do you feel somewhat anxious or depressed? Look for cognitions such as, "If I were a good therapist, he'd have done his assignment," and challenge them. Homework assignments can indeed be diagnostic tools.

ing model, urging their clients to take large rather than small steps. Although the theoretical model is clear, the practical reality is that it is often desirable to go back down the hierarchy of difficulty a step or two in order to find a task which the client is willing to confront. Remember that the goal is to get clients to *do* their behavioral challenges, and a little patience and creativity in breaking down difficult assignments into smaller steps may be important in accomplishing this goal. Thus, if the client is a dependent adult who has always phoned her mother every day and yet wants to sever some of these ties, she may be unwilling to refrain from calling her for a week but may contract for a two-day hiatus at first. Success at an easier task will make it more likely that she will attempt harder tasks.

Similarly, the therapist will want to investigate the *response cost* of the assignment. Perhaps the client will be more likely to listen to a tape than to read a book. Perhaps an adolescent is more likely to read a smaller book than a larger one. Perhaps a woman will practice relaxation exercises twice a week but "cannot find the time" to do them nightly. While the therapist will want to continue to urge the client to work steadily and concertedly, it is wise to praise the client for any accomplishments at first; learning is, after all, a gradual procedure. Nevertheless, the therapist may confront clients with reality; that is, the less they do, the slower their improvements will come. Clients always have a choice, but the therapist can be sure that they understand the consequences.

A common problem encountered among patients who do not do their homework is the *mañana contingency* (Ellis and Knaus, 1977). The patient continually makes excuses for not beginning the assignment today and ardently vows to begin it tomorrow; when tomorrow comes, the cycle is repeated. For example, "Today is too hectic—I'll relax tomorrow" or "I'm too anxious to study today—I'll really buckle down tomorrow."

A related problem is the *double-bind contingency* (Ellis and Knaus, 1977). Here are some examples. An anorexic client complains that she has no friends. Although her stated goal is to cultivate a friendship, the therapist finds out that she has turned down two invitations from a fellow bridge player to visit after the bridge game. Why? Food might be served at the other woman's house, and being anorexic, the patient believes that she is still overweight and needs to lose ten pounds. A more common illustration is the smoker who wants to give up cigarettes and also lose some weight. Neither goal is accomplished because he fears that if he gives up cigarettes he will eat more and if he diets, he will smoke more.

Problems such as the above illustrate a philosophy of Low Frustration Tolerance and are best treated by a direct confrontation, a determined course of action, and perhaps the addition of a program of external contingencies. It might be pointed out to the smoker in the example above that he has three choices for change: (1) he could stop smoking and not worry about his weight for the first few difficult weeks of withdrawal; (2) he could work very hard at losing ten pounds and then begin his smoking cessation program; or (3) he could do both at the same time, which is *merely harder.* Thus, the patient is confronted with the fact that the two problems can be treated independently. Once a goal is selected, a strategy can be outlined.

Getting clients to do the homework is critical for the therapeutic process, and almost anything the therapist can do to get them to comply is therapeutic. It is particularly important that clients understand this, and that wherever possible, rewarding contingencies be established for the successful completion of homework. This does not mean that clients have to "succeed" in the homework by getting what they want, but rather succeed in the sense of doing what they have been assigned. It is even desirable, when clients repeatedly "cop out" on their homework for reasons of Low Frustration Tolerance, to make the next appointment contingent upon the client's completion of a homework assignment. Of course, this plan had better be administered with clinical judgment, and certainly would be contraindicated with the depressed patient or others whose problems require regular attention.

Phasing Out the Therapist

A terminal goal of therapy is to have clients function independently and to acquire the cognitive and behavioral skills to be their own therapist. To achieve this goal, the therapist can gradually fade out his or her role as the active agent in assigning homework projects and encourage clients to think of their own assignments. Thus, when clients report on their previous week's progress, the therapist can ask, "What could you do *next* week to follow up on that?" By gradual shaping and fading of directions, clients will acquire the ability to design their own self-help homework.

12 The Course of Therapy

Let us review what we have learned so far. The therapist has identified a problem situation (A), a distressing emotion (C), and the irrational concepts held by the patient (IB), and has attempted to dispute these irrational notions. Of course, clients will typically have more than one A or C on which to work. If you have seen Ellis' demonstrations of therapy, you may have an oversimplified image of the process of rational therapy, for in these demonstrations, Ellis purposely focuses on one or two problems. In ongoing therapy, it is also appropriate to focus on one problem at a time, but clients typically have multiple problems. The error that the novice RET therapist may make is to try to condense the client's problems into one. Instead, we recommend that you work on each problem separately but develop a *treatment plan* to assure that you don't neglect any and don't become mired in the client's complaints.

Treatment plans are frequently used at mental health clinics and psychiatric hospitals; they will probably be required by many third-party payment systems (e.g., APA-CHAMPUS program) and appear to be an inevitable development in professional peer review systems. Treatment plans are best developed from a problem-oriented record system such as the one outlined below. Realize that not every therapist constructs treatment plans, nor will it be necessary to do so for each of your clients. We offer this as a model to help you understand the ongoing therapy process and as a guideline for formal requirements to document treatment.

To begin a treatment plan, list each of the client's excessive emotional reactions, behavioral excesses, and behavioral deficits; these are the emotional and behavioral aspects of the C. Look for relations between these components and between the C's and their accompanying cognitions.

A Sample Treatment Plan

Problems	Emotions	Cognitions	Behaviors
1. Relationship with boss	Anger, anxiety	He shouldn't criticize me. It would be terrible if the boss doesn't like me.	Talking angrily to boss. Inefficiency at work due to time spent catastrophizing. Lack of assertive responses in repertoire.
2. Problems in dating	Anxiety	No one will ever like me. It's awful to get rejected.	Avoidance of social contact. Lack of social skills.
3. Relationship with parents	Guilt	I should visit my mother more often. I'm not a good son.	Daily undesired phone calls to mother. Undesired Sat. night dinners at mother's house
4. Obesity	Agitation (when not eating), depression (after eating)	I've got to have what I want (LFT). It's hopeless; I'll never control it; I'm no good.	Overeating.

The next step is to arrange these problems in order of priority, which can best be done in consultation with the client. For each problem identified, plan behavioral and cognitive strategies to implement. In addition, we recommend that you try to plan ahead for your next three sessions with the client, organizing how you ideally will utilize your therapy hour in blocks of time. Realize that your plan will best be kept flexible, so that you remain sensitive to your client's immediate concerns, yet be aware that you'd best guard against distractions. If your client brings in a new problem every week, you may lose sight of your original goals. Another purpose of a treatment plan, therefore, is to help the therapist remain on track.

The following is a treatment plan constructed after four sessions with a new client; you may find this useful as a general model.

Session 5

Problem 1   1. Check on homework assignments from previous week.
                2. If client was successful, reinforce him; if unsuccessful, trouble-shoot.
                3. Continue disputing irrational demands creating anger at boss.
                4. Dispute awfulizing about obtaining boss's approval.
                5. Teach and role-play some assertive responses to use at work situation.
                6. Give homework assignment: (a) read *Your Perfect Right* (Alberti and Emmons, 1974), (b) implement the behavior rehearsed in session with the boss, (c) monitor work efficiency; when off-task, use as a cue to do ABCD homework sheet on catastrophizing.

Problem 2   7. If time, begin inquiry into anxiety in social situations.

Session 6

Problem 1   1. Check on homework assignments from previous session, reinforce or trouble-shoot.
                2. Review disputation of IB's leading to anger or anxiety in work situations.
                3. Role-play assertive response to a different work situation to increase generalization.
                4. Give homework assignment: (a) continue to read *Your Perfect Right* and begin *Overcoming Frustration and Anger* (Hauck, 1974), (b) continue to do homework sheets on anger/anxiety when work efficiency drops.

Problem 2   5. Dispute awfulizing about rejection.
                6. Give homework assignment: do ABCD homework sheet disputing fears of rejection.

7. Summarize major points in sessions and review homework assignments for coming week.

Session 7

Problem 1
1. Review homework assignment; reinforce or trouble-shoot.
2. Briefly review disputation of anger-producing beliefs.
3. Homework assignments: continue monitoring work performance and do homework forms as needed, and continue trying to implement new assertive responses as needed.

Problem 2
4. Check homework sheet disputing fears of rejection. Reinforce or trouble-shoot.
5. Do REI in dating situation to uncover anxiety and do in-session disputing.
6. Begin social-skills training: role-play asking a woman for a date.
7. Homework assignment of risk taking: attempt to get 3 rejections this coming week; if distressed, do homework sheet(s).

Problem 3
8. Dispute beliefs about self-worth causing guilt.
9. If client appears to understand the disputation, check veracity of perception of the A.
10. Summarize major points of session and review homework assignments for coming week.

After reading over the above treatment plan, you may find it overwhelming; how could any therapist accomplish that much in any session, and do clients really move that quickly? Rest easy; the sample above is somewhat exaggerated and was used to make three major points:

1. It is important to work *consistently* on each of the problems outlined by the client. Notice how the therapist continues to work on the first problem across succeeding sessions. Although the percentage of time spent on this problem is reduced over sessions, therapeutic follow-up is built into the system.

Therapist attention to this problem is faded slowly, principally by assignment and review of homework tasks, as the client improves.

2. New problems are introduced systematically into treatment as the more significant problems show improvement.

3. Note also the multiplicity of treatment strategies implemented. Some of these strategies will be discussed below.

While all of these steps might be taken in an actual therapy case, the number of steps per problem, number of problems per session, and number of sessions required to accomplish each goal will probably vary widely from client to client and for the same client at different points in therapy.

Note that each session begins with a review of homework (usually a written disputation by the patient) and a review of a previous disputation in session; in both instances the therapist is checking to see whether or not the client has thoroughly understood the D. If your client has not comprehended or is having problems with the homework sheet, trouble-shooting is called for (see p. 142).

A frequent problem in new therapists is impatience or even anger at the client who makes mistakes. Monitor your reactions in this situation. If you are impatient, look for your own irrational beliefs—specifically, that the client *should* have felt better or at least have performed better. Be careful that you are not rating *yourself* by your client's behavior. Disputation involves subtle and sophisticated philosophical points and taps skills that clients do not ordinarily use. Give yourself and your client permission to be beginners.

If your client has successfully worked out a homework sheet and has experienced a reduction in emotional stress during an in-session dispute, you may recognize one of two possible outcomes at this point in therapy:

1. The client may continue to experience the old C somewhat regularly and will use this as a cue to utilize his or her RET skills as modeled in therapy. Disputation thus serves as a coping technique.

2. A new C may emerge. If the patient has truly been able to replace the old IB's with more rational philosophies, the original A events will automatically be followed by more appropriate

emotional reactions. When well practiced, the new RB's will tend to become as automatic to the client as were the original IB's.

Continuing Therapy

In many cases, after the client's presenting problem has been resolved, the patient will continue to make appointments or will request a continuation of therapy. What do you do then? You listen. Very often the behavioral changes made in therapy will present clients with new social situations which they may not have the skills to handle. For example, the formerly obese man may now find himself confronted with issues of dating or find that others have higher expectations of work output from him. The formerly nonassertive, reclusive housewife may encounter new problems as she adjusts to the working world. In other words, although there may no longer be evidence of psychopathology, the client may profit from continued work with the therapist.

In other instances, clients may bring up new problems when they experience some relief from the original ones. This pattern may be viewed as a figure-ground effect; as the primary problem (figure) gets resolved, it recedes and minor problems (background) come into relief. This is not an example of *symptom substitution*, a term which implies that curing one problem leads to an increase or development of other problems. Rather, the client may now have the time to focus on less pressing issues. With low socioeconomic status clients, who seem to lead "crisis management" lives, the "figure" presented to the therapist may be a new one each week.

When clients do bring in new problems they may, at some point in therapy, become discouraged and morose, making dire predictions of a gloomy future filled with problems for which they must get professional help. At such times, it is useful to have the patients recollect their earlier problems, now in the background; point these out to them and reinforce them lavishly for the progress already achieved. An analogy such as the following may also be helpful: "If you go to your physician with fourteen splinters in your hand, even after five are out, your hand may still hurt because nine more remain. It just takes more work." But remember, your patient's confidence in allowing you to go on removing "psychological splinters" may waver unless you point out that five have already been removed. Another analogy, pointing out the figure-ground effect discussed above, might be useful. If you have a minor cut on your finger, sore feet, and a dull headache, and then receive a punch in the nose, you probably won't notice the first three troubles until the pain of the last one recedes.

Periodic progress reviews such as the above may, in fact, be recommended as a routine part of therapy. Patients come in to therapy because they are in pain, and as soon as it is alleviated, they tend not to think about it or how the relief was accomplished. We all tend to forget the stone that was in our shoe yesterday. If patients are made aware of the pain reduction and how it was accomplished, they may be more likely to use the same techniques in the future. If you think that patients have made gains which are not clear to them, you needn't hesitate to point these out and show how you think they were accomplished.

Also, ask your clients for periodic feedback on the therapy experience. They can usually recall what preceded their "Aha" reaction and may be a rich source of information for you. In addition, their comments may reinforce your helpful therapist behaviors. Ask the following kinds of questions: "How did I help you? How could I have helped you more? Was there anything I did which interfered with my helping you?" Some therapists (e.g., Beck et al., 1978) ask such questions at the end of every therapy hour, not only for personal feedback but also to identify any lingering irrational beliefs or to correct any misperceptions.

The periodic review may also serve as a good preparation for the client's termination. Terminating is often uncomfortable for clients; for example, they may feel that they need an excuse to do so or that they cannot function independently. When it is time for a review, therefore, you may also ask: "How are we coming in getting you toward your goals? How much longer do you want to work? When shall we schedule our next review?"

Termination of Therapy

In a sense, good therapy provides a continual preparation for termination. RET in particular, following an educational model, attempts to teach the client rational self-analysis skills which, hopefully, can be generalized to new problem situations. As the client improves, the therapist can do less of the disputing in the session and leave more of it to the client. We recommend that as sessions progress, you remain as active as ever but shift the content of your speech.

In early sessions, you will talk more about the IB's and why they are irrational. Toward the final sessions, you will comment more about how well your clients are disputing their own IB's. Thus, by the end of therapy, most patients have acquired some basic understanding of the theory of emotional disturbance and have learned some skills to combat it, so that you can serve merely to guide them through its application to specific problems.

When patients announce that they feel ready for termination and you agree that the goals outlined at the beginning of therapy have been met, you may wish to inquire if they have any new goals or issues that they wish to discuss. Such an invitation may be helpful to clients who feel inhibited about bringing up what they view as minor or unrelated problems. Occasionally, you may believe that clients are terminating before they are ready; the original goals may have been met, but the clients may have a number of other significant issues with which you may help. However, if clients do not contract to work on these, you may be making an ethical error in insisting that they remain in therapy.

You may have to deal with your own perfectionistic standards. Do you have a "should" about how clients will perform at the end of therapy? Clients will not always arrive at the end points you'd prefer, and little will be achieved by pestering them or worrying whether or not they "got their money's worth." It is possible and acceptable for therapy to terminate before ultimate goals are accomplished. In fact, some clients report that major gains occur after therapy is terminated; there may be a significant lag time between learning the principles and deciding to implement them wholeheartedly. Of course, you may suggest to clients that you perceive them to be selling themselves short, and the pro's and con's of working on further problems can be discussed. Ultimately, however, it will be the client's choice.

Some clients come in after just a few sessions announcing complete success. In such instances of "flight into health," it will be extremely important to ask the patients how they account for the change. Have they improved because they have really applied RET principles? Have they changed for the wrong reasons (e.g., to please the therapist)? Have they improved because the obnoxious A's in their lives are less frequent? As a check on clients' improvement, you may ask them to think of examples of problems that they used to upset themselves over but now do not *and* to explain why. The latter part of this question highlights cognitive change and enables the therapist to evaluate whether or not the client is thinking more helpfully.

If the client terminates abruptly, without notification, what is the appropriate course of action? Many clinics send the client a letter noting the failure to keep the appointment and offering further treatment if desired. Phone calls are acceptable in most cases; although they are more intrusive, they may be more informative to the therapist and helpful to the client. If you do not know the client well, however, phone calls may be less desirable. For example, some patients may have kept their foray into therapy a secret from family members; leaving a message may prove awkward, and even if they are at home, they may not feel able to talk openly. In any case, it is recommended that you contact no patient more than once, since this may be legally viewed as harassment.

In many instances, because of external factors, clients will terminate therapy before either they or you feel they are ready. It would be helpful for you to stop and ask yourself: "This may be my last session to work with this patient. How can I structure the session so that it will be of maximal value to him or her?" Here are some suggestions:

1. Ask the clients what they want to accomplish in the final session(s).
2. Try to elicit a recapitulation of the therapy: why they originally came to treatment, what they have learned, and what they still want to change. You may then compare your own ideas on these three questions and share them with the clients.
3. Suggest a continuation of behavioral assignments to bridge the gap after therapy. Assignments may also serve as a reminder to patients of the concepts you have taught them.

If clients are terminating because of a move to a new community, you can discuss the pro's and con's of reinitiating therapy there. It may even be possible for you to make a referral to another professional in the new locale or to suggest how patients can go about locating a new therapist. The Institute for Rational-Emotive Therapy has a referral list of RET therapists in the United States and abroad. This list may be ordered by writing to the Institute at 45 E. 65th Street, New York, N.Y. 10021, and sending a dollar to cover mailing costs.

It will also be helpful to point out to the client that the move itself may be a life stress. In this way, patients may be given an *explanation* for backsliding, if it occurs, and may be prepared for it. Otherwise, they may view any new emotional distress as evidence that they are *never* going to get better, which may induce further panic, depression, or a decision to stop working at it. Understanding their backsliding may help them to move forward in their future work with therapy.

At termination, some patients may not discuss their reactions to this change but may act in a depressed manner. In this instance, you may respond to body language and voice inflection cues and comment on this behavior. Later, you may wish to add: "You know, if you hadn't been my patient, I have a feeling we could have been good friends. I feel badly about not seeing you in the future. How do you feel about our terminating?" If you avoid such a confrontation, the patients may never have gotten this message or the opportunity to discuss what may have been a very important relationship in their lives.

Booster Shots

After your clients have terminated therapy, they may find occasional reasons to call for an appointment or to resume therapy for a brief period. Before termination is completed, therefore, be sure that they understand that there is no stigma to coming back for further work, which you may suggest is analogous to getting immunization booster shots. The future will inevitably hold new challenges which they may want to discuss with you, and it would be incorrect to assume that *no* further problems will emerge in the future or that the clients will *always* be *absolutely* rational.

13 A Rational Approach to Marriage and Divorce Counseling

Couple counseling is analogous to running a very small group, consisting of two clients and a therapist. Couple counseling using RET is easier to understand, as is all RET group therapy for that matter, if you remember that *the individual is the target of change.* Couple counseling in joint sessions, however, is much more difficult to conduct than individual psychotherapy for several reasons. First, there are added distractions provided by having two people in the room. Second, the interactions or arguments between the clients may be distracting. Third, there are more problems to be dealt with: his, hers, and theirs. Fourth, most therapeutic maneuvers have repercussive effects on the partner; a change in one partner may provide a significant Activating event for the other and result in pleasure or displeasure. Fifth, a major difficulty in couple counseling is that the two clients may have different agendas; the therapist may have a hard time assessing and meeting these incompatible goals.

As a therapist, you had better be clear about whom you are serving: him, her, or the marriage. Professionals refer to this area of work as "marriage counseling," as if the *marriage* or the *relationship* is the party being served. In the view of the rational therapist, however, the two individual parties (or three, if you're dealing with a group marriage) are the clients, not the marriage. This viewpoint had better be made clear to the clients; they may then understand that you are serving them as two independent adults, and that the goals of counseling are to help each one maximize his or her happiness, whether this means living with or separating from the partner. Unless you make these goals clear, allegiances can be blurred and trouble can emerge.

We suspect that much of what goes on in marriage counseling is actually divorce counseling. A review of the research in marriage counseling (Fodor, 1978) indicated that most of the studies to date have focused only on mildly to moderately dysfunctional couples. These people are basically compatible but have problems in one or a few areas and lack the skills to negotiate these conflicts. In our experience, however, these individuals are unrepresentative of the typical couples who arrive for therapy. Many couples seem to be basic mismatches, and by the time they come for marital counseling, the partners have experienced substantial bitterness, diminished sexual involvement, and strained communications. One of the partners may already have decided to leave the marriage, and the relationship could profit from counseling on how to separate amicably. You may provide little help to such clients if you believe that you have "failed" if the couple divorces. Such a belief reflects an underlying value judgment on your part.

Value judgments frequently arise in marital and divorce counseling, for you and for your clients. Our society as a whole is undergoing a period of rapid change in the mores of marriage and divorce. Most of us do have strong positions on many of these issues, although we may never have verbalized them clearly to ourselves or others. Before you begin to do marriage counseling, we strongly recommend that you examine your own value systems of the ethics and mores of relationships. The following questions may be important in clarifying these for you. Consider each carefully:

1. Is marriage better than no marriage?
2. Is a bad marriage better than no marriage?
3. Is a long marriage better than a short one?
4. Do you want to teach your client how to live in a bad marriage?
5. Do you readily encourage couples to separate?
6. Does this reflect a belief in the value of divorce?
7. Do you encourage clients to stay together regardless of how dysfunctional their relationship is?
8. Does this reflect a bias in favor of marriage?
9. Are you tolerant of different living arrangements, such as open marriage or communal marriage?

10. Do you believe that affairs are always destructive to marriage?
11. Do you believe that people are capable of making their own decisions?
12. Do you feel comfortable helping them to achieve a goal which you yourself may believe is unwise for you? For them?

Regardless of what type of relationship *you* prefer, or what type you believe fosters the "common good," you can best help your clients if you are tolerant and accepting of them. Your chances of helping people resolve marital and divorce problems are greater if you dispel your own "shoulds" in this area. If you *do* have biases and your values dictate one therapeutic goal over another, make your goals clear to your clients and see that they are comfortable with those goals.

A quick insight into your value system about marriage and divorce is to examine what you say when a colleague or acquaintance announces that he or she (or a mutual friend) is getting a divorce. Do you typically offer condolences, even when you know nothing of the state of the marriage?

Clarification of ethics and values can arise in marital counseling if you have previously seen one of the partners in individual therapy. After you have developed a relationship with that client, can you then be objective and help the spouse as well? Will you try to "get the best deal" for your client? Even if you decide that *you* can be objective, there may still be problems. Will your previous client expect special consideration and protection? Will the client be overly offended if you criticize him or her or agree with the spouse's comments? Feelings of betrayal can arise in such situations if clients are not prepared for the change in contract beforehand. The new member of the trio may also have some reservations about seeking marriage counseling with the spouse's therapist. The spouse may have made changes while in individual therapy, some of which may have resulted in marital conflict; the new party may feel resentful. In addition, the new client may not believe that you will adequately listen to his or her side of the story.

Problems such as the above may be minimized by stating the new contract clearly; make sure both parties understand that you will now serve them both, and any "special relationship" has ended. Some therapists believe that one should avoid these problems altogether by sending the couple to another therapist, never seeing the couple together if you have worked with one partner individually. We believe that such rules or "shoulds" are unwise. A decision to see a couple under these circumstances can best be made on an individual basis. The important point is that the above issues be shared with the couple before embarking on joint sessions.

Another important ethical issue that arises in couple counseling is that of *confidentiality*. Some therapists demand that partners keep no secrets from each other or from the therapist; everything is grist for the mill. Other therapists inform clients that nothing that is told to them in individual consultations will be kept secret from the spouse; this therapist wants no burdens. Still other therapists promise strict confidentiality to both parties. What is the best way to proceed?

The decision to never allow secrets and to provide no privileged communication between the therapist and one of the marriage partners seems foolish to us. How many individual clients would confide in you if they learned you had a "no secrets" rule? In marriage counseling, such a rule forces the client to keep secret what may be valuable clinical information or to reveal it even though this may have unnecessary and unfortunate consequences. Therapists who insist on complete disclosure between the partners and who encourage the unburdening of secrets usually believe that it is the secrets themselves (A) which cause marital disturbance (C).

We suggest, again, that moderation is the best path to follow. Few rules will apply to every case. What you can do is to share your rules with the clients beforehand and then negotiate. If one party is willing to share information with you in return for confidentiality, it is wise to listen. Such information is likely to be important to the client, and you are usually in a better position to help both parties if you know such important facts. Thus, we recommend that a certain degree of confidentiality be given to each client, and that the advantage of having clients openly discuss their problems with the therapist outweighs the disadvantage of having to remember what is secret and what is open for discussion.

We believe that the position of no secrets in marriage is of questionable value. How many marriages would survive if all the BLACK TRUTHS (the opposite of white lies) were told and no secrets were allowed. Would yours?

Assessing the Clients' Agendas

Now that you've thought through some of the ethical and moral issues in marriage, you are ready to see your first couple. The first task in marital counseling is to assess the situation and discover the agenda of each party involved. People come to marriage counseling for a variety of reasons, some of which are listed below:

1. To help improve the relationship. This is the most obvious reason, but by far not the only one.
2. To help the spouse form a relationship with a therapist in whose hands he or she plans to leave the spouse on departing.
3. To sabotage the therapy in order to provide an excuse to leave (e.g., "You see, even marriage counseling can't help us; we'd better get a divorce").
4. To obtain help in deciding whether or not they want to stay together.
5. To get a third party's opinion on the advisability of staying married or getting married (premarital counseling).
6. To get permission to leave.
7. To help keep their infidelity a secret or to arrange a contract wherein such behavior is allowed.
8. To get their spouse to stop engaging in extramarital affairs.

If you assume that all couples come in with the same agenda of improving their relationship, you may waste many sessions working on the wrong problem. It is also unwise to assume that clients will divulge their true agendas with their spouse present. They may be quite frightened of the repercussions or too timid to seek what they actually want. In order to assess the agendas, we suggest that the therapist see the couple together for a session but then see each partner individually for a half, full, or several sessions to assess what each desires, which is best accomplished by openly asking the client for his or her goals. Here is a transcript of a therapist starting an individual assessment session:

> "Well, Mr. Jones, when we met last week with your wife, you said you were coming here to help your marriage. What I'd like to do now is to ask you if there are things you would like to tell me in confidence without your wife present. Now before you answer, let me explain something. People usually come to marriage counseling for lots of reasons. Some come for permission to separate, or to help one another stop having extramarital affairs, to sabotage the therapy in order to provide an excuse for leaving, etc. So I would like you to tell me just what your feelings are and what you would hope to gain from these sessions. If there is something troubling you that you do not want your spouse to know, please tell me now and we can keep it confidential."

When the therapist asks to see each person individually, each will probably be curious about what the other has said. For example, if the therapist is helping a husband to deal better with his wife or to leave her, and the patient tells this to the wife, she may upset herself about the news and the progress of therapy may be halted. To avoid problems of miscommunication, be sure to instruct your client that if the spouse asks what was discussed in therapy, he or she can say, "We just talked about my problems." The spouse is usually satisfied by such an answer, since it indicates that the therapist is aware that the partner has problems, and is usually willing to allow privacy for those sessions, at least temporarily.

If both parties have the same agenda, you can proceed to see them together. If they don't, what options do you have? The therapist's job obviously becomes more difficult, and issues of confidentiality and allegiance become more prominent when the agendas are incongruent. Obviously the therapist cannot help one client make the relationship better while knowingly helping the other client to leave. The situation is worsened if the spouse has revealed in confidence his or her plans to leave and does not wish the other party to know yet. Such problems are shown in the following case. We present this case as an example of problems that arise when a therapist tries to do joint counseling when the parties have incongruent agendas:

Sam and Jean were a couple in their mid-thirties who had been married for ten years and had three children. After an argument concerning Sam's suspicion that Jean was having an extramarital affair, Sam moved out. They had been separated for two weeks when Sam suggested that they go for marital counseling. Sam reported that he knew his suspicions were false. He had a quick temper and frequently exploded. He was sorry and wanted to be forgiven and to return home. Jean refused to accept him back. She reported that Sam was a strict and rigid man who always criticized her housework and was generally disapproving of her family. Sam retorted that Jean had many faults too. She frequently deceived him about financial matters and sided against him in family arguments.

At this point, the therapist decided to see each of them alone. Sam reported that he loved his wife. He was aware that their marriage had been deteriorating over the past years, and he recognized that his rigid, compulsive behaviors had contributed to this. He would do anything to keep Jean. Jean reported that she was disgusted with Sam's criticisms and compulsive neatness. She had never engaged in extramarital sex with her accused lover, although she did see the man and was very fond of him. Jean wished to leave the marriage and responded negatively to suggestions of how they could improve their relationship. Jean did not want to tell Sam of her decision for fear of his wrath. Her biggest fear, however, was not his reaction, but that of her parents and their children. She believed that these people would view her as the wrongdoer and reject her. Thus, Sam, and especially her family, must never know of her wish.

Jean was seen for one further session. She reported that she would seek a divorce when she could figure out a way that all blame could fall on Sam. The therapist had agreed to keep this information confidential. The three parties then proceeded to work together. During these sessions, as one would guess, Sam was most cooperative. After Jean had identified his behaviors that most annoyed her, Sam worked diligently at changing them. He listened carefully to all advice and followed all behavioral assignments exactly. Jean, on the other hand, would admit to no wrongdoing, expressed no commitment to change, and denied any anger or unpleasant feelings toward Sam. Jean never mentioned her anger at Sam or her plans to leave the marriage; this area was off-limits to the therapist because of the pledge of confidentiality. The joint therapy was terminated after several unrewarding sessions.

This case was particularly disturbing to the therapist, primarily because Sam was being deceived. While Sam was working very hard at the goal of improving his marriage, the therapist and Jean knew that this was a hopeless endeavor. She had decided to take Sam back after a short stay in marriage counseling, resume the marriage for a while, and then provoke him into leaving. Thus, he would receive all the blame, and family and friends would not reject her for getting a divorce. While it could be argued that Sam did receive many benefits from these sessions, they were not the ones for which he had contracted. He did correct his compulsive neatness, which had offended many other people in addition to his wife. He definitely reduced his anxiety about being single. He learned better social skills, among them the ability to communicate more effectively with his wife and other women. All of these things could be of benefit to him whether or not he stayed married. But, again, he had not contracted for these gains. It appears in retrospect that the therapist made an initial error in taking this case on for marital therapy because there was a clear conflict between the agendas of the two parties.

Individual sessions were subsequently recommended to Sam and Jean to help correct the problems that had arisen. The therapist suggested to Jean that her decision to leave could have been based on intense anger at Sam. If she changed her demanding philosophy and as a result relinquished her anger, she might feel differently about leaving. Once this issue had been discussed, Jean decided that she still wanted to leave, but the fear of rejection from her family remained a problem. This problem was worked on for a significant period of time, and its resolution made Jean's decision easier. Concurrently, the therapist worked individually with Sam at some of his goals: overcoming his demandingness, his anxiety about rejection, his compulsive neatness, and his poor social skills. While Sam believed these things would make him more attractive to Jean, the therapist stated that they were good for Sam and would help make him more attractive either to Jean or to *other* women; the therapist was not helping Sam directly to get Jean back.

Therefore, when conflicts of agenda arise, we believe it is best to see each person (or one person) individually. Persons undecided about staying, or too guilty or fearful to leave, can be helped to work out their individual emotional problems and then be helped to make a decision. It appears unlikely that people will freely talk about such problems in joint session. Thus, the problems remain unsolved, and the marriage counseling sessions may be wasteful.

The Decision to Separate

Clients such as Jean, who desire to separate or divorce but are emotionally blocked from doing so, are not uncommon. Frequently, what keeps people "stuck" in undesired relationships is *anxiety*. Clients often worry about rejection by family and friends if there is a divorce. They may fear that they will be unable to find another mate ("I'll never find anyone as good as the louse I've got now") or will be rejected when they encounter the singles' scene. In each of these instances, the irrational belief causing the anxiety is some variant of the dire need for love and approval. The disputations discussed in Chapter 7 are relevant for your work with such a client.

In addition, it is also helpful to do a hedonic calculus for such clients. For example, when dealing with clients who are afraid of leaving because of loss of approval from others, the therapist can ask the following kinds of questions:

1. Are the frustrations and losses of staying in a bad relationship over a number of years really worth enduring to avoid the disapproval from people? Especially when this disapproval may have to be endured for a short period of time?
2. Will the disapproval really be that great, given the general acceptance of divorce in our culture now?
3. What would it take to make you leave? A physical assault? Nonsupport? How would you cope with the disapproval of others then?

Similarly, people anxious about finding a new mate could benefit from other solutions, such as assessing their ability and probability of chances for success and improving their social skills and social desirability.

Guilt is another emotion which can prevent people from leaving a marriage. A typical case involved Ron, who arrived with his wife, Elaine, for marriage counseling. When seen alone, Ron reported that he wanted to leave the marriage but just couldn't. Elaine would be "crushed—she just couldn't take it." How could he hurt someone who had been so good to him, he moaned. People in this quandary usually have three misconceptions that lead to their guilt. First, their mate will "fall apart" if they leave. Second, they are totally responsible for their mate's feelings. Third, and most important, they are worthless and horrible people if they do such a horrendous thing.

Let's discuss how you, as a rational therapist, could attack each of these beliefs. For the first belief, that the spouse will fall apart, it is important to ask the client exactly what "fall apart" means. Does it mean "commit suicide"? Does it mean "having a psychotic episode requiring hospitalization"? Does it mean "crying a lot"? Does it mean "not being able to keep up a daily schedule for a period of time"? The terms "falling apart" or "having a nervous breakdown" are quite vague, and it is important for clients to identify just what consequences they expect. Yes, Elaine will probably experience pain, and this is likely to last for a long time. But most people do recover from divorce. Many people, especially chauvinistic men, exaggerate their spouse's need for them and their spouse's reaction to their leaving. It is somewhat reassuring, yet grandiose, to believe that someone loves you so much that he or she will "fall apart" when you leave. If, however, the client has considerable evidence that the spouse will behave very badly and react with significant psychopathology, the motivation for such behavior had better be investigated. It is possible that the spouse's depressive or hysterical behavior is reinforced by the client's willingness to stay. Thus, rather than being an accurate reflector of psychopathology or fragility, the depression may be viewed as adaptive, although unpleasant, behaviors which *work* in the sense that they preserve the marriage.

In discussing the belief that one's spouse will "fall apart" and her life will be miserable, it may also be helpful to attempt a hedonic calculus for the partner. While it is true that Elaine may undergo a significant degree of pain right after the separation, other questions remain. How much is *Elaine* missing by staying in a marriage with a partner who doesn't choose to live with her? What is that worth? Is this long-term cost worth the initial short-term pain of separation? The long-term payoff for Elaine may be better if she experiences the initial pain and then has the choice of finding a compatible partner with whom she could find happiness. In any case, Ron is preventing Elaine from making that decision and assumes that he knows what is best for her and that he can figure out *her* hedonic calculus better than she can.

The second belief, that you are responsible for your mate's upset, is only partially true. While Ron has provided the Activating event for Elaine, it is her beliefs which are causing most of her disturbance. If her thinking were rational, she would experience some sorrow and displeasure over his leaving. For this, he may be responsible; but any additional pain that she may be feeling is of her own doing. Just as Ron's thinking is responsible for his guilt, Elaine's thinking is responsible for her depression.

The third belief is most important. Even if Elaine does have a psychotic episode after Ron leaves and even if he is responsible for a large percentage of her pain, does that make him a bad or worthless person? Again, all the disputation strategies discussed in Chapter 7 can be used here to persuade clients to give up their beliefs about self-worth and self-rating. Once clients have changed these beliefs, they can reach a decision on the basis of the relationship and not the guilt.

Inability to Make a Decision About the Marriage

So far, we have discussed conflicts in agendas which involve one party leaving the marriage. A more difficult problem, however, exists when a partner is undecided about whether or not to stay. When clients are uncertain, the therapist may choose to see them separately and not as part of a couple.

There are usually several areas of emotional conflict that prevent clients from deciding on a marital status. The decision of which problems to work on may represent a value judgment by the therapist concerning directions to be taken in the marriage. That is, clients can remain in the marriage but may have emotional problems and irrational beliefs which make this decision difficult. On the other hand, they can leave the marriage but have emotional problems and irrational beliefs which prevent them from doing so. Which is the therapist to work on? If you choose the first, you may be enforcing your value judgment that all marriages must be saved, or that at least one must *try* to save them. If you choose the latter, you encourage divorce and may enforce the value judgment that transient or short-term relationships are more valued. Regardless of your convictions and regardless of how good your reasons are for making such a value judgment, we believe that the decision of whether or not to remain married is best made by the client. That decision will be easier to make if you work on both areas simultaneously.

You can discuss with clients the Activating events which might occur if they decide to stay in the marriage, their emotional reactions to these events, and the irrational beliefs which lead to these emotions. Conversely, you can have the clients discuss what would result if they decided to leave the marriage. The client is standing at a crossroads; each path at the fork is a life option, but the patient cannot accurately evaluate the option if its path is littered with the stones of irrational beliefs and emotional turmoil. Once the stones are removed from both paths, the client can more rationally decide which path has a greater probability of maximizing his or her long-range happiness. Removing the stones, of course, is the job of disputation.

A key irrational belief to watch for is that the individual *needs* the partner and remains in the relationship largely because of a fear of leaving the "other half" behind. Such a belief is not only debilitating to the client but extremely unflattering to the partner. How would *you* feel if you knew that your wife (or husband) were staying in the marriage only because she was afraid of leaving you? It is not pleasant to think that the only reason your spouse stays is neurotic.

If this irrational belief can be challenged, clients may realize that they have the option of leaving. If they choose to stay in the marriage, it will be because of its positive qualities and their affection for the partner. This realization can be an important building block on which both parties can reconstruct the relationship.

After the therapist has disputed the sets of irrational beliefs, it would be helpful to lead the client through a hedonic calculus of the pro's and con's of staying in or leaving the relationship. The advantages and disadvantages of each alternative can be outlined and discussed to help the client assess the individual value of each factor.

Even if clients have overcome any irrational beliefs about staying in or leaving the marriage and have done the hedonic calculus and decided which alternative would be most desirable, there may be one additional problem. The clients may be blocked from making a decision because of excessive *anxiety about decisions*. In such cases, there are two common irrational beliefs that make the decision difficult. The first problem falls under the rubric of LFT; making a decision to do something entails deciding not to do something else. The unwillingness to face the discomfort of sacrificing the "something else" may keep the client stuck at the decision point. Such was the problem of a client recently seen individually after a request for marriage counseling had been made:

> Peter was a thirty-year-old business executive who was uncertain whether to stay with his wife. Peter and Marlene had been married for five years. Marlene felt totally committed to Peter and cared for him dearly. Peter, however, had wanderlust for women and places. He wished to experience new relationships and desired to travel extensively. After computing the hedonic calculus, Peter decided that he wanted Marlene more than anything else. But if he chose her, other women and travel were restricted. Peter continued to whine about his decision; he felt depressed and cheated. Although he clearly identified Marlene as his top priority, he failed to make a decision to become committed to the marriage. After discussing the matter, he admitted believing that he was unwilling to give up *anything*. In effect, he demanded to have his cake and eat it too. He wanted Marlene, and he wanted other women and he wanted to travel.

The key irrational belief in such cases involves self-statements such as, "I must have everything I want; I must not be deprived of anything." In Peter's case, the therapist tried to show him that (1) he could not have it all, and (2) if he gave up his demandingness and accepted the limitations of any decision he would be much happier, regardless of the choice. Once his pernicious irrational beliefs were disputed, Peter's anxiety about making a decision diminished and he was free to work on improving his relationship with Marlene.

A second major irrational belief which makes decision making difficult is a belief in the *need for certainty*, which results in anxiety. The client believes that somehow there should be evidence for the Perfect Decision, one with no chance for a mistake. This belief is quite destructive to a marriage. While one's mate may be highly desirable, the chances are that since that mate is human, he or she will have some faults and be just as imperfect as the rest of the human species. Even with a highly desirable mate, there are no guarantees of the future. Your mate may decide to leave you; the chance always exists that your union, regardless of how desirable, will end. If you could predict the future, which you can't, and you knew your marriage would remain happy, some doubts could still remain. There is always the possibility that a more desirable companion will come along one day, or that you could have been happier with someone else.

When beliefs for certainty cause anxiety which is blocking the clients' decision, rational therapists dispute the needs for certainty and dispel the myth that certainty exists. None of us can foretell the future, and time machines have not yet been perfected. All of our decisions will lack certainty. Uncertainty is a basic fact of life, and clients will be less disturbed if they accept that fact. To help clients stop catastrophizing about the uncertainty, you can have them imagine all the possible negative consequences of the decision. Then each of these negative consequences is put into an ABC analysis so that they do not catastrophize about them. Once clients accept certainty as myth and no longer awfulize about the errors in decision making, they can proceed to choose an alternative.

Improving the Relationship

Assuming that both parties have similar agendas and they desire to work to improve their relationship, the rational therapist can commence with joint marital sessions. Ellis (1962, 1977a) believes that disturbed marital relations result in large part from "should" statements or unexamined demands. Husbands and wives produce trouble between themselves when they hold unrealistic expectations for themselves, for their mates, or for the marriage. Many disturbances occur when one or both believe that the spouse should always be affectionate, always be considerate, always do what pleases them, and never make demands; marriage, in other words, should always be happy and enjoyable. Your primary role in such situations is to dispute these beliefs and replace them with a more tolerant and accepting philosophy.

Admittedly, couples do not present themselves to you saying, "We're holding unrealistic and demanding philosophies." More likely, they will tell you that they have difficulty communicating, that they argue a lot, or that their sexual relationship is deteriorating. Sometimes couples diagnose themselves and may do so incorrectly. Many seem to diagnose themselves on the basis of what they have read in Sunday supplements or magazine articles. For example, a couple may complain of poor communication, when what they really mean is that they are ineffective in influencing each other to produce the behaviors they are demanding. You would do well to carefully evaluate the couple's self-diagnosis and make sure that you agree with it. Communication, for example, really means the transmission of a message from one party to the other; it does not mean that the receiver will necessarily comply with the sender's wishes.

The RET therapist assumes that the couple's problems stem from distressing emotions such as anger, anxiety, jealousy, or guilt—and these, in turn, are based on the individual's irrational thinking habits. When one or both partners are thinking irrationally and are in emotional turmoil, they are quite likely to experience a series of relationship difficulties. If a husband believes that his wife should always please him, and he is in a state of anger, he will probably:

1. Distort reality (e.g., "She never pleases me," when in fact she does).
2. Be poor at social problem-solving skills, such as alternative-solution thinking (e.g., "What could I do to get her to please me? Nothing!").
3. Be inept at communications (e.g., sulking or having temper tantrums).
4. Be experiencing little pleasure in the relationship.

The rational therapist does not assume that once people learn to think rationally, they will automatically be able to communicate, negotiate, or problem-solve. Rational thinking, however, will increase their chances of learning and practicing these skills.

In conducting a joint session, you may begin by having the couple present their major problems briefly, but avoid getting into a prolonged history-taking or complaint-hearing discussion. Then, as soon as possible, focus on one member of the couple (in the other's presence) and help this mate identify and dispute his or her irrational philosophies. Periodically focus your gaze or nod at the observing partner in order to convey the message, "Pay attention—I want you to learn this, too." The observer typically relishes this phase of the session; thus, a husband may conclude that the therapist is a "genius" since he or she obviously recognizes that the problem lies entirely with the wife and that he is clearly the "better half." Soon, however, when the initial disputation has been completed, the therapist will shift the focus to the husband in order to examine *his* emotional excesses and point out and dispute *his* irrational thinking.

While this shifting of focus from one partner to the other sounds simple, it contains several difficult aspects. First, the therapist had better realize that triads are extremely unstable groups which easily break into a dyad and an isolate. Unless the therapist is skilled at avoiding it, couples counseling can be perceived by one (or both) partner(s) as the therapist and the mate siding together against the focal client. As pointed out above, some clients welcome an alliance with the therapist because it "shows that I'm right." A simple solution to help avoid this trap is to address roughly equal numbers of remarks to each person; show that *both* are creating their own feelings, that *both* think irrationally when they blame the other, and that blaming leads to anger.

In order to do a complete ABCD analysis on each partner and spend about equal amounts of time on each, time is of the essence. The novice therapist who is less skilled at basic RET techniques may find that time runs out before he or she has had a chance to balance the session. To avoid this problem, you can explain your strategy to both clients beforehand. Thus, you might say:

> Well, Mr. and Mrs. Jones, I've listened to both of you outline your problems. You both have some difficulties which lead to your arguments. Mr. Jones, you appear to be angry whenever your wife

criticizes you and you react nastily, which in turn is rather annoying to her. Mrs. Jones, you appear to be upset and depressed whenever your husband does act obnoxiously, and you draw the conclusion that he doesn't love you and you make yourself more depressed. Now, both of you had better change these ways of acting and thinking if you're going to get along better. I would like to discuss each of these problems with you in turn, and show you, Mr. Jones, how you are needlessly making yourself angry, and how you, Mrs. Jones, are needlessly making yourself depressed. Now, who would like to go first?

The therapist then proceeds to discuss the problem with the individual in the presence of the other.

There are distinct advantages to disputing with the client in the presence of the spouse. First, by modeling, the spouse can learn about irrational beliefs and how to dispute them. Second, the spouse can learn from you how to help the partner correct his or her irrational thinking. Third, the spouse can actively engage in the discussion and help the partner overcome irrational beliefs right in the session.

Communication Problems

Poor communication patterns between marriage partners are often a result of emotional blocks. If you have successfully reduced the emotional stress by disputational sessions, the couple may still exhibit communication problems because of old habits or skill deficits. Problems can exist on the part of the sender as well as the receiver. The most common problem seems to be the transmission of vague or ambiguous communications (Rausch, Barry, Hertel, and Swain, 1974).

Ambiguous communication occurs when there is a discrepancy between the verbal and nonverbal parts of a message. For example, the spouse may deny feelings of anger, yet speak in a cold and distancing tone of voice. There are several possible reasons for this dishonest communication, such as fear of rejection, reprisals, or loss of control, or simply lack of know-how; the client may have had poor communication models and not know how to communicate directly. Receivers of such communication may aggravate the problem by either getting upset at the sender or by simply failing to ask for clarification. Their failure may be the result of similar fears or skill deficits as plague the sender. These interpersonal problems result in an inability of each partner to predict the other's behavior and may initiate a cycle of distrust.

Once you have uncovered and disputed the irrational beliefs which interfere with direct and honest communication, you may then move to retrain communication skills. While space does not permit an elaborate discussion of the communication-training literature, the reader is encouraged to become familiar with the training techniques such as those described by Raush et al. (1974) and Jacobson and Martin (1976).

One exercise which communication skills trainers have found useful is to have the couple take turns filling out the following two sentence-stems. They continue alternating as long as they can.

I appreciate it when you . . .

I resent it when you . . . .

Increasing the Pleasure in the Marriage

While the partners are caught up in their anger or hurt at one another, neither will want to take the first step of doing something positive for the other in order to make the relationship better. It is for this reason that the rational therapist does sufficient disputation to reduce the emotional "highs," which may then allow the parties to think about making their relationship more fulfilling. The RET therapist recognizes, however, that cognitive change may not be sufficient to build a happy marriage. "Absence of emotional distress" does not equal "a good marriage." A fulfilling marriage entails many rewarding experiences for both partners.

Behavior therapists have conceptualized marital discord as a problem of unbalanced or low-frequency reinforcement. When the partners are giving each other very few positive "strokes" and are attempting to manipulate each other by negative control tactics, the relationship will be very unsatisfying to them. One way to conceptualize marriage, admittedly not a romantic one, is derived from social-exchange theory (Thibault and Kelley, 1959). The partners are simply not exchanging many positive reinforcers. Thus, even if clients are not emotionally upset, a lack of sufficient positive encounters may make the relationship less desirable.

One technique used by behavioral marriage counselors to increase the pleasure of marriage is the use of *contingency contracting*. Contracts are written agreements between the spouses which are designed to rearrange the balance or increase the overall frequency of reinforcement. Each partner describes behavior changes that he or she wants in the other, trying to limit the contract to positive behaviors to be increased (rather than focusing on negative behaviors to be decreased). The reason for this focus is that it is difficult to notice or reinforce the nonoccurrence of a behavior, and the therapist hopes to train the partners to notice and reinforce those behaviors they find pleasing. Questions that clients may ask themselves in order to prepare written contracts are:

> What characteristics would a new partner have to have that Joe (or Ellen) doesn't have?
> What changes in Joe's (or Ellen's) behavior would make him (or her) more acceptable?

The therapist may also have to retrain the partners in how to say nice things to one another; "pleases" and "thank-yous" may not come easily at first.

Contracting skills will be directly useful in helping the couple learn to negotiate other decisions; e.g., "We'll go to see the movie you want this weekend if we can go to see the opera next weekend." In this way, partners learn to make decisions more equitably, and thereby each maximizes his or her reinforcement potential in their joint ventures.

Rational therapists utilize these behavioral procedures after disputation, as a way to help the clients change their Activating events. As we pointed out in the work with individual clients, changing the A's is more effectively done after the client is thinking rationally.

Sexual Enhancement

Once marriage counseling is under way, whether or not the couple has brought it up for discussion, the therapist had better check on the couple's sexual relationship. Poor marital adjustment and poor sexual adjustment do not necessarily correlate; a couple could have a disturbed marital relationship and function quite well sexually, while couples with sexual dysfunction can often relate well in nonsexual areas. The presence of marital conflict, however, may have arisen because of a sexual problem *or* may have resulted in one. Regardless of the etiology, it is advisable that attempts be made to improve the couple's sexual adjustment. Sexual contact is a very reinforcing segment of a relationship for many people. A good sexual relationship may provide added reinforcement to motivate the partner to work at other areas of the relationship, and sexual contact can become a cue for other romantic behaviors as well.

The RET therapist focuses attention on sexual disturbances rather than solely on a sexual dysfunction; that is, the emotional upset is the target, whether it is the cause or the result (or both) of a sexual problem. You can help clients to decatastrophize their sexual problem and simultaneously work on improving their sexual skills. We strongly advise that if you have clients with sexual problems, and you have not received training in sexual therapy, that you consult with or refer the client to a skilled sex therapist for the sexual retraining portion of the work. References for further reading in this area are given in the Appendix.

Summary

In summary, the rational therapist does not assume that marriage counseling entails simply reconstructing relationships. The first step of good rational marriage counseling is to assess the goals of the clients and to see if the husband and wife both have congruent agendas for therapy. If the agendas are incongruent, we recommend that you see each individual alone to help him or her achieve personal happiness goals. When agendas are congruent and you decide to conduct joint marital counseling sessions, the focus of therapy is still on each individual client. You do not initially work on the relationship or the system, but work on helping each member cope better, think rationally, and experience as much happiness and as little emotional distress as possible. The core disturbance that the rational therapist looks for in achieving this end is the partner's shoulds—unrealistic expectations or demands on themselves, the other, or the marriage. Once these shoulds are disputed and emotional distress is reduced, you can also assist the couple by helping them to improve their communications and improve their interpersonal relationship so that they maximize the pleasure that each contributes to the other.

Appendix:
Selected Readings
for Therapists and Clients

In this Appendix we present an annotated bibliography of books, articles, and tape recordings that the RET therapist-in-training may wish to draw upon when confronted with specific clinical problems or may wish to recommend to clients. Although this list is far from complete, we hope it will provide an initial list of therapist resources and a basis for continued study of cognitive-learning therapy. This chapter is organized as follows: Under the major topic headings, we provide, first, a list of professional references, and second, materials appropriate for the client to listen to or read. Some of these materials (especially the pamphlets and tapes) can be purchased only from the Institute for Rational-Emotive Therapy, 45 E. 65th St., New York, N.Y. 10021; many of the books are also available through bookstores. The first group of recommended readings are general writings on rational-emotive therapy and other cognitive therapies.

INTRODUCTORY MATERIALS: RET AND OTHER COGNITIVE THERAPIES

For the Professional

Cognitive Therapy and the Emotional Disorders by A. Beck. New York: International Universities Press, 1976. Traces the development of Beck's cognitive approach to psychopathology and psychotherapy, an approach very similar to RET. Discusses how cognitions relate to emotions; deals specifically with depression, anxiety, phobias, obsessions, and psychosomatic disorders.

Growth through Reason by A. Ellis. North Hollywood, Ca.: Wilshire Book Co., 1971. A series of verbatim therapy transcripts conducted by Ellis and other prominent rational therapists, including Ben Ard, Jon Geis, Paul Hauck, John Gullo, and Maxie Maultsby. The selection of cases is quite interesting, including a marriage counseling session with a couple who had not had intercourse in thirteen years of marriage; a young man who was afraid of becoming a homosexual; a masochist; the use of RET with a culturally deprived teenager; and depression and severe phobic reactions.

Humanistic Psychotherapy by A. Ellis. New York: McGraw-Hill Book Co., 1973. An update of Ellis' original thinking on rational therapy, including such topics as a comprehensive approach to rational-emotive therapy, self-awareness and personal growth of the psychotherapist, and cognitive approaches to behavior therapy. This book contains examples of the treatment of alcoholism problems, phobic reactions, and borderline psychotic states.

Reason and Emotion in Psychotherapy by A. Ellis. Secaucus, N.J.: The Citadel Press, 1962. The original text by Ellis, the first major work identifying the theory and practice of rational-emotive therapy. It focuses on such issues as the origins of RET and the essence of rational therapy, and includes discussions of marital therapy, group therapy, sexual dysfunction, schizophrenia, and psychopathy.

Handbook of Rational-Emotive Therapy by A. Ellis and R. Grieger. New York: Springer Publishing Co., 1977. The latest and most comprehensive collection of papers on rational-emotive therapy. The book has five major sections: theoretical and conceptual foundations of RET; dynamics of emotional disturbance; primary techniques and basic processes in RET; additional and more specialized techniques, such as group counseling; and RET applied to children. Contributors include Arnold Lazarus, Aaron Beck, Michael Mahoney, and Donald Meichenbaum.

Pamphlets: The following series of four pamphlets published by The Institute for Rational Living may be important reading for the therapist to handle specific questions about general principles of rational-emotive therapy. (1) "An Answer to Some Objections in Rational-Emotive Psychotherapy," by A. Ellis, originally appeared in *Psychotherapy: Theory, Research and Practice*, 1965. This paper may be particularly useful before you face your first client or your first class in which you try to defend RET. (2) "Showing Clients They Are Not Worthless Individuals," by A. Ellis, was reprinted from *Voices* and originally appeared in 1965. It outlines Ellis' position on human worth. (3) "The Neurotic Agreement in Psychotherapy," by P. Hauck, originally appeared in *Rational Living* in 1966. This paper is particularly good reading for the new therapist because the neurotic agreement to which Hauck refers is the psychotherapist's irrational notion that all of his or her patients must get better swiftly, a belief that the author disputes nicely. (4) "What Really Causes Psychotherapeutic Change?", by A. Ellis, originally appeared in *Voices*, 1968.

Tapes: There are two tape recordings which may be ordered from the Institute which the new therapist will find interesting as background listening. The first is a general lecture delivered by Ellis in 1962 entitled "Theory and Practice of Rational-Emotive Psychotherapy." In it Ellis traces the development of RET, his own development as a psychotherapist, and the evolution of the theory. The second tape, "Fun as Psychotherapy," is a lecture by Ellis given at the American Psychological Association convention in 1976. In this tape Ellis speaks of the many advantages of the use of humor in therapy (with illustrations), including reductions to absurdity, paradoxical intention, puns, irony, whimsy, provocative language, slang, and the "deliberate use of sprightly obscenity." The tape makes interesting listening as well as good sense.

For the Client

A New Guide to Rational Living by A. Ellis and R. A. Harper. Englewood Cliffs, N.J.: Prentice-Hall, 1975; North Hollywood, Ca.: Wilshire Books, 1975. An updated version of *Guide to Rational Living*, available in both hardcover and paperback. Ellis and Harper give an introduction to rational-emotive theory and explain how the techniques can be used in helping nonprofessionals solve their emotional problems. Included are such topics as "how far can you go with self-analysis?", "how you create your own feelings," "recognizing and attacking neurotic behaviors," "overcoming the influences of the past," "controlling your own destiny," and "conquering anxiety." This is probably the most commonly recommended self-help book used by rational-emotive therapists.

Help Yourself to Happiness by M. Maultsby, Jr. New York: Institute for Rational Living, 1975. Explains the system of rational behavior training and how clients can use this approach as a self-help technique. There is specific emphasis on the problems of alcohol and drug abuse.

You and Your Emotions by M. Maultsby, Jr., and A. Hendricks. Lexington, Ky.: Maxie C. Maultsby, 1974. A cartoon version of rational behavior therapy which gives examples of how RET can help clients overcome their emotional problems. It has many illustrations and easy readability and is useful for less educated clients.

A Rational Counseling Primer by H. Young. New York: Institute for Rational Living, 1974. A useful brief introduction to the basic concepts of RET, often prescribed by rational therapists as preliminary reading. It is particularly useful for adolescents, who find its style and illustrations quite interesting. It is also an important resource for adult clients whose reading skills are limited.

Pamphlets: Two pamphlets are recommended for clients who want a very brief introduction to RET. The first is "The No Cop-out Therapy" by A. Ellis, reprinted from *Psychology Today*, 1973. A somewhat shorter paper is "The Essence of Rational Psychotherapy: A Comprehensive Approach to Treatment" by A. Ellis. A pamphlet that may help your client prepare written homework assignments is "Techniques for Disrupting Irrational Beliefs (DIBS)" by A. Ellis. It provides clear models for filling out a self-help form and beginning a disputation.

Tapes: Two tapes available from the Institute may be useful for clients who are unwilling or unable to do reading assignments. The first, "Solving Emotional Problems," is a talk that Ellis gave to a college audience. This thirty-minute recording is a basic review of the ABC theory and its application to emotional disturbance. The second, "Rational Living in an Irrational World," was made by Ellis in 1963. It shows Ellis at his delightfully irreverent best. He discusses acceptance of those irrationalities which we cannot control and points out that we do have some ability to control or at least select our environment. He reminds us that we can be happy in an often unpleasant and quite irrational world.

BEHAVIOR THERAPY

For the therapist who is not well schooled in the theory and practice of behavior therapy, the following references are useful:

Clinical Behavior Therapy by M. R. Goldfried and G. R. Davison. New York: Holt, Rinehart and Winston, 1976. A good reference for therapists who wish to learn more about behavior therapy and its techniques. It includes chapters on relaxation training, systematic desensitization, behavior rehearsal, cognitive re-labeling, problem solving, and reinforcement procedures. Chapters are also de-voted to specific clinical problems, an extended case illustration, and ethics of behavior change.

Multi-Modal Behavior Therapy by A. A. Lazarus and contributors. New York: Springer, 1975. Lazarus presents his acronym for his sytem of therapy: BASIC ID, which stands for Behavior, Affect, Sensation, Imagery, Cognition, Interper-sonal relations and Drugs. Lazarus' theme is that the assessment and treatment of clients in behavior therapy had better be far ranging, covering many aspects of their psychological, behavioral, and physiological functioning.

Clinical Guide to Behavior Therapy by S. R. Walen, N. Hauserman, and P. Lavin. New York: Oxford University Press, 1977. A comprehensive, problem-oriented text that focuses on twenty-eight specific symptoms or syndromes. Each topic includes a discussion of the problem, relevant statistical information, the nonbehavioral treatments most commonly used, and the behavioral treat-ments described for the new practitioner. Each chapter includes illustrative case histories which describe the clinical problem more concretely, provide detailed instruction on the application of a specific behavioral technique, or discuss pit-falls to avoid. Major headings include: eating problems, bladder and bowel problems, addictive behaviors, fearful behaviors, sexual problems, repetitive dysfunctional behaviors, and physiological problems.

Also helpful is the tape recording "Cognitive Behavior Therapy," a talk by Ellis given in 1972 at the Association for the Advancement of Be-havior Therapy annual meeting. Ellis emphasizes the connection be-tween behavior therapy and rational-emotive therapy and points out the interactive view of human activity. That is, we perceive, cognize, emote, and act, each of these behavioral elements affecting the other. Each, therefore, is an appropriate focus for a cognitive-behavior therapist.

RET AND SEXUAL PROBLEMS

Professional References

The Art and Science of Love by A. Ellis. New York: Lyle Stewart, 1960. Perhaps one of Ellis' original important writings, useful for both therapist and client. It includes discussions of the entire range of sexual issues, from a description of human sexual apparatus to techniques of sex play to overcoming sexual inadequacy, as well as such topics as sterility, fertility, pregnancy, and birth control.

The New Sex Therapy: Active Treatment of Sexual Dysfunctions by H. S. Kaplan. New York: Brunner/Mazel Publishers, 1974. A comprehensive treatment of sexual problems, with a review of basic concepts in human sexuality, etiology of sexual dysfunctions, and their treatment. Although the author is a psychiatrist with psychoanalytic training, her approach to sex therapy focuses directly on the relief of the sexual problem and is more akin to cognitive and learning-theory approaches to this clinical population. This book is very well illustrated.

Handbook of Sex Therapy, edited by J. LoPiccolo and L. LoPiccolo. New York: Plenum Press, 1978. An integrated sourcebook covering a broad range of therapy approaches designed for the rapid treatment of sexual dysfunctions. It is a collection of articles reprinted from professional journals and books, plus ten contributions prepared especially for this volume. Major section headings are: An Overview of Sex Therapy; Female Orgasmic Dysfunction; Dysparunia and Vaginismus; Male Orgasmic Dysfunctions; Male Erectile Dysfunction; Sexual Dysfunction in Special Populations: Group Procedures; Comments on Sex Therapy and other Therapeutic Approaches to Sex Dysfunction; and Professional Issues. We would recommend this book to therapists who wish to increase their expertise in the rapidly expanding field of sexual counseling.

Human Sexual Inadequacy by W. H. Masters and V. E. Johnson. Boston: Little, Brown and Co., 1970. A classic reference for the professional new to the field of sex therapy. The book presents the now-famous study of sexual dysfunctions and the treatment procedures used by Masters and Johnson at the Reproductive Biology Research Foundation in St. Louis. The authors' dual-therapist model for treatment of the couple is introduced, using both physiological and psychological methods of treating impotence, ejaculatory incompetence, premature ejaculation, orgasmic dysfunction, vaginismus, and painful intercourse. Although the authors are perhaps not the clearest writers, the therapist-in-training should certainly review this landmark book.

For the Client

For Yourself: The Fulfillment of Female Sexuality by L. Barbach. New York: Doubleday and Co., 1975. Outlines a step-by-step program for educating women to their bodies and their sexuality. The author discusses sources of sexual confusion, describes female anatomy and physiology, prescribes special exercises, explores the role of the partner, and much more. The book shows how women can achieve orgasm and strive for greater fulfillment of their sexual potential. The book is based on experiences of many of the women who attended female sexuality workshops with the author. Their insights and comments are included as useful models and examples.

Our Bodies, Our Selves: A Book by and for Women by the Boston Women's Health Book Collective. New York: Simon & Schuster, 1976. Written for women and helps to teach them about their bodies in order to control them. Topics covered include: the anatomy and physiology of sexuality and reproduction; sexuality; sexual relationships; gay women; rape; self-defense; venereal disease; birth control; abortion; parenthood; menopause; and women and health care. This book is recommended for any female client, especially one with health or sexual concerns.

Liberating Masturbation by B. Dodson. New York: Bodysex Designs, 1974. A consciousness-raising discussion about female sexuality and masturbation. It presents a very positive and healthy view of masturbation, with many examples and quotations from women who have learned to be more sex-positive. The author is also an artist and includes many lovely illustrations of women's genitals, depicting the variety of anatomy and encouraging acceptance of one's own body.

One of Ellis' unique contributions to the topic of sexuality has been his willingness to write for the lay public, to explain and to teach about human sexuality, its problems, and ways to deal with them. The following books are among his most helpful in this series:

The Art of Erotic Seduction by A. Ellis and R. O. Conway. New York: Ace Books, 1967. A useful primer for men who have never had their basic questions about sexuality answered. This brief paperback is unique, addressing itself to questions discussed in virtually no other source: questions such as "How do you kiss?" "What is meant by light petting?" and "How does one remove a woman's bra gracefully?" These are the kinds of questions that young men are often too embarrassed to ask their fathers yet are supposed to know automatically. Although this book has a chauvinistic slant, we nevertheless recommend it as an important skill builder.

Sex and the Liberated Man by A. Ellis. Secaucus, N.J.: Lyle Stewart, 1976. A more advanced and more contemporary hardcover version of the above, including a much broader and more detailed set of topics. The focus is on male sexuality, but the book is equally valuable for female clients. It discusses such topics as masturbation, the sexuality of women, how to handle sex problems, and how to avoid sexual disturbance.

Sex Without Guilt by A. Ellis. North Hollywood, Ca.: Wilshire Book Co., 1977. Attacks the myths and misconceptions with which patients unfortunately upset themselves on topics of sexuality. The focus of the book is permission giving and guilt reduction. Topics include premarital sexual relations, adultery, justification of sex without love, sexual censorship, sex education, myths about love, and the right to sexual enjoyment.

The Civilized Couple's Guide to Extra-Marital Adventure by A. Ellis. New York: Pinnacle Books, 1972. Discusses the pro's and con's of extramarital sexuality. It does not recommend extramarital adventuring but rationally discusses its advantages and disadvantages in various settings. It describes how to handle some of the problems that may arise from extramarital sexual encounters, as well as how one can be happily monogamous in a nonmonogamous world.

There are also three items (published by the Institute for Rational Living) of interest for therapists interested in *feminist therapy* and how RET relates to women's problems. The first is a pamphlet by J. Wolfe entitled "Rational-Emotive Therapy as an Effective Feminist Therapy," reprinted from *Rational Living,* 1975. In this delightful paper, Wolfe analyzes some of the problems which prevent women from maximizing their happiness in love-sex relationships. A second pamphlet by Wolfe is "How to Be Sexually Assertive," published in 1976. In this pamphlet, the author specifically discusses the irrational beliefs which prevent women from assuming responsibility for their own sexuality, their own sexual pleasure, and their own orgasms. It is very helpful for women with sexual concerns. The third item is a tape recording entitled "Rational-Emotive Therapy and Women's Problems" by Wolfe, in which she proposes a new model for consciousness-raising groups that incorporates RET and is conducted by trained leaders. Wolfe discusses some of the problems of women, including love needs, sexuality and sexual expression, guilt, and assertiveness issues.

There are a number of tape recordings on the topic of sexuality which your clients might find useful. "The Psychology of Sex," by Ellis, is a talk originally given in 1971 in which two major irrational ideas are discussed: a problem of men ("I must have gigantic erections to satisfy women") and of females ("I must have a man or I'm nothing"). In this talk, Ellis disputes these irrational notions and then answers questions from the audience. A second tape is called "Sex, Sanity and Psychotherapy," an address to the American Humanist Society in 1960. Ellis addresses the issues of guilt and shame about sexuality and disputes the irrational beliefs which lead to these two problematic, sexually inhibiting emotions. A third tape by Ellis is called "Harmful Sexual Myths and How to Exorcise Them." This extended recording analyzes the most commonly held misconceptions about male and female sexuality and shows how one can enhance sexual pleasure by liberating oneself from their crippling influence.

RATIONAL-EMOTIVE THERAPY IN MARITAL COUNSELING

For the Professional

Handbook of Marriage Counseling by B. N. Ard and C. C. Ard. Palo Alto, Ca.: Science and Behavior Books, 1976. Consists of fifty chapters grouped under the following major subheadings: the place of philosophy and values in marriage counseling; theoretical issues and viewpoints; joint marriage counseling; group marriage counseling; premarital counseling; special techniques in marriage counseling; counseling regarding sexual problems; professional issues and ethics; divorce counseling; and technical assistance for the marriage and family counselor. The contributors represent the disciplines of psychiatry, psychology, sociology, social work, medicine, law, and the ministry. The book is a convenient and comprehensive reference for marriage and divorce counselors.

Two items useful for the marriage counselor are, first, "The Nature of Disturbed Marital Interaction" by Ellis, originally presented at the American Psychological Association convention in 1964. In this paper Ellis gives his view of the causes of disturbed marital interaction, stressing the importance of irrational premises leading to disturbed emotions. The second item of interest is a tape recording by Ellis entitled "RET and Marriage and Family Counseling," a talk originally given in 1972. This outlines a typical rational-emotive counseling session, including discussion of the use of rational-emotive imagery, self-management, and other techniques in treatment of marital and sexual difficulties. In the example described, the couple present emotions of anger, depression, and resentment, as well as diminished sexual involvement. Ellis illustrates how he keeps the focus on the individuals, each in turn, in order to improve their relationship.

For the Client

A Guide to Successful Marriage by A. Ellis and R. Harper. North Hollywood, Ca.: Wilshire Book Co., 1974. Discusses topics such as gauging marital compatibility, problem solving in marriage, sexual preparation for marriage, non-monogamous desires, communication in marriage, and divorce. It also lists a directory of marriage counseling services and has a good selection of suggested readings for the therapist in marriage counseling training.

Marriage Is a Loving Business by P. A. Hauck. Philadelphia: The Westminster Press, 1977. Shows what marriage can be when both husband and wife understand it as a partnership. Hauck describes the real reason why people form such a partnership and what pitfalls the couple is likely to encounter. The book includes many case histories and examples drawn from Hauck's private practice and is written in an easy-to-read style that makes it appropriate reading for clients.

"How to Be Happy Though Mated" is a tape recorded lecture given by Ellis at the Institute. Ellis rationally evaluates the advantages and disadvantages of being mated and points out cognitive blocks to happy mating and some solutions to these blocks. He provides valuable insights and practical solutions to the myriad communication problems and conflicts that beset the mated or about-to-be-mated.

RATIONAL-EMOTIVE THERAPY WITH CHILDREN

For Professionals and Clients

Instant Replay by S. Bedford. New York: Institute for Rational Living, 1974. This small paperback is illustrated with cartoon drawings and offers an example of what the author calls a "rough spot," a situation that results in unpleasant emotions. The story describes how the child recognizes a feeling, teaches the child to replay the situation descriptively in order to teach more accurate perception, to understand what the child was thinking at the time of the event, to come up with other behavioral options for handling the situation, and to evaluate the consequences of the various options. The book, therefore, illustrates a combination of RET and social problem-solving approaches.

I Have Feelings by T. Berger. New York: Human Sciences Press, 1971. Geared for a young audience (ages four to nine) and presents seventeen different feelings, both good and bad, as precipitated by different life situations. Each feeling is then explained in a rational therapeutic approach and is illustrated by sensitive and realistic photographs. The book would be useful for children to read themselves, or preferably to serve as a basis for discussion with therapist, parent, teacher, or counselor.

How to Raise an Emotionally Healthy, Happy Child by A. Ellis. North Hollywood, Ca.: Wilshire Book Co., 1977. A retitled version of the 1966 text "How to Prevent Your Child from Becoming a Neurotic Adult." It illustrates how rational-emotive therapy can be directly applied to helping children overcome specific problems. Chapter headings include: Helping Children Overcome Fears and Anxieties; Helping Children with Problems of Achievement; Helping Children Overcome Hostility; Helping Children Become Self-disciplined; Helping Children with Sex Problems; Helping Children with Conduct Problems; Helping Children with Personal Behavior Problems; and How to Live with a Neurotic Child and Like It. This book shows parents how to teach their children to cope with a harsh world, to refuse to catastrophize about dangers, to accept themselves as worthwhile human beings even when they fail, and to prepare them to enter adolescence and adulthood with maximal self-acceptance and a better ability to overcome the stresses of modern life.

Homer the Homely Hound Dog by E. J. Garcia and N. Pellegrini. New York: Institute for Rational Living, 1974. This children's story is illustrated with line drawings and is appropriate for children from about five to ten years of age. Homer the homely hound learns how to overcome his shyness and self-downing attitudes with the help of his canine friends, who suggest both cognitive and behavioral techniques to help Homer overcome his problems. This is a good book for therapists to recommend, to stimulate discussion between the child and his or her parents or teacher.

The Rational Management of Children by P. A. Hauck. New York: Libra Publishers, 1967. Written for the parent, this book discusses techniques of child management, habits of kindness and firmness, and discipline. It includes five chapters on fears: of people, of failure, of injury, of rejection, and of ridicule. Further chapters deal with anger, worry and depression, lack of self-discipline, and undesirable habits. The book presents, in clear language, treatment methods for the most commonly encountered problems of early childhood through the teens.

Pamphlets: "Counseling Strategies with Working Class Adolescents," by H. Young, is a paper presented at the first National Conference on Rational Psychotherapy in 1975. The author discusses how to develop a relationship with this client population, defining the problem, teaching the principles of rational thinking, and encouraging change.

For the Teacher

Rational-Emotive Education: A Manual for Elementary School Teachers by W. J. Knaus. New York: Institute for Rational Living, 1974. Discusses the nature of rational-emotive education as applied by teachers in a classroom setting. This paperback includes many examples of activities and exercises which the teacher can use to teach the following concepts: feelings, the art of challenging irrational beliefs, challenging feelings of inferiority, challenging concepts of human worth, and challenging philosophies of demanding and catastrophizing. It also deals with the special topics of responsibility, stereotyping, teasing, bullying, and friendship patterns. The book would be appropriate for use with children of ages seven to thirteen.

PROBLEMS OF ANGER

For the Professional and the Client

How to Live With and Without Anger by A. Ellis. New York: Readers Digest Press, 1977. The rational-emotive theory and therapy for anger control, comparing this technique to other points of view and thus giving a comprehensive and critical analysis of the problem of anger. Chapter headings include: Looking for Self-angering Philosophies; Disputing Your Self-angering Philosophies; Acting Your Way out of Your Anger; Ripping up Your Rationalizations for Remaining Angry; Accepting Yourself with Your Anger.

Overcoming Frustration and Anger by P. A. Hauck. Philadelphia: The Westminster Press, 1974. An easy-to-understand explanation of the ABC's of angry emotions, the thinking process that is the common human denominator of anger. Hauck points out that by blaming people or events and reacting with anger, hostility, and rage to frustration, reactions will backfire and ultimately be self-destructive, preventing one from handling the problem and producing emotional distress. The book presents RET techniques for correcting blame cognitions and suggests techniques for coping with frustration and for being firm without being angry.

A pamphlet on anger is Ellis' "Healthy and Unhealthy Aggression," originally presented at the American Psychological Association convention, 1973. Ellis discusses the meaning of the term *aggression*, pointing out its ambiguous use by others. He attempts to distinguish healthy forms of aggression (those that are based on rational cognitions) from unhealthy ones (those based on irrational cognitions). He states that if we educationally and psychotherapeutically help ourselves to understand what our goals and purposes are, and how certain forms of aggression tend to either encourage or block these goals, and if we incisively change the intolerant cognitions by which we create unhealthy forms of aggression, we may well survive more happily.

PROBLEMS OF ANXIETY

How to Master Your Fear of Flying by A. Ellis. New York: Institute for Rational Living, 1978. Describes how the author overcame his own fear of flying, thus providing a useful model for the application of rational-emotive therapy to a specific fear. An important contribution of this book is a discussion of anxiety about death and dying. Ellis discusses techniques for acting against anxiety and for confronting the specific fears of the individual who has an airplane phobia.

Overcoming Worry and Fear by P. A. Hauck. Philadelphia: The Westminster Press, 1975. Gives practical techniques for relaxing uptight feelings and learning to take problems in stride. Hauck explains rational-emotive therapy and teaches how fears and worries are generated by irrational beliefs. In the case of fear, the major irrational belief that is challenged is that if something is dangerous or fearsome, one ought to think about it at all times, dwell upon it endlessly, and never let it out of one's mind. The book gives numerous examples of persons who have learned to question their faulty philosophy and to handle situations with a feeling of calm and accomplishment. The book is useful for both therapist and client.

A useful paper for students who suffer from test anxiety is "Overcoming Test Anxiety" by R. Oliver, reprinted from *Rational Living*, 1975. Oliver discusses and disputes irrational beliefs which maintain test anxiety and gives both cognitive and behavioral techniques for overcoming test anxiety. The paper is easy to read and well organized, with subheadings which make its points clear to the student.   ·
    A tape recording on anxiety by Ellis is entitled "Twenty-one Ways to Stop Worrying." Ellis reviews a large number of palliative techniques to stop worrying, some more helpful than others—all, however, temporary and inelegant diversionary techniques. He then discusses a more

elegant series of procedures that the anxious individual can use to diminish anxiety and teaches the listener how to engage in anti-awfulizing cognitive and behavioral techniques.

PROBLEMS OF DEPRESSION

Cognitive Therapy of Depression: A Treatment Manual by A. T. Beck, A. J. Rush, B. F. Shaw, and G. Emery. Copyright, A. T. Beck, 1978. Recommended to therapists working with depressed clients. Chapter headings include: The Therapeutic Relationship; The Initial Interview; Session by Session Treatment; Application of Behavioral Techniques; Cognitive Techniques; Specific Techniques for the Suicidal Patient; Homework; and Termination of Therapy. The manual is detailed and provides many concrete suggestions for the therapist, including segments of therapist-patient dialogues.

Overcoming Depression by P. A. Hauck. Philadelphia: The Westminster Press, 1976. Shows the reader three main reasons for emotional depression and what one can do about them. The first reason is self-downing, the second is self-pity, and the third is other-pity. Hauck discusses techniques for attitude change, ways to correct these three erroneous beliefs and thereby to reduce depression. This book is an excellent and readable sourcebook for clients as well.

Pamphlets: The following three papers may be helpful to clients. (1) "Thinking and Depression" by A. T. Beck, reprinted from *Archives of General Psychiatry*, 1963. Beck discusses the kinds of cognitions that lead to depression, including low self-regard, ideas of deprivation, self-criticisms and self-blame, overwhelming duties, self-commands and injunctions, and escape and suicidal wishes. (2) "Coping with Depression" by A. T. Beck and R. L. Greenberg, 1974. This paper is particularly useful for clients, helping them not only to examine their cognitive systems with a checklist of negative thoughts but providing space for a weekly activity schedule and seven simple solutions to the problems of depression. It is a simple and very portable self-help paper. (3) "An RET Theory of Depression" by P. A. Hauck, reprinted from *Rational Living*, 1971. This is a brief review of the three sources of depression outlined by Hauck in his book described above, and may be a useful reminder sheet for the client.

ASSERTIVENESS TRAINING

Your Perfect Right by R. Alberti and M. Emmons. San Luis Obispo, Ca.: Impact Press, 1974. A classic book on assertiveness training, including not only a complete discussion of assertive behavior but a description of therapist preparation for beginning assertiveness training, diagnosis of assertiveness problems, instruction on how to run an assertiveness group, and applications of assertiveness training to various populations and in various settings.

Responsible Assertive Behavior: Cognitive-Behavioral Procedures for Trainers by A. Lange and P. Jakubowski. Champaign, Ill.: Research Press, 1976. An excellent resource for the therapist who wants to learn more about problems of nonassertiveness and therapeutic techniques for dealing with them. Chapter headings include: Structured Exercises; Cognitive Restructuring Procedures; Behavior Rehearsal Procedures; Modeling and Behavior Rehearsal Procedures; Planning and Conducting Stages in the Life of an Assertion Group; Theme-oriented Assertion Groups; Assertion Training and Consciousness-raising Groups; Specific Applications of Training Groups; Assessment Procedures; and Ethical Considerations. The book is unusually comprehensive and well organized.

I Can If I Want To by A. Lazarus and A. Fay. New York: William Morrow and Co., 1975. This book discusses a number of erroneous notions with which individuals block their own assertiveness and outlines an easy-to-read, step-by-step program of change. The three steps are (1) understanding basic mistakes that ruin your life, (2) understanding the faulty assumptions underlying these mistakes, and (3) applying techniques to combat the mistakes by changing your thinking and your behavior. The book is clear and concise and is organized for quick reading and easy reference.

PROBLEMS OF PROCRASTINATION

Overcoming Procrastination by A. Ellis and W. J. Knaus. New York: Institute for Rational Living, 1977. Defines procrastination and its main causes, as well as teaching a rational approach to overcoming the problem. Chapter headings include: Overcoming Procrastination Stemming from Self-downing; Overcoming Procrastination Resulting from Low Frustration Tolerance; Overcoming Procrastination Resulting from Hostility; Overcoming Other Emotional Problems Resulting from Procrastination; Behavioral Methods of Overcoming Procrastination; Emotive Methods of Overcoming Procrastination; and Impediments to Overcoming Procrastination. The book concludes with a verbatim psychotherapy session with a procrastinator.

Two items by William Knaus may be useful to the client. One is a pamphlet entitled "Overcoming Procrastination," reprinted from *Rational Living*, 1973. In this paper, Knaus outlines the irrational bases for procrastination, points out why people resist changing their procrastination tendencies, and then discusses specific procedures for overcoming procrastination. Second, Knaus can be heard on tape; the recording is called "Overcoming Procrastination" and is a discussion of the problem as given at one of the public education workshops at the Institute. Knaus discusses the dynamics of procrastination and provides a host of techniques to help one stop goofing and start living.

PROBLEMS OF BAD HABITS

Permanent Weight Control: A Total Solution to the Dieter's Dilemma by M. Mahoney and K. Mahoney. New York: W. W. Norton & Co., 1976. Focuses on both a cognitive and a behavior approach to problems of overweight and outlines a step-by-step program for gathering information about eating habits and attitudes and changing both. Chapter headings include: The Elements of Successful Self-Control; Cognitive Ecology; Engineering a Slim Environment; Reducing with Reason; and Troubleshooting and Maintenance.

Pamphlets: Two papers on weight loss may be recommended. The first is "A Rational Approach to Obesity" by I. Greenberg. The author outlines various reasons for obesity and for excess food consumption, emphasizing the dieter's inability to tolerate deprivation, an irrational belief which he disputes. The second pamphlet is "The Psychology of Dieting" by J. Geis. Geis outlines thirty-two techniques to help the dieter stay on task, including both cognitive (tackling your "need" to eat) and behavioral (using principles of reward, penalty, response-cost, and self-monitoring) methods.

Tapes: For the individual who is trying to give up a bad habit, whether smoking, drinking, overeating, or any other, the following tape recording will be very helpful. It is "I'd Like to Stop But..." by A. Ellis, and deals with the need for immediate gratification, overcoming the "tomorrow" and "I deserve to have it easier" attitude, and how not to down oneself for one's bad habits. Again, both cognitive and behavioral procedures are described and illustrated for the patient.

References

Alberti, R. and Emmons, M. *Your Perfect Right.* San Luis Obispo, Calif.: Impact Press, 1974.

Allen, G., Chinsky, J., Larcen, S., Lockman, J., and Selinger, H. *Community Psychology and the Schools: A Behaviorally Oriented Multilevel Preventive Approach.* Hillsdale, N.J.: Erlbaum, 1976.

Beck, A. T. *Cognitive Therapy and the Emotional Disorders.* New York: International Universities Press, 1976.

Beck, A. T., Rush, A. J., Shaw, B: F., and Emery, G. *Cognitive Therapy of Depression: A Treatment Manual.* Copyright by A. T. Beck, 1978.

Camp, B. Verbal mediation in young aggressive boys. Unpublished manuscript, University of Colorado School of Medicine, 1975.

Carkhuff, R. *Helping and Human Relations: A Primer for Lay and Professional Helpers.* New York: Holt, Rinehart and Winston, 1969.

Cautela, J. and Baron, M. Covert conditioning: A theoretical analogy. *Behavior Modification,* 1977, *1,* 351–368.

Davison, G. C. and Neale, J. M. *Abnormal Psychology: An Experimental Clinical Approach.* New York: Wiley, 1974.

Dyer, W. *Your Erroneous Zones.* New York: Funk and Wagnalls and Avon Books, 1976.

D'Zurilla, T. and Goldfried, M. R. Problem-solving and behavior modification. *Journal of Abnormal Psychology,* 1971, *78,* 107–126.

Ellis, A. Requisite conditions for basic personality change. *Journal of Consulting Psychology,* 1959, *6,* 538–540.

Ellis, A. *Reason and Emotion in Psychotherapy.* New York: Lyle Stuart, 1962.

Ellis, A. *The Essence of Rational Psychotherapy: A Comprehensive Approach to Treatment.* New York: Institute for Rational Living, 1969.(a)

Ellis, A. A cognitive approach to behavior therapy. *International Journal of Psychiatry,* 1969, *8,* 896–900.(b)

Ellis, A. *Growth Through Reason.* No. Hollywood, Calif.: Wilshire Books, 1971.

Ellis, A. Helping people get better rather than merely feel better. *Rational Living,* 1972, *7,* 2–9.

Ellis, A. *Humanistic Psychotherapy.* New York: Crown Publishers and McGraw-Hill Paperbacks, 1973.

Ellis, A. The education and training of a rational-emotive therapist. *Voices,* 1974, *10,* 35–37.(a)

Ellis, A. The treatment of sex and love problems in women. In V. Franks and V. Burtle (Eds.), *Women in Therapy.* New York: Brunner/Mazel, 1974.(b)

Ellis, A. The biological basis of human irrationality. *Journal of Individual Psychology,* 1976, *32,* 145–168.

Ellis, A. The basic clinical theory of rational-emotive therapy. In A. Ellis and R. Grieger (Eds.), *Handbook of Rational-Emotive Therapy.* New York: Springer, 1977.(a)

Ellis, A. *How to Live With—and Without—Anger.* New York: Reader's Digest Press, 1977.(b)

Ellis, A. Conquering low frustration tolerance. Cassette Recording. New York: Institute for Rational Living, 1977.(c)

Ellis, A. Fun as psychotherapy. Cassette Recording. New York: Institute for Rational Living, 1977. Also in A. Ellis and R. Grieger (Eds.), *Handbook of Rational-Emotive Therapy.* New York: Springer, 1977.(d)

Ellis, A. Research data supporting the clinical and personality hypotheses of RET and other cognitive-behavior therapies. *Counseling Psychologist,* 1977, *7,* 2–43.(e)

Ellis, A. Discomfort anxiety: A new cognitive-behavioral construct. Invited address to the Association for Advancement of Behavior Therapy Annual Meeting, November 17, 1978. New York: BMA Audiotapes and Association for Advancement of Behavior Therapy, 1978.(a)

Ellis, A. Rational-emotive therapy and self-help therapy. *Rational Living,* 1978, *13,* 3–6.(b)

Ellis, A. Rational-emotive therapy. In R. J. Corsini (Ed.), *Current Psychotherapies,* 2nd edition. Itasca, Ill.: Peacock, 1979.(a)

Ellis, A. *Theoretical and Empirical Foundations of Rational-Emotive Therapy*. Monterey, Calif.: Brooks/Cole, 1979.(b)

Ellis, A. A note on the treatment of agoraphobics with cognitive modification versus prolonged exposure *in vivo*. *Behavior Research and Therapy*, 1979, in press.(c)

Ellis, A. and Abrahms, E. *Brief Psychotherapy in Medical and Health Practice*. New York: Springer, 1978.

Ellis, A. and Grieger, R. *A Handbook of Rational-Emotive Therapy*. New York: Springer, 1977.

Ellis, A. and Harper, R. *A New Guide to Rational Living*. Englewood Cliffs, N.J.: Prentice-Hall, 1975.

Ellis, A. and Knaus, W. *Overcoming Procrastination*. New York: Institute for Rational Living, 1977.

Eriksen, M., Rossi, E., and Rossi, S. *Hypnotic Realities*. New York: Irvington Press, 1976.

Eysenck, H. *Experiments in Behavior Therapy*. New York: Macmillan, 1964.

Fay, A. *Making Things Better by Making Them Worse*. New York: Hawthorn Press, 1978.

Fodor, I. Cognitive behavior therapy and couples conflict. Paper presented at the Second National Cognitive-Behavior Therapy Research Conference, New York, 1978.

Goldfried, M. R. and Davison, G. C. *Clinical Behavior Therapy*. New York: Holt, Rinehart and Winston, 1976.

Goldstein, A. J. and Chambless, D. L. A reanalysis of agoraphobia. *Behavior Therapy*, 1978, *9*, 47–59.

Harlow, H. F. The nature of love. *American Psychologist*, 1958, *13*, 673–685.

Hauck, P. A. *Overcoming Depression*. Philadelphia: Westminster Press, 1974.

Hauck, P. A. *Overcoming Frustration and Anger*. Philadelphia: Westminster Press, 1974.

Horney, K. *Our Inner Conflicts*. New York: Norton, 1945.

Jacobson, N. J. and Martin, B. Behavioral marriage therapy: Current status. *Psychological Bulletin*, 1976, *83*, 540–556.

Johnson, W. *People in Quandaries*. New York: Harper and Brothers, 1946.

Kassinove, H. and DiGiuseppe, R. Rational role reversal. *Rational Living*, 1975, *10*, 44–45.

Kelly, G. *The Psychology of Personal Constructs*, Volumes I and II. New York: Norton, 1955.

Kimmel, J. The rational barb in the treatment of social rejection. *Rational Living*, 1976, *11*, 23–25.

Kubler-Ross, E. *On Death and Dying*. New York: Macmillan, 1969.

Lazarus, A. A. *Behavior Therapy and Beyond*. New York: McGraw-Hill, 1972.

Lazarus, A. A. *Multimodal Therapy*. New York: Springer, 1976.

Lazarus, A. A. Film: Broad-Spectrum Behavior Therapy in Groups. Available in rental from Pennsylvania State University, University Park, Pa. 16802.

Lazarus, A. A. Tape recording: Learning to Relax. Available from the Institute for Rational-Emotive Therapy, 45 E. 65th St., New York, N. Y. 10021.

Lembo, J. *The Counseling Process: A Rational Behavioral Approach*. New York: Libra, 1976.

Luria, A. Speech and formation of mental processes. In M. Cole and I. Maltzman (Eds.), *A Handbook of Contemporary Soviet Psychology*. New York: Basic Books, 1969.

Mahoney, M. Personal science: A cognitive learning therapy. In A. Ellis and R. Grieger (Eds.), *A Handbook of Rational-Emotive Therapy*. New York: Springer, 1977.

Marks, J., Boulougouris, J., and Marset, P. Flooding vs desensitization in the treatment of phobic patients. *British Journal of Psychiatry*, 1971, *119*, 353–375.

Maultsby, M. *Help Yourself to Happiness*. New York: Institute for Rational Living, 1975.

Maultsby, M. and Ellis, A. *Techniques for Using Rational-Emotive Imagery*. New York: Institute for Rational Living, 1974.

Meichenbaum, D. Therapist manual for cognitive behavior modification. Unpublished manuscript, University of Waterloo, 1973.

Meichenbaum, D. *Cognitive Behavior Modification*. New York: Plenum Press, 1977.

Morris, K. T. and Kanitz, H. M. *Rational-Emotive Therapy*. Boston: Houghton Mifflin, 1975.

Neisser, V. *Cognitive Psychology*. New York: Appleton-Century-Crofts, 1967.

Novaco, R. W. *Anger Control*. Lexington, Mass.: Heath, 1975.

O'Leary, D. and Borkovec, T. Conceptual, methodological, and ethical problems of placebo groups in psychotherapy research. *American Psychologist*, 1978, 33, 821–830.

Powell, J. *Fully Human, Fully Alive.* Niles, Ill.: Argus, 1976.

Protinsky, H. and Popp, R. Irrational philosophies in popular music. *Cognitive Therapy and Research*, 1978, 2, 71–74.

Rachman, S., Marks, I. M., and Hodgson, R. The treatment of obsessive-compulsive neurotics by modelling and flooding *in vivo. Behavior Research and Therapy*, 1973, 11, 463–471.

Raimey, V. *Misunderstandings of the Self: Cognitive Psychotherapy and the Misconception Hypothesis.* San Francisco, Calif.: Josey-Bass, 1975.

Raush, H., Barry, W., Hertel, R., and Swain, M. *Communications, Conflicts, and Marriage.* San Francisco, Calif.: Josey-Bass, 1974.

Rogers, C. *Client-Centered Therapy.* Boston, Mass.: Houghton Mifflin, 1951.

Rogers, C. The necessary and sufficient conditions of therapeutic personality change. *Journal of Consulting Psychology*, 1957, 21, 459–461.

Sobel, H. Panel discussion, presented at the Second National Cognitive-Behavior Therapy Research Conference, New York, 1978.

Spivack, G., Platt, J., and Shure, M. *The Problem-Solving Approach to Adjustment.* San Francisco, Calif.: Josey-Bass, 1976.

Thibaut, J. and Kelley, H. *The Social Psychology of Groups.* New York: Wiley, 1959.

Tosi, D. J. *Youth: Toward Personal Growth.* Columbus, Oh.: Merrill, 1974.

Tosi, D. J. and Reardon, J. The treatment of guilt through rational stage directed therapy. *Rational Living*, 1976, 11, 8–11.

Vygotsky, L. *Thought and Language.* New York: Wiley, 1962.

Walen, S. R., Hauserman, N., and Lavin, P. *A Clinical Guide to Behavior Therapy.* New York: Oxford University Press, 1977.

Wegner, D. M. and Vallacher, R. R. *Implicit Psychology: An Introduction to Social Cognition.* New York: Oxford University Press, 1977.

Wessler, R. and Ellis, A. Supervision in rational-emotive therapy. In A. K. Hess (Ed.), *Psychotherapy Supervision.* New York: Wiley, 1979.

Wolfe, J. L. Rational-emotive therapy as an effective feminist therapy. *Rational Living*, 1975, 11, 1–6.

Wolpe, J. *The Practice of Behavior Therapy.* New York: Pergamon, 1973.

Yates, A. J. *Behavior Therapy.* New York: Wiley, 1970.

Answer Key

Chapter 3:

1. I did poorly on that exam—*Activating event.*
   Oh, I'm such a failure—*self-evaluation.*
2. No one talks to me—*Activating event.*
   I just can't stand being so alone—*hedonic evaluation.*
3. My mother's always picking on me. I know she hates me.—
   Activating event (no evaluation stated).
4. Doctor, the most terrible thing happened last week—*evaluation of Activating event.*
   My wife told me she wanted a divorce—*Activating event.*
5. I ate like a pig—*Activating event.*
   You see, I know now that I'm really no good—*evaluative conclusion about self.*
6. I only make $30,000—*Activating event.* (The word "only" implies an evaluation, however.)
   Do you call that success? How can I be satisfied with that?—*evaluation of Activating event expressed as rhetorical questions.*
7. I had a marvelous time with George—*Activating event.*
   It makes me feel so important that he loves me—*self-evaluation.*

Chapter 5:

All statements in the exercise are *rational beliefs,* expressing an evaluation but not an absolutistic demand.

Chapter 8:

Sample cognitions leading to *depression:*
>   I'll never be able to get what I want.
>   Others have it better than I.
>   I can't cope.

Sample cognitions leading to *pity:*
>   How awful not to get what I want!
>   Poor me!

Sample cognitions leading to *mirth:*
>   It's great to be alive!
>   What a wonderful time I had!

Chapter 10:

Sample coping statements:

(a) 1. Yelling won't help anything. Try to state your ideas clearly without yelling and sounding angry.
  2. Calm down a little. When I raise my voice, it's a sign I'd better calm down.
  3. It's working! I'm not escalating the argument.

(b) 1. There is nothing here that can hurt me. Pretending that there is won't help anything.
  2. I feel afraid but I can cope with that. It's OK for me to feel that way; it's not so bad.
  3. I feel better now. I can do it!

(c) 1. Don't worry. Worry won't help anything. She will probably be satisfied if I take my time and learn what she likes.
  2. This fear is what I expected. It reminds me to focus on enjoying myself and my partner, and not on what she might think of me.
  3. It's working! I can control how I feel! And the more I relax, the sexier I feel.

(d) 1. I'm not sure how to begin. Just speak up as best I can. The worst that can happen is that she might fire me, and I can cope with that.

2. I can feel anxious about disagreeing with her and still speak up. My anxiety won't stop me unless I let it.
3. It's getting better each time I try. I'll probably feel even more in control next time.

Chapter 11:

Activating event: I went for a job interview *and* was turned down.
   (Client incorrectly included part of the A as a Rational Belief.)
Rational Belief: I did not like getting turned down. I wanted the job.
   (Incorrectly stated by the client; the therapist provides a likely guess.)
Irrational Belief: It is horrible that I didn't get the job.
   (Correct. There may be others, but additional Irrational Beliefs can be sought later.)
Emotional Consequence: I felt depressed.
   (Correct. The emotion appears to be appropriate to the Activating event and Irrational Belief. There may be other feelings, but these can be sought later.)
Disputing: Why is it *horrible* that I didn't get the job?
   (The client's statement, "I didn't care that I didn't get the job," is a rationalization, not a disputational question. Depression often follows frustration unless the client questions the "horror" of the frustration. The resulting beliefs, at E, would probably be something like the folllowing:)
New effect: It is unfortunate that I didn't get what I want, but it is clearly not horrible. There is no evidence that it is more than unfortunate and disappointing. I'd better look for another job rather than indulge myself in self-pity.

Index

A. *See* Activating event
ABC model, 13–14, 21, 38
ABCDE model, 21–22
Acceptance of distress, 127–28
Activating event (A), 13, 36–50
  beyond therapist's expertise, 47
  challenging client's perception of,
    40
  changing the client, 205–9
    social problem solving, instruc-
      tion of, 205–9
  changing the environment, 201–5
    contingency management, 203
    conflict resolution training, 202
    discrimination training, 201, 202
    problem-oriented set, 202
  clarification of, 41–42
  client errors in perceiving, 194–201
  confirmable reality and, 37
  dealing with, 194–201
  identification of, 37–41
  large numbers of, 45–47
  perceived reality and, 37
  symptom stress, 47–48
  vagueness in reporting, 43–45
Active-directive therapist style, 32,
    164–65
Active listening skills, 144
Affect
  avoidance of, 55, 60

flat or inappropriate, 54–55
lack of during session, 54, 60
Agendas, client assessment of, 247–50
Anger, irrational beliefs in, 94
Anxiety, irrational beliefs in, 92–93
Attention training, 172
Assertiveness Training, 209–12
  guidelines for assertive behavior,
    211
  suggested readings in, 277–78
Avoidance behavior and awfulizing,
    129
Awfulizing statements, 125–30

B. *See* Belief system
Beck, A. T., 40, 93, 196–98
  cognitive triad in depression, 93
  magnification/minimization, 196
  patient's distortion of events,
    196–98
  selective abstraction, 196
Behavior modification, 103–4
Behavior therapy, marriage counsel-
    ing and, 260–61
Belief system (B), 13
  confusion with C, 56–57
  identification of, 86–92
    techniques in, 88–90
    therapist suggestion, 88